MEKONG MUD DOGS

The Story of: SGT. Ed Eaton

EDGAR W. EATON

MEKONG MUDDOGS.COM
&
EDTHESNIPER.COM

Cover picture: 2nd Plt. of Bravo Co. 3/60th 9th Infantry Div.

ISBN: 0615965180
ISBN 13: 9780615965185
Library of Congress Control Number: 2014902775
Ed W. Eaton, North Charleston, S.C.

Contents

PREFACE

Yes, I am one of the lucky ones whose story has been told. As we in the brotherhood know, there are many more out there whose stories will, unfortunately, never be told. Nevertheless, their bravery and fortitude will always be in the hearts of us who know and those who will come to know the brotherhood.

Why I started writing this book in 1979 I'll never know, just as I'll never know why I decided to finish it thirty-five years later. The one thing I do know is that it's one of the toughest things I've ever had to do.

I'm not a writer by education or employ, so please excuse some of my ways.

What I have tried to do is to tell you the way it was in the Mobile Riverine Infantry in the Mekong Delta for a young man from small-town Oregon, who, like so many others during that time, just wanted to go, see, be a part of, and be a soldier for his country.

For most of us, our memory allows us to recall only what it has saved. I apologize in advance for those who feel left out or those who see things in their own way.

In the past, I have chosen to discount, ignore, and disown remembrances, only to find out thirty years later at a Mobile Riverine reunion that they were true after all. I once challenged the truth of a war story at the reunion, thinking it was outrageous, only to have three or four of my brothers get in my face and try to remind me that I was a main player in the story. I had blanked the story out of my mind. And by just being ten yards away from or closer to the incident, one can attain a completely different point of view.

My own pride and morals will not allow me to tell you anything I believe to be false—this is my promise to you. I have not researched exact dates, names, circumstances, or logistics. I'm not one to wait for outside indulgence from the rear. However I have had fellow members of Bravo Co. help me with getting it right in reading the manuscript and with their views. The way I saw it and felt it will not change from after-action reports. After action reports are seldom correct and are usually nothing more than a daily chore to get out of the way. And, throughout the years I have had many brothers from those days with Bravo Company help me with their point of view and knowledge. By taking notes since 1971, I've managed to remember more than most.

I hope that you appreciate the effort these men gave while serving their country in times when others went to great lengths not to. These men were my brothers, and I shall never forget them and their bravery. I can only dedicate this book to those who bled and died in Bravo Company, 3/60th Ninth Infantry Division, Vietnam.

"You've watched Roy Rogers and John Wayne, read Superman comics, your father served in WWII and Korea, your Uncles served in the military, you played cops and robbers as a kid; this is who you are; and you're not about to destroy your American ideals and morality easily."

Ed Eaton

FAMILY HISTORY

Ed's family history includes northwest pioneers on both sides. His great-grand-father John Eaton was the son of Levi Eaton, who was mortally wounded at the battle of Franklin while serving with the Forty-Fourth Missouri Infantry during the Civil War. John and his brothers would come to Washington State soon after the war and settle in southeast Washington. Walter, one of John's sons would settle in the northern Blue Mountains and raise a family of eight with his wife, Pearl, who was one of the first women to attain a college education within the state of Washington. Pearl was the school teacher at the Echler Mountain School near where Walter settled. They soon met, and Walter (president of the Columbia County Literary Society) would give her buggy rides to the monthly meetings. They married soon after. Their firstborn was Otho, Ed's father. Otho was raised in a simple cabin at over four thousand feet elevation, where the winters were de-manding and restrictive. They survived by farming on land they cleared among the surrounding forest of pine and fir. Their meat was from hunting and trap-ping. Oftentimes after the deer and elk had moved to lower elevations due to the deep snow; snowshoe rabbit was their only meat in the late winter months. Their only vegetables at times would be turnips and cabbage. Times were tough as all children didn't even have beds, so they would use the floor as their sleep-ing space. Walter was a tough, one-eyed, hardworking man, and as a father, he demanded the best from all his children. Otho remembered once being caught in a snowstorm with his little brother Norman while running his snowshoe trap line with skis. A blizzard had him confused and lost for hours into the late January night. When they finally reached the safety of the cabin, he could only think of how upset his mother must be, so he broke into the dark cabin as soon as possible to let everyone know they were all right, only to be met by an angry and physical father who threw them back outside for tracking in snow that they had not cleaned from their snow-matted, gunny sack-wrapped feet.

Education was a must in his mother's eyes, so when Otho was of age to go to high school, he was sent to live with a family fourteen miles down the mountain in the little town of Dayton, Washington. When school was over each Friday, he was expected to walk home with whatever provisions the family needed from town and then do family chores and his homework Saturday and Sunday before walking back to Dayton. Weather was no excuse; snow depth was the only excuse that allowed Otho his sports opportunities in high school. He was an excellent boxer, and his father, Walter, would revel in the opportunity to watch him fight. Walter would hitch up the buggy and go to town, watch Otho fight on Friday nights, and bring him and the store-bought provisions home, saving him from the walk. These were some of the few times Otho felt close to his father in early life.

Walter himself would walk to Dayton when he was without a horse and as times demanded. He was known to bring back sacks of flour over his shoulder up the fourteen-mile, four-thousand-foot mountain. Ed talked to an old-timer once, who told him that he offered Walter (who was carrying a sack of beans over his shoulder) a ride up the mountain in his buggy, only to be turned down. "It's a nice day, and the walk will do me good," Walter said. He was a proud man. Although missing the one eye from an accident in earlier years, he never tried to hide his wound and always walked proud.

As the cabin got even more crowded and the last of the eight was born, Otho could no longer deal with crowded conditions and the crying new baby brother. He decided to build himself a treehouse one summer to have his own privacy, which worked out well until one night a black bear decided to come visit. Otho was then glad to be back in the cabin with crying baby Johnny and all.

As with many American men, after the attack on Pearl Harbor, he used the opportunity to leave home and serve his country. Otho joined the Marine Corps and was on his way.

The Marines trained him as a machine gunner and put him in Marine Corps Air. They soon sent him to the Pacific, where he was a rear machine gunner in a Douglas Dauntless dive bomber.

The battle of Midway was his first heavy combat. While concentrating on a Japanese Zero with his machine gun, Otho's line of fire went through his plane's rudder and severed it, forcing the plane to discontinue the mission and creating enough drag and instability that the plane ran out of fuel before getting back to its field, so the crew had to ditch in the ocean.

Otho would later be put in a Helldiver that would also later ditch, this time not his doing. He would put in over four years in the Pacific, bouncing around from job to job and island to island before being discharged. He returned home, where he met his wife to be, Dona Zimmerman. They would settle down and have Eddie, the oldest, and his sister, Karen, before the Korean War. Otho went back in the corps soon after the Korean War started and was put in a helicopter company in Korea. He returned to Dona and the kids; they soon had two more boys, Gary and Billy.

After his tour, Otho went back to school/college, but life was not the best for the Eaton's, as Otho suffered from post-traumatic stress disorder (PTSD) and had a drinking problem that stayed with him the rest of his life, breaking up the family more than once after many efforts to make the best of it.

Ed's mother, Dona, also came from pioneer stock, as her grandfather and grandmother would journey from Kansas to Oregon in a horse-drawn wagon in the early 1900s, leaving their Sod home behind. They would, however, soon go back to Kansas, but the Oregon experience was a part of them.

Dona's father, Ed Zimmerman, was the third of a family of eleven. Ed married his wife of over sixty years in the 1920s. Lulu Shaul was a tough farmer's daughter from western Nebraska. They would make their way to Oregon in the '30s, where Ed would go to work in the logging industry. They would later make the small, eastern Oregon town of Milton-Freewater their home, where they would finish raising their five children, of which Dona was the eldest.

Dona was an outgoing girl held to high standards by her mother. She went to a Christian school most of her school years prior to meeting Otho. While Otho took time with Eddie in his early years, teaching him how to hunt and fish in the Rocky Mountain Blues, it was Dona who held the family together, oftentimes taking on two jobs to make ends meet. Eddie's early summer years found him spending time with both grandparents.

Eddie was forced to work early himself to help with the family needs, sometimes taking on two part-time jobs during school months and twelve-hour-a-day jobs in the summer months to make ends meet. Despite the hard work, Eddie had a wonderful life in Eastern Oregon/Washington. He was a cub scout and a boy scout. He loved his family and friends and enjoyed playing football and a little baseball. However, his greatest memories were of the hunting opportunities he had in Eastern Oregon and Washington. Pheasant, Duck, Goose, Grouse, Chucker, and Quail were all on the table when he was successful. Then it was on to Deer and Elk to fill out the year. Springtime would find him in the mountains again hunting for edible mushrooms and later his favorite; huckleberries. Eddie never thought of himself as coming from a poor family; in his mind there was always someone in deeper need.

He didn't think he couldn't afford college, so he changed jobs every chance he got to attain more real-life experience. Some summers he would have as many as ten different jobs with only three or four employers. However, in the fall of '66, after graduation from high school, he did attend junior college for one semester. This reasserted the need for financial help with his education, so he began thinking of active duty, as he now had a hernia, which made finding work more difficult.

Ed, as Eddie now preferred, had joined the Oregon National Guard in 1965 during his senior year of high school. The Vietnam War was ramping up, the Guards had few slots in the Army's National Guard training schedule. So Ed continued to be a lowly private until volunteering for active duty in late '67. He went to Ft. Lewis, Washington, in early 1968, where his hernia was repaired, and he went through basic training and later infantry training before being sent to Vietnam. Ed thought that his earlier experience as an ambulance attendant would be enough for the army to want him as a combat medic—the job he really wanted—but the army needed grunts, so he became a combat infantryman and sniper.

Ed: Senior class photo

Chapter 1

GOING TO VIETNAM

It was late in September during my advanced infantry training when the Army issued us our OD (olive drab) underwear when it really hit me: I was slated to go to Vietnam. It was then that I first questioned my choice to leave the National Guard for active duty, all because I had a need to see for myself.

As my leave ended, Vietnam got closer, and it was time to go. My mother decided to drive me to Portland to catch the plane for Oakland. We were leaving our sleepy little eastern Oregon town when a police car pulled out in front of us and blocked traffic so that a funeral procession could cross the main street on its way to the cemetery. However, it wasn't just anybody's funeral—it was my friend Rich's funeral.

Rich and I were high school friends, and as the procession passed, I wondered if I had made the right choice to not be present. My thoughts went back to when I had pulled a prank on Rich in which I had faked anger and pulled my .30-06 up and fired a blank round at him. The look of surprise and shock that filled his face haunted me as I wondered if that was the look that he had before being killed in Vietnam. I felt terrible about what I had done then and now for not going to his funeral.

My mother's silence was piercing as the drive took on a feeling of false hope and the inability to communicate with my best friend, my mother. We made bad jokes and conversation for the sake of conversation. As we proceeded to the departure area in the airport, the air became very cold, and I wondered if this was what it was like when my mother and father parted as he left for the war in Korea. The flight attendant touched me and brought notice that the plane was waiting on me. Mom grabbed me in an embrace meant never to end and broke down in tears as I had never seen before. It was all I could do to act strong and stay in control as I tore her arms away and firmly said, "I'll come home; don't you worry!" I then turned, and the tears flowed as I walked down the aisle at attention and took my seat in erectness, fighting back the tears while looking without variance at the back of the seat before me. I hated myself and those responsible for my mother's hurt. I had made myself a promise earlier when my father left that I would do everything possible to help her raise my brothers and sister. I had selfishly thought that the money I could send home would help. My god, how wrong was I to think money would overcome this kind of hurt, not to mention the real possibility of what my death would bring to my family.

I reaffirmed my attributes to myself: I was raised by a combat marine; I had hunted since I was eight; and I was an excellent shot. I played football and baseball and understood the importance of being on a team. I was an American.

Arriving in Saigon, as we disembarked, we could smell the stench of death in the tropical air at Ton Son Knut. I was in Vietnam, no doubt. We proceeded to a large building where a brief statement was made as to what to expect in the next few days. We were forced to turn in all US dollars for MPC (Military Payment Currency), which was to be used for our entire tour. It all looked like funny money to us. We were then bused to Long Binh for further processing.

The army had its processing down in Long Binh, and we were in no time at all in a holding area with hundreds of others awaiting orders to our next destination. Relationships were a dime a dozen as the faces changed every few hours. You couldn't trust anybody and needed to keep your valuables close by. I had little as I had spent it getting drunk in the Philippines while awaiting repair of our plane. We would hold formations during which names were called out, and those named would promptly leave for their new home. I would soon find myself going to a place called Bear Cat, the home of the 9th ID (Ninth Infantry Division).

I spent a few days in Bear Cat, once again going through orientation and procedure training before receiving my final orders for my new home in the Mekong Delta. The army was building a new base camp, Dong Tam, in the delta for the 9th ID. I was heading for Dong Tam and was to link up with my new unit: Bravo Company, Third of the Sixtieth Ninth Infantry Division (B 3/60th 9th ID). I was elated as I was told that they were part of the MRF (Mobile Riverine

Force) and as such were based onboard navy ships. My mind immediately had visions of air conditioning, hot food, white sheets, and hot water—what luck, I thought!

As our Caribou C-7A descended into the crosswind pattern I could see the base camp called Dong Tam, which was hugging to its south by the river My Tho, a finger of the great Mekong Delta. It immediately bordered what was once rice paddies and coconut groves, beyond which was the land of Charlie. The base camp was larger than I had imagined, and it was obvious that a lot of construction was going on. The base camp itself took one of the largest efforts the engineers had undertaken during the entire war. Massive movements of dirt fill and river sediment was moved to make the base camp acceptable to vehicles and aircraft.

The Caribou entered base and then final, in a radical nose down attitude with full flaps and power cut, we leveled out with the countryside close by. The new tropical flora became evident and made one realize that he was in a less-than-secure area. The main wheels touched down as the power was poured on to the reversed props. The sound and the inertia were incredible as I watched pieces of the runway surface (linked metal strips of PSP) break away from the ground and fly past the tail section of the plane. I could see privates running from the sideline to the segmented metal pieces of PSP, obviously to relink them with the runway surface. It was a violent landing that an Alaskan bush pilot could appreciate. We deplaned and immediately sank into the freshly rained upon soil. It was obvious now why the artificial surface was necessary.

We were loaded up and transported into the base camp and to our holding barracks. Once inside Dong Tam, we drove by a company of off-duty infantrymen in their company area. My self-questioning continued: these guys looked as though they were of a different army. They didn't look like those in training or in the movies. They were physically beaten up and had a death-camp look about them. There was no macho look there in the discolored jungle fatigues, just a look of insensibility and stupor as they looked right through us. Is this what I was to become? The thought shook me to the bone.

While waiting for orders, we confronted the incredible humidity and smells of the Mekong Delta, a smell that seemed to be semiliquid as it hung in the air with touches of smoke, human waste, rotting flora, and stagnant water, a blend sautéed in the one hundred-degree humidity awaiting our virgin nostrils—a smell that I shall never forget.

We were finally given bunk assignments and given a night of freedom until the morning formation. A group of us FNGs (fucking new guys) decided that we should get to know Dong Tam a little better. We didn't have to go far, and we ran into our first shit-burning detail. What a sight! We couldn't believe it—these guys were pulling out the pots (fifty-gallon drum barrels cut in half) from under the individual shitters, pouring diesel into the pot, lighting them on fire and then mixing the concoction with four by one boards. What a sight! We laughed all the way to the EM club (enlisted men's club—for all under the rank of sergeant). As we approached, we could hear the hoopla and roaring from the building. It was like no military bar I had ever been in. It was huge and sleazy with slot machines, beer all over the tables and floor, and plastic cups strewn all over hell. The atmosphere was one straight from the Wild West. Exuberant, loud conversation attempted to overcome the jukebox. Everyone felt closeness and camaraderie. Everyone wanted to know your outfit and where in the world (the United States) you were from. The infantrymen wanted to know others of their MOS (Military Occupational Specialty) and especially wanted to find someone from their new unit. I was dying to find anything out about what it was like to be in the MRF.

I soon made myself at home with a can of Budweiser and found conversation with another FNG; we all knew each other's fears and got right to them. He was another 11Bravo (infantry MOS) and, like me, was also assigned to the MRF. He informed me that we would be stuck in Dong Tam for another two days as the unit was on operation in the southern part of the delta. We would have to wait until the ships got back to the Dong Tam area. As we partied, men of our company were dying.

We found a table of grunts who had MRF patches on their left pockets. We approached them and were given a seat at the table. They were courteous and answered our questions, but it was evident that they didn't want to know us. They were, after all, combat infantrymen with their CIBs (Combat Infantry Badges) on their chests. They were from Alpha Company and drunk on their asses. We soon got the feeling that we were not one of the guys and that they didn't really care about us. However, I had to ask them what they knew about Bravo Company before finding friendlier drinking partners. They informed me that Bravo had been having a bad time of it and had recently taken on casualties in the last couple of operations. One in particular took their lives wholesale.

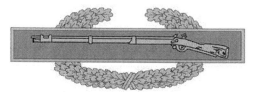

Combat Infantry Badge

I went back to the bar and started hammering the drinks down wholesale. Disappointed in my false sense of good luck, I decided to forget the recent information and concentrate on Budweiser for the moment.

The next morning found my comrades and me in a painful way as our sergeant demanded an early rise and gave us a detail filling sand bags after breakfast. We were soon wishing we had the detail of burning shit.

It didn't take long and we realized that our sergeant in charge of our details had his office in the NCO club (Noncommissioned Officers Club). We soon found ourselves back at the EM club killing our pain. The days continued that way until Halloween eve, when we were put on a navy boat and given a ride out to the USS *Westchester* 1167 a World War II LST used in the Pacific campaign. This is where Bravo Company was hanging their helmets.

There were about eight of us altogether with our duffel bags standing on the barge, which was attached to the starboard side of the ship. Not knowing where to go, we soon found our berthing area in the bottom of the ship.

U.S.S. WESTCHESTER COUNTY

LST with River Division attached

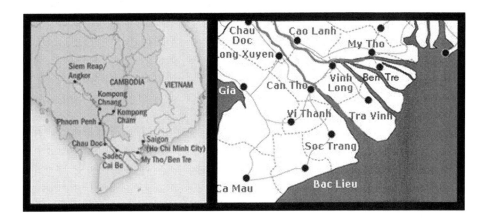

Chapter 2

TRICK OR TREAT

As we made it down to the bowels of the ship, we found empty bunks in our berthing area and marked them with our duffel bags; the reality of being in a combat infantry company started setting in. We all huddled and tried to make small talk while keeping an eye on the few men who had remained behind, as the rest of the company had gone out on a mission. Some with bandages, some not, but all keeping to themselves and busy with a card game while paying no attention to us, pretending we weren't there, talking to us only to answer questions. The company clerk seemed to be the only one interested in our presence and our welfare. The company was to come in any time now, and we were to get a look at our comrades soon.

Getting hosed by the Navy

Then the news came in that the guys were arriving and without all, as they had been hit hard. The lightly wounded went topside to meet their brothers as we held together awaiting the unknown. Soon they started to trickle in one by one. All came in with worn-out boots and faded uniforms that were wet, muddy, and dripping brown trails of water from being washed down by a fire hose prior to being allowed onboard. Once the overall perusal of their condition was finished, my eyes went straight to their hollow-looking eyes—eyes I had not seen before. There was a noncommittal, faraway look that seemed to look right through us but passed by us at the same time. I was shaken to the bone. These weren't the hard-core grunts I was expecting. They looked totally worn out, lean to the bone from lack of food and too much humping (on the move-loaded down). I needed big brothers to protect me and be my mentors not these worn out guys.

Soon the area was full, and elbow room was at a minimum, as every rack was taken. The berthing area was meant for troop carrying, not comfort. The new guys were relegated to the lower racks that hit the bottom of the now wet and muddy floor. Small talk was now abounding, and the awful truth of loss within the company ranks was part of it. A couple of guys asked what platoon we were assigned to, a question we couldn't answer. They then went on their way.

Soon a raw-boned Texan came up to me and introduced himself as Sergeant Reed. He informed me that I was now in Second Platoon, assigned to his squad and that I would be his new RTO (Radio Telephone Operator), and then he went on his way.

Some of the other FNGs (Fuckin' New Guys) and I found our way out of the berthing area and up to the ship's galley, just trying to get some breathing room away from all the overwhelming sights, sounds, and smells that arrived with the company. It gave us all a chance to talk about our new platoons and jobs within. We all had reservations and wished we had paid better attention to our classes in infantry training that pertained to our new obligations. There were about eight of us FNGs, including a new RTO for the FO (Forward Observer), a well-built football player from New Jersey by the name of Ed Ziek. Soon chow was on, and we as a company enjoyed a hot meal in the galley alongside the ship's company. There was finally a small sense of belonging to this group as we segregated ourselves from the sailors.

We went back down the hatch in the floor and down the ladder to the bottom hole of the USS *Westchester*. We wriggled our way through the mess of a torn-up area strewn with dirty uniforms, sleeping grunts in precarious positions, and duffel bags. I finally pulled and worked my way down to my bottom bunk, which would hit bottom, my clothes absorbing moisture every time I moved. I finally fell asleep wondering what tomorrow would bring. This was no treat for Halloween, I was thinking.

At 3:30 a.m. a large explosion rocked the ship, and I was immediately awakened by diesel fuel filling up the area. For some unknown reason, I stuffed my billfold in my mouth as I arose from the floor and the diesel fuel that was fast filling up the berthing area. One wall in the area had collapsed, pinning men in their racks, condemning them to their last breaths. Men were yelling for help, some screaming, but most just trying to make it to the hatch and then to the vertical ladder leading to the hatch on the upper level. Within seconds, the level of fuel was to the top of the room, leaving only a cushion of air among the pipes and cables attached to the ceiling. The duffel bags, mattresses, and all floatable material further became obstacles to our progress to the exit. The main lights were off, and the emergency lights dimly lit the room. Panic was setting in, and I was a part of it as I swam, pulled, clawed, and reached for a way out.

Finally, Sergeant Reed took command, controlling the exodus in a steady, sure voice, demanding orderly control of ourselves. He saw that I was panicking and pulled me to the hatch, which was now below and under the diesel level. With a reassuring voice, he said, "Take a deep breath, pull yourself down and through the hatch, and then up the ladder." I was on it like stink on shit; I wanted the fuck out of this Poseidon Hellhole. However, mentally, I was only prepared for the same level of diesel on the other side as I had experienced on the berthing area side. As I pulled myself up the ladder, I could see the light of the hatch hole above where Fourth Platoon's berthing area was, but there seemed to be no end to the diesel as the pressure had pushed it up into the ladder well to a much higher level than the level below in the berthing area. I panicked and gave a big pull of the ladder rungs, throwing my hands ahead of me. I soon broke out and was immediately grabbed by my arms by John Beck, Dan Hendricks, Willy Perez, and others from the Fourth Platoon, and then I was thrown across the room into the pile of those before me. As we made it to our feet and tried to make sense of our environment, through our now fogged and burning eyes, it was evident that there was a fight going on between the army and the navy. The navy personnel were trying to close the hatch to save the ship from sinking, and the Fourth Platoon guys were not having anything to do with that. As the navy personnel were physically ejected, I took it upon myself to grab a naval officer and pull his shirt out for a rag to wipe the diesel from my eyes. He just kept going, and I just kept wiping to no avail as I made it through the ship with burning, fouled eyesight, following those who knew the route. As we made it to the top deck, I could hear the loudspeaker order us to the port side, what the hell ever that meant. We soon found our way to the high side of the listing *Westchester*, where we huddled in a naked mass of diesel-drenched bodies still rubbing our eyes, hoping for our sight back. The ship had hit the bottom of the river Song My Tho and had listed forty degrees to its right side, making standing difficult.

Reed stayed in the bottom hole until the last capable man was out. He then returned to the area and found three men with broken limbs and internal injuries. He helped them navigate the obstacles as they dived and clawed their way to the hatch. Reed got all the men out and went back a third time to search for any survivors. He disregarded his own safety and the possibility of fire. Reed managed to do what none of the rest of us would. He found deep inside a way to disregard his own fears for the good of the brotherhood. Reed was truly our hero on this night of Poseidon Hell. Without his calm leadership and returning bravery, the story would be different for many of us. Larry later received the prestigious Soldier's Medal for his action this night.

The navy ship's crew was busy as we just tried to keep out of their way; they were in search-and-rescue mode. Gunboats circled the wounded *Westchester*, dropping charges into the water to deter any enemy divers who might be in the area. They shone their searchlights, looking for survivors as the attached River Division of gunboats and Tango boats detached themselves from the attached barge on the right side of the ship. The blast had blown a hole the size of a large room just under the waterline now visible because of the listing of the ship. The blast was a direct hit on the navy's first-class berthing area. Bodies were askew in torn and dismembered state within as the navy tried to put a Tango boat inside the hole for rescue. While we didn't appreciate the actions of the navy trying to close our hatch, we now understood that they were trying to save the ship and the rest of the crew as procedure would require in open ocean. The ship, however, was in a shallow river. We were impressed with their attention to the job at hand as they did everything they could outside and inside the ship to rescue their brothers. The night was busy as we contemplated our chemically burning bodies and our fortune at the same time. We had no water to wash the fuel away from our skin; the experience was miserable.

As the sun rose and hopes of some attention to our dilemma rose, we could see the rashes growing on our bodies. Finally able to see, we were put in formation for a body count. Rows of naked men with distorted scrotums, at a forty-degree angle to the deck was a somber sight with no humor to be found. Our losses were estimated at six, all from my small berthing area. I stood there with my only possession, my billfold. For some reason I had put it in my mouth when I was awakened. I then noticed Willy Perez had retrieved his pictures. It cracked me up for a second. Why would anyone care about such things when survival was at such a premium?

The rising sun only made the matters worse. Few of us had any issued underwear; I had kept my socks on but threw them overboard because they were soaked with fuel. Fuel-soaked clothing only made skin irritation worse, but cover was needed from the burning sun that only made the burns grow. Those with light skin were hit the worst, I noted, when seeing a redhead's scrotum blowing up to grapefruit proportions. The misery continued as the sun rose with the temperatures rising and rising. We didn't want to complain because we knew there were still hopes of finding survivors, and every man was needed for the rescue. The navy was now growing weary from exhaustion and fruitless efforts as they estimated their losses at over twenty.

We had no communications with battalion, as all of our gear and radios were now on the bottom of the river from being blasted off the barge by the mine. But it was now time for us to be attended to. We were thirsty, and our burns grew with the rising afternoon sun: scrotums, lips, and eyes were swelling up to unrecognizable proportions. Our officers were demanding that we be taken off the ship and soon.

It was almost twelve hours after the blast when relief came in form of clothing and a trip to the USS *Washtenaw* 1166. Our Poseidon Hellhole Halloween nightmare was over.

Later we would find out that VC scuba divers had swum two fifty-gallon neutrally buoyant barrels full of explosive to the sides of the ship and connected them with a detonation cord and then ran the detonation line to the banks before charging. As luck would have it, only one went off. The other was located only feet from our only exit in the bottom hole of the USS *Westchester* 1167.

Ltc. Pete Peterson & Reed

Chapter 3

FIST MISSION

2nd Platoon: Circa Oct. 1968

It was my first mission, and I was nervous and anxious with my new job as an RTO for Sergeant Reed. I was asking anyone who seemed to listen about my expected load. How many smoke grenades, high-explosive (HE) grenades, C rations, M-16 magazines, batteries, water, among other things, would I carry? I mostly watched the other RTOs and then loaded up as we were on our way and then soon boated by navy Tango boats to a large rice paddy on the bank of the main river, the Song My Tho. Within minutes, we had configured into groups for each expected Huey helicopter. I found myself in the middle of the cargo floor as the Huey took off and made a southerly heading away from the large river. I could see the sun dipping and close to falling below the horizon as we made our descent into what seemed to be an awfully small rice paddy for the nine Hueys. Huey gunships were on each flank and strafing the wood line as our airspeed slowed to a hover, and then, before a complete landing, all hurried off and ran toward the wood line with no hesitation. My job was simple: follow Sergeant Reed wherever he goes. We soon made a perimeter in the wood line and started setting up positions with a field of fire for protection. This was it? This is where we're staying? What now?

Heuys landing in PZ   Huey Cobra

I was already scared and uncomfortable with the night, my first as a combat infantryman in the Mekong Delta. The smell of rotting humus and tropical stench were among the new smells invading my nostrils. My position was just a few feet from my squad, and we now shared the radio. I was to have last watch and told to get some shut-eye. I had selected, on purpose, a small stand of dried sugar cane, complete with mosquitos, next to our position for its ability to give me a noisy awakening if an invader was to walk on the dry, crisp leaves but I thought surely no one would come in here. Yet, to my amazement, as the darkness set in and all was quiet, there was no mistaking the sureness of the sound of a stalker. My heart started pounding as never before as my respiratory rate increased with the fear that was mounting to a degree I had never experienced before. My fear mounted higher as I realized that I, too, was going to have to make noise in order to get my weapon to a ready position. I knew he couldn't see me, as I had the best of positions, and the night was as black as the proverbial ace of spades. He was getting so close. Could he hear my heart beat? It was now too late for me to ready myself for firing without giving my position away. God, did I fuck up or what? I'm going to have to quick draw when I can see him; he sounds so close. Then it happened; he charged my position—but where was he? Oh my God, I was paralyzed with fear and was one dead son of a bitch! My body almost exploded with horror as he stepped on my hip and ran up on my face and then fell inside my mouth. Goddamn, a fucking rat! I sat up and purged my mouth with saliva! My squad became excited; they were at first pissed at my noise and then amused at my dilemma.

My heart was still pumping like crazy minutes later as it pushed the adrenaline around, my mind now developing more fear than before. Is this the way I am going to react to a real attack? Am I really as afraid as I was when our ship was blown up with us in the bottom hole? I'm never going to make it unless I change. How in the hell did I get here anyway?

As dawn approached, all started to stir, and the quiet became relaxed conversation as all broke into their C rats for breakfast. I had peaches and pound cake, a favorite of mine in infantry training. The mosquitos had done a job on me: my face was swollen, and my lips were so numb from the bites that my water and the juices from the peaches ran down my chin from lack of feeling. But I felt good—nobody had shot at us yet.

We were soon loaded up and on our way single file, walking through the countryside. My eyes were taking in all the new sights of the Mekong as my nose was taking in all the new smells that were uniquely those of the tropical Mekong Delta. My body and mind tried to balance their attention to the needs of where to step, what to look for, how close to one another to be, the orientation of my M-16, and so on. My straps started cutting into my shoulders, with the heavy load getting heavier as the sun started penetrating with its ever-increasing temperature. Reed warns me about drinking too often, as the sun was overhead and my water was hot. It was over one hundred degrees, and there were no breaks in the constant push to plod forward to wherever. As the heat rose, the chatter on the radio lessened. My job was simple in that I only needed to know the code signs for the other leaders and be close to Reed. The code signs went like this: if you were a squad leader, you would take on your platoon's number and your squad's number. For example; the squad leader of First Squad, Second Platoon would be B-2-1 and so on. The platoon sergeant would be B-2-5 the platoon leader (usually an officer) would be B-2-6. The company commander would be B-6. All radio operators (RTOs) would take on their leaders' call sign and add an O or *Oscar* to it. So the RTO for the platoon sergeant of Second Platoon would be B-2-5-Oscar and so on. I was Bravo-Two-One Oscar.

We stopped for lunch, but it was all I could do to down a couple of bites. I just wanted to enjoy the absence of the cutting straps on my shoulder as I elevated my legs and positioned myself away from the searing Mekong sun under the shade of a coconut tree. I was no sooner all set when we loaded up and continued the merciless grind. This infantry shit is brutal, I was thinking.

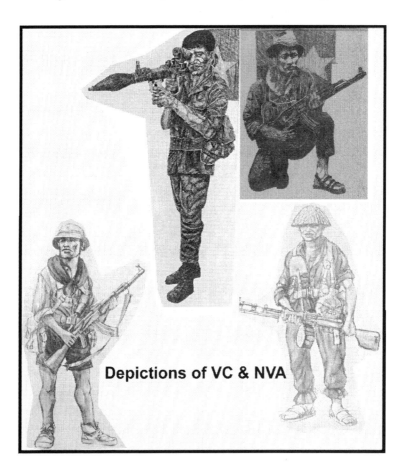

Depictions of VC & NVA

Soon into the afternoon we received rifle fire from our flank and all hit the dirt. Was this an attack? But the firing was short, and it was directed more toward the point platoon than at us and deemed to be far away enough to just be harassment, so we continued with a sigh with relief. The sweat was pouring down my face to the point I was constantly wiping it off with my wet sleeves; I was totally wet from perspiration as we marched on.

The sun finally started dropping, and the temperature slowly went below one hundred. I can't wait to call it a day. Surely we would stop soon and set up our night perimeter (Remain Over Night, or RON). But we continued, even as the shade turned to dusk. Then it was Second Platoon's turn to walk point as dusk turned to night. Were we ever going to stop? What the fuck was this? Then the CO told us to look for a good location to set up. Finally, I think, just a few more steps! However, the point man who was just three ahead of Reed and myself stopped in his tracks, and all became quiet. We could hear the snorting of an animal and the stomping of its hooves. A huge, black shadow started moving toward the point element and then suddenly charged as Ramos the machine gunner opened up. The tracers went only ten to fifteen feet and then into the black mass as the tracer rounds exited at every angle possible as their trajectory was changed from glancing off the bone mass. The animal stopped at the foot of Ramos and in the middle of the dark trail. We all maneuvered ourselves over the carcass of the huge, dead water buffalo. Because of the firing, we had to go on a little further than planned, as surely every VC in the area now knew our location if they weren't already following us.

We finally set up inside the wood line. Reed positioned us in three-man positions. Two others and I kept the radio as Reed set up close to the platoon leader and his RTO. We were in a coconut grove, and the tide was coming in, filling the canals where we were to take cover. I laid my PRC 25 radio up against a tree before us, and we all got into the canal with the water up to our chests. It felt fantastic. My body was beat, and this cooling down was needed badly, as it was still hot out. We positioned our rifles next to us but up on the dry dike. I took the first watch as the other two tried to get some shut-eye. It was just the mosquitos and me, a lonely feeling as our positions were farther apart than the night before. At least the mosquitos only had my face and head to work on, but they were fierce, and I had to strain to keep my eyes open from all the swelling.

About two hours into my watch, I could hear something or someone directly before me. As my heart started to race, I could see shadows only thirty feet away. Was it another squad? Why were they in front of me? As my eyes became tuned in to the movement, I could see rockets and a tripod as the intruders set their machine gun on it. I was really friggin' freaked at this point. What the hell should I do? My first thought was to radio someone about what I was seeing, so I reached up out of the canal and grabbed my handset, pulling it toward my hidden frozen body. I was now not even sticking my head up, and I needed the handset to reach down to me, so I kept pulling it to the point that I ripped it away from the radio and its connection. I now had no radio—fuck! Then all hell broke loose as rockets ripped through the air just inches from my head, landing just feet behind me in the area of the command post (CP), only to be followed by heavy machine-gun and AK-47 fire ripping through the foliage. I was frozen as they pounded us with green tracers. Then the firing suddenly ceased, and the clanking of their weapons disappeared into the night.

My God, what had I done? They surely killed and wounded many of us and all because of me. I could have forewarned everyone. I could have shot at them, thrown a grenade, anything but what I did. Nobody was able to return fire as we were in between them and Charlie. Surely I would be court martialed. How was I going to look anyone in the face after this? Everyone had to know now that I was a coward. I wanted to throw up, and I was shaken to the bone. Pretty soon Reed made his way over to us ask if everyone was OK, and then he returned, leaving us there with the broken radio. I couldn't sleep a wink for the third straight night. I had never felt this way before. Everything about me was a now a lie. I had no worth. Was this the way I was going to die—a coward?

The thought of facing the men in the morning was terrifying. What would be the consequences?

Finally, dawn crept into the grove, and the men started stirring. I hadn't eaten anything substantial since yesterday morning; I now didn't even try as my stomach surely wouldn't keep it down. The swelling was even worse today: I could barely see, I couldn't feel my lips, and now my fingers were swollen to the point I could barely feel my trigger. The guys next to me were busy pulling leaches off their bodies; they looked like they had been gut shot by .00 buckshot. I didn't even look for any on myself; I just didn't care. I was still in complete shock.

We were soon ordered back, and the inevitable was here; I was going to have to face the music. But there were no wounded or dead, and to my surprise no one is looking at me or paying any attention, as though nothing happened. Then one of the old-timers says, "That must have been pretty scary, being your baptism by fire and all." I had no reaction as he chuckled. As we headed out once again, I was relieved to know that no one knew about my actions or lack of and, most important, no one was hurt because of it. However, I was still nauseous and sick to my stomach knowing what I had done, and having had no sleep for three days with little food wasn't helping.

Was I to go on for an entire year being sick to my stomach, being a coward? It is a hell of a way to die, I thought to myself. I couldn't go on this way. I had to grab myself up by the bootstraps and get a grip on the reality of all this. This was the last thing I thought would happen to me. I was sure I could and would perform. To what degree I didn't know, but never did I think of myself as a gutless coward. I had to do something and fast. I'd been given a reprieve, and I couldn't be that person ever again. I hated that person; no, I loathed that person. Every step I took I couldn't shake the thoughts of what I did.

Within hours I had decided I was going to do something about it. I kept imagining being fired at again and again and returning fire time after each time. Every likely ambush point we came upon I imagined Charlie being there, and I would stand up to him and fire back. Once again the heat was upon us like stink on dung, and I was running out of water. We didn't get any resupply that day, as we had used little ammo. Rationing was now being talked about, but I didn't have shit to ration. Between the heat, the mosquitos continuing their rampage, and my consuming thoughts of my next reaction to Charlie, my head was nauseously spinning.

Just before lunch break, we were attacked again from the right flank. This time we were on point, and they were just yards away. As everyone hit the dirt, I whirled my rifle to my shoulder and fired at the muzzle flashes with full automatic. As I went to change magazines, I was tackled hard to the ground. Reed was on top of me yelling, "What the fuck do you think you're doing?" After the brief firefight, Reed apologized for the hard hit, but he let me know that under no circumstances was I to do that ever again. "Always hit the dirt, and then return fire" was his order. We dusted ourselves off, and on we trudged again, but now I was only tired, hot, and thirsty, with swollen lips and fingers; my stomach ache had gone away, and I had made a statement to myself. I could almost smile again: "Maybe I won't die a coward after all."

We broke for lunch, and I ate all my fruits because I not only needed the nourishment but also the juices. I notice that some of the guys were opening their fruits and just sucking the juices out then throwing them away. We were all thirsty. It was well over one hundred again. Another FNG had tried to put down some food, but he upchucked it immediately. I was praying mine stayed down. I notice that the old-timers weren't even swollen from the mosquitoes, and they didn't even bother to wave them off their faces. Evidently, they had gotten immune to them. Incredible, I thought; will I ever get that way, I wondered?

We pushed on, and in no time we were held up as one of the guys had passed out from heat stroke. Doc got as much paddy water on him as possible, and he soon regained consciousness and was able to take in some water, but he was delirious. The decision to medevac him off was made. It gave us a few minutes of much-needed rest and the hope for a resupply of water. But we hoped to no avail, as the Dustoff came and went without leaving so much as a drop. Within the next hour, we had two more guys go down and then another Dustoff, and yet again, no water as our frustrations grew. On we dragged our beaten bodies. We soon came upon a hooch with a large rain barrel. We looked into it and saw that it was three-fourths full but with a scum of mosquitos a quarter-inch thick. Then one of the guys stuck his canteen down into it while brushing the mosquitos aside as he filled his canteen. Doc Schuebel warned us all of its possible diseases, but his words fell on deaf ears as one by one we all took some of the infested water. I just stuck my head in as others had done and sucked it down, straining the mosquitos with my teeth. It was great! It tasted better than any Coca-Cola I had ever drank.

As we plodded on, another FNG was down, but this time it was a seasoned troop that was the casualty of heat exhaustion. While waiting for another Dustoff, the morale took another dip, as we all couldn't understand why no water was being flown in.

As we waited for the Dustoff, another FNG was determined to be in need of extraction. This made a total of five casualties due to heat exhaustion. Soon we were on our way again with legs cramped and the pace even slower. Would the sun ever lower?

Another sniper attempted to slow us down, but this time most just kept on going as though nothing was happening, or was it our way to just say, Fuck it. Who cares?

We came upon a drying, muddy canal, and as the point man made his way into it, he was immediately stuck, too exhausted to fight it, he just lay there and waited for help. As the slack man and machine gunner attempted to help him out, the mud also took them. We all tugged on them for what seemed to be an eternity. One of the other FNGs, Zane, who was even more pathetic than I, lost his balance while tugging and fell even further into the quagmire. As others started to pull him out, Reed made the decision to leave him there and use him as a stepping stone. As each one crossed, his body became more and more submerged in the slime and mud. The entire company crossed and proceeded as the Second Platoon stayed back to retrieve their men and give First Platoon its turn on point. It took ropes and the last of our energy to extract Zane, whom we were now calling Super Private in a demeaning manner.

Another hour of humping and two more men were down with heat exhaustion. Once again, there was no water on the Dustoff.

It was rumored that the CO had had it with Battalion and gave them an ultimatum, which garnered a decision to bring us in. However, we would have to head to the main channel in order to meet with a navy Riverine Division (RivDiv), which had space in its Tango boats and was heading down river to Dong Tam. We were told that this would mean that we would have to pick up the pace.

Not much to cheer about as we all wondered how much was left in us. We had already lost seven men in just a few hours (four would have permanent damage to the brain and never return).

We trudged on the best we could, but it was just a matter of time and we would slow down once again. I was really hurting and thinking about how to fake heat exhaustion. After an eternity, the word came back that the beach had been reached, but it was too late for me. I just couldn't go any further as I laid down in what moisture I could find in the Nipa palms. I told Reed I'd be right there, but I knew in my mind I wasn't going any further as the rest of the squad passed me by and asked if they could help to which there was no response from me. I just didn't seem to even have the energy to talk. Then the very last man stopped and wanted to know what the problem was. He was a sergeant, and this was his very last mission. He was a small, slender young man who had some words for me. He told me how tough it was for him when he was a FNG and that, believe it or not, it actually got easier as time passed. He told me that he would take my radio and pack it to the river but that he wasn't going to help me any further. He went on saying, "This is a terrible way to die. You can't expect anybody else to come back and help you. You are on your own. You have it in you—just make up your mind." And he went on his way.

I laid there watching him disappear as I realized I was truly by myself— Charlie to the rear and salvation just meters away. I really didn't want to move, but I also really didn't want to be left to Charlie's ways. For whatever reason, I got myself up and plodded to the beach. I walked straight to the river while dropping my weapon and walked into neck-deep water. Here I was dying of thirst and water all around me. And while the water was cooling my body to a normal temperature, it wasn't quenching my thirst. We had been sternly warned about drinking from the river and were told about the hundreds of thousands of people whose feces and urine was dumped directly upriver into the Mekong. *Fuck it. I'm thirsty and maybe a disease will get me out of this shit hole*, I thought as I gorged myself with the brown water. As I cooled down and went to the beach, a large turd floated by. Oh well!

As we boarded the boats, I was elated to be going in but at the same time realized that I still hadn't seen the type of firefights that the old-timers talked about.

This was going to be hell if I made it and hell if I didn't.

No doubt that our cherry asses had been made a little tougher. But you've got to remember we dusted off a bunch of guys for heat exhaustion, and some were old-timers. I'll never forget that my cup of hope went from half full to empty as a bone. I couldn't believe that after years of playing football and my infantry training that I wasn't ready physically, and I was shocked to the bone as to my lack of mental preparedness. It made me sick to my stomach once again.

ATC Tangos beached, awaiting Infantry

Coming in from a mission.

Unloading River Division and boarding ship.

Chapter 4

F I R S T   K I L L

RTO Ed Eaton next to Tango Boat

We awoke before the sun rose, took our early morning piss, and made our way up to the galley. My butterflies were evident as I forced down the greasy eggs and bacon. This was going to be my second mission, and I now knew what was before me, and my body didn't like it.

This time on the barge when I was collecting my gear and rations, things were going to be different. Less food and more water, I thought, as I scrounged two more canteens. My load of smoke grenades was going to be attached differently than before—no more unnecessary rubbing. No more food that didn't have lots of water in it. Fruit was the only thing I was going to carry this time. It was the only thing that would go down and stay down anyhow. I wanted more bullets, more magazines. I wasn't going to be caught without.

We loaded on the Tango boats and were soon heading up river to a beach unknown to all but the officers, and then they really didn't usually know anything other than a grid coordinate.

River Raider/Mud Dogs unloading Tango.

Tangos beached and ready to load.

We unloaded unscathed and made our way online into a wood line bordered by a small rice paddy. Second Platoon was pulling point, and our squad was the lead element. This was a beautiful area, I thought, nothing like the last mission. The fields were well manicured. It was a tropical garden of sorts with coconut groves, banana trees, and paddies, with the occasional thatched hooch of the farmer and his family.

We were only one hundred meters inside the wood line when we came upon a hooch that obviously was being used as a VC training classroom, as the chalkboard in front of the benches testified. We were all checking it out, taking turns looking inside with curiosity. After taking a look, I followed Reed back outside where he was engaging in conversation about which direction to take from there. I then heard a Loach (Hughes 500 helicopter) approaching overhead. As I looked in the direction of the noise, to my amazement I saw two VC, one with his AK-47 lying in the crotch of a tangerine tree, with the weapon pointing directly at the now visible Loach only fifty meters away. Without hesitation or words, I brought my 16 up to my shoulder and took deliberate but quick aim at the would-be ambusher. I fired and fired again and again as he fell to the ground, and his partner hit the canal next to him. The rest of the squad was now firing and attacking the position of the other VC. As they fired and ran to his position, he popped up a few feet from where he previously was and was now on the run with Reed, Kloph, Middendorf, and others on his tail like stink on shit. I followed to the edge of the sugarcane where they had gone, hampered by my heavy load of PRC 25 radio and gear, only to see them returning with disappointment on their faces. They had lost him, but they thought that maybe he had received one of our M-16 rounds before disappearing. Everybody was on edge, with weapons at ready as I stood over my first kill, thinking how close the two men in the Loach were to certain death.

At first I just stood there looking at him. His camouflage helmet was askew and his body contorted, lying on his back with his eyes open and weapon at his side. There was a sense of relief as I absorbed the fact that I had made my first kill. I could do it, I now thought. And maybe I was now part of the team. Without hesitation, I leaned down to him, rifling through his pockets and tearing his Chinese-made ammo belt off and then his helmet. These were going to be my souvenirs. I didn't want the AK or anything else, just those two items, which I tied on to my radio. I then heard Lieutenant Wolfer say to Doc Schuebel, "I think you had better watch that guy. He's not normal." I assumed he was taken aback by my lack of fear of a dead VC. Oh well, it's not the dead ones you should be afraid of. The lieutenant didn't know my father was a mortician and that I had been around the reality of death since I was a young boy.

Lieutenant Wolfer was a New York boy who looked sixteen and was slight of build. His demeanor was laid back as he allowed the platoon sergeant to be a large influence in the decisions made, a strong point of his. He was always on the ball when it came to staying in contact with the CP, being on top of our logistical needs, and knowing what was going on, a true asset to the platoon and a likeable guy.

Hughs 500/OH-6 (loach) landing on LST.

Soon we were on our way with caution, humping in the noonday sun of the Mekong Delta. In no time, I was feeling the heat as the sweat poured down my face and into my eyes. This day was going to be hell, I thought. Would I ever get used to this? The old-timers weren't even sweating yet as one foot went before the other. The water was lowering as the tide retreated, and we put some klicks (kilometers) behind us.

The morning's action kept with me as I tried to keep focused on my surroundings, as I now knew that my eyes were needed for my survival. The protection I garnered from the old-timers was no longer there as it was before. Whether I liked it or not, I was part of a team. As we plodded along further, I was starting to get a sense of what was going on. Being an RTO really helped me understand the theory of the day and the continuing problems of getting a group of men from one point to the other in this ever-changing, godforsaken environment.

There were families in the hooch's this time. As we approached a hooch with caution, the point man would stick his head in and appraise the situation and then call for the evacuation of the bunker within the hooch. A lame attempt at saying "come here" in Vietnamese and pointing his M-16 would usually suffice.

We would then move on our way as the area was cleared. The family would squat in a corner with wide-open eyes of fear as they watched us move on our way. My eyes were taking it all in, the cooking area, the eating utensils, the mats for beds, the clothing, and the whole environment of the Vietnamese Mekong hooch. If your eyes couldn't tell you, then the smell could tell you that these were poor people living with fear every day. Such a contrast: the beautiful paddies with lush Nipa palm borders broken by coconut groves and the occasional citrus trees, and then fear and poverty intertwined within the dried, brown woven bamboo and Nipa palm hooch's. We dragged on with fear in our hearts, sweat pouring down our faces, and the never-ending question: What's around the next corner, bush, hooch, paddy, river crossing, or grove? And on and on we go with the fear continuing in our hearts and an occasional sniper round overhead as we searched in hopes of finding nothing.

Another canal to cross

The mode of operation became clear as our days were all about getting in the enemy's face. Helicopter insertions were the main mode of transportation to probable enemy locations. The terrain would change with each flight. One hour you're in deep, dark jungle, the next in an open rice paddy, the next in rivers and canals, and the next in agricultural groves.

The next two days of the mission were relatively quiet. As we awoke in the morning haze, we were hoping it was time for us to go in, as the ringworm and emersion foot were starting to break out on many of the men.

As we awaited marching orders, we had time for breakfast, but for the most part, eating solid meals in the field was nearly impossible. The heat and the physical demand left one almost nauseated at the thought of food. We usually stocked up on the fruits from the B-1 units for our lunch and dinner meals. The pound cake from B-2 units, crackers, and a little peanut butter were usually saved for breakfast. We would, however, usually take one meal of solid food with us for those rare occasions when we would cool down and our appetites would allow for solid foods. One day when we had cooled down, I noticed others heating their C rats with lit pieces of C-4 explosives. Having never seen this practice before or done this before, I decided to try it. So I pinched off a piece of C-4 and lit it. I opened up my can of spaghetti and put it above the flame. From time to time I would stick in my finger and see if it was hot. All of a sudden the bottom of my can disintegrated, dropping all the spaghetti on the C-4 and the ground. Why didn't this work for me, I wondered? The old-timers laughed at my dilemma. Apparently one needs to stir the food or the C-4 will burn through the can like an acetylene torch, as the heat provided by the C-4 was in the four-digit range. Oh well, live and learn.

C rats (combat rations) were designed for issue in the field. Each complete meal contains approximately 3600 calories. Each menu contains one canned meat item, one canned fruit, bread, or dessert item. One B unit contains an accessory packet containing cigarettes, matches, chewing gum, toilet paper, coffee, cream, sugar, salt, and a spoon. Four P-38 can openers are provided in each case of twelve meals.

Ed having Breakfast

As we headed out, we got a call from an air force FAC (forward air controller) that a heavy bunker complex to our flank had been spotted and that F4 Phantoms were on their way with one thousand-pound HE bombs aboard. The air controller requested that we immediately evacuate the area. The fastest route was to take a hard right through a large coconut grove. The only problem with this route was that we had to go against the grain, so to speak. This meant that we had to cross the irrigation dikes at a ninety-degree angle by jumping from one to the other. The heat and the jumping soon were taking a toll as some started to just wade across the four-foot canals instead of jumping. About this time the F4s came on station, and although we weren't out of range yet, they took it upon themselves to make a practice run on the bunkers as we watched. To our amazement, Charlie was firing on them as they came in. Tracers were flying on both sides of the F4 as the pilot pulled his stick back to gain altitude. Then the next one came in with his twenty-millimeter Vulcan cannon firing, only to meet some more tracers head on. These guys have some balls, I thought.

Charlie was firing into the face of a Vulcan cannon and then retreating to his bunker at the last moment. The F4 pilots were coming in unnerved by all this, and my knowing that they couldn't yet release the thousand pounders due to our proximity gave me more respect for them. It seemed to be a game with them as they shot it out with each pass.

F-4 Phantom

Soon we gave them the OK to drop their bombs as we took up positions behind the coconut trees. I was amazed as the ground shook and the shrapnel whistled and buzzed over our heads. After a few passes, the tracers from the ground ceased, as trees and debris were thrown into the sky. A large piece of shrapnel the size of my finger fell next to me on the last strike. Not knowing any better, I picked it up, only to find my hand blistered with pain by the intense heat of the metal. Just what I needed, more anguish—and on my trigger finger.

Soon we were on our way again, fighting the canals as most all had been reduced physically to wading across each canal instead of jumping by them. As we jumped into the mud, the man ahead would turn around and lend his hand and give the man behind a tug out and then you would do the same for the man behind you as his boots would break the suction of the mud. With my burned hand and the exhaustion of all this, I thought once again I was going to die from heat exhaustion as the canals seemed to never end and the sweat continued to pour into my eyes, making everything a blur visually as well as mentally. Again, I can't understand why I'm not physically ready. I reflected on the time that some angry mothers and congressmen had come to Ft. Lewis demanding that the army quit treating their kids with the inhumanity of its demanding cruel training. Thank you, moms and congressmen, for making me less capable of surviving, I thought to myself. You're killing us with your kindness.

We hit a small booby trap on the way to our awaiting Tango boats, but the damage to the point man was light, and he chose to continue with us.

We were loaded onto Tango boats for a short ride to Fire Base Truman on the south side of the channel. There, we configured in the rice paddy for our first PZ (Pickup Zone) of the day as the sun rose, warming our bodies for the upcoming insertion. I sat on the paddy dike with my boots in the water, watching leeches suck on the boot leather as my stomach churned with a bad case of what I thought was butterflies. I pulled my leech-ridden boots out and into the sun, watching the leeches dry up like raisins, all the while still latched onto my boots as though there was something in it for them. My stomach was getting worse, and I wondered if this was butterflies or the real thing.

Helo Co.: 167th Vultures coming in for PZ

Soon the choppers could be heard and then seen descending upon our position. I started to throw up my breakfast uncontrollably. Without hesitation, Reed ordered my gear removed, and I was stripped of my radio, extra battery, my C rats, and some of my smoke grenades. All the while, I was throwing up without end in sight. I watched, writhing in the paddy, with pain and confusion as my company boarded the birds and ascended into the hot, humid, morning delta sky, leaving me all alone in the middle of this large paddy to my own problems. With fear of being closer to the wood line than the actual fire base, I moved my pitiful self a little closer to the river and to a defensible position.

Within a half hour, my body was purged of all the poison, and I walked over to the artillery barges that made up the firebase, all the while wondering why no one had come to see how I was doing. I was met indifferently as I found a seat on the edge of the command barge and proceeded to wash myself off.

I soon felt much better and was hungry again as my stomach growled for food. Straightening out myself, I presented myself to the battery commander, requested some C rats, and asked if there was any way back to my ship or Dong Tam. He told me that I was on my own; however, supply boats and an occasional chopper passing through might give me a ride back.

As I sat there, I thought maybe this was my chance to get rid of the radio. I hated that job—the radio was cumbersome, and the job itself didn't lend to reacting on my own, as my job was to stay by Reed's side. I wanted to be a rifleman, even though it meant that the security of being an RTO would be forsaken.

Soon there was a fire mission and orders were yelled out to the gunners for a specific grid coordinate. The lazy, relaxed atmosphere had turned 180 degrees as the men hustled and the orders being shouted out were acted upon. The guns fired, and the barges rocked from side to side. I got closer to the guns for a better understanding of the process because I couldn't understand how they could be firing accurately with the rocking of the barges. To my amazement, the lanyard was being pulled when the bubbles on a set of levels were at center. I couldn't believe that they could be that accurate, and I immediately assumed that they must be firing at a good distance from any friendly troops. Soon the mission was over, and the relaxed atmosphere returned. I asked a lieutenant what the fire mission was all about. He informed me that the mission was for Bravo Company, as they were briefly in contact with Charlie. I asked the distance from the troops, and the answer shocked me when he told me they were shooting as close as thirty meters to Bravo Company. My moral plummeted as I realized this was what we got most all of the time for fire support, cannons on barges floating in the river. Amazing!

Early afternoon came around as a brand-new Loach landed on the barge's pad. I saw this as a great opportunity to get a ride on one of these things and asked at first chance for a ride back. The warrant officer told me he was going on a recon mission first and then to Dong Tam. I had lunch and then a major and the pilot came out of the command enclosure waving me to come with them. They occupied the seats in front as I took the right rear seat, and off we went. We flew up river to Ben Tre and then hung a right and descended to the river cutting through Ben Tre. Flying on the deck, the pilot made sharp turns following the river north. As the river bends increased, he would grab the collective, popping the bird up and then turning violently back into the river while lowering the collective for another on the deck look. This was a never-ending process and one hell of a ride, one that my stomach couldn't take as my stomach problems came back. I grabbed the headset that was hung in front of me only to find it not working. I still had some paper and my extra pencil, which I swiftly took out and wrote the words "I'm getting sick" all the while in the acrobatic mission. I leaned over the major and held the note in front of the pilot just as I purged while trying to keep my mouth closed. The force was too much for my lips as my stomach contents were expelled with great force into the cabin and onto the instrument panel while the open-door bird allowed the swirling wind to grab the vomit and throw it around and on everything, including the pilot and the major. The pilot immediately grabbed the collective and climbed to altitude and then flew straight and level to Dong Tam.

We landed, and while the rotors were still whipping around, the pilot jumped out with puke all over him. He turned to me and yelled, "Get the fuck out of my chopper!"

As I found my way back to the ship, I couldn't help but chuckle and at the same time condemn myself for ruining a possibly great ride.

There was always a new experience with each mission. Most were terrifying, but all were a learning experience.

ED WITH POPULAR FORCES AND RECAPTURED TV

One day while strolling through the boonies of the delta, we linked up with a company of Vietnamese Popular Forces, commonly called PFs. To our amazement, they had a TV slung under a bamboo pole. We were at least twenty miles from the nearest electricity and wondered what in the hell a TV was doing down in the delta. It was time for lunch break, so Bravo Company and the PFs joined one another for lunch. The American advisor and I ate together. He told me that the TV had been stolen from an American base camp that had been overrun over two years ago. While he knew his men would not be able to use the TV and that it had no real value to anyone other than those in the rear and near Saigon, he allowed them to encumber themselves with the heavy load strictly for morale purposes, as they were sure it had value. I also couldn't imagine how the VC thought it had any value and why they would have dragged it around all that time.

I soon found out that he was also from Oregon and that he used to hunt in areas familiar to me within the Blue Mountains. I told him that I would get out of the army the week before elk season and that I couldn't wait to buy myself a decent hunting rifle. He promptly informed me that all that has changed. He said that once you've hunted human beings, the thrill of hunting unarmed animals will have lost its challenge and excitement. We argued about that for some time. But he assured me I would be a different person once I got home. I didn't believe him but allowed him to have a say anyhow. I had my picture taken with the men and the TV; we shook hands as we went on our separate ways.

Chapter 5

WALKING SLACK

An M-79 is a very effective and important weapon for the infantryman for many reasons. And because of this, many infantry companies, platoons, and squads had their favorite form of employment for the grenadiers within their various groups.

Second Platoon used the grenadier in the slack position. Slack was the back-up for the point man, walking in the number two position directly behind the point man. The third position was usually a rifleman/ammo bearer for the machine gun, which was usually in the following position. So we had up front in the main four positions all the basic weapons used by the US Infantry.

I had been thinking about my job as RTO for some time. It had its benefits in that you didn't pull point, and if your squad leader became the platoon sergeant, you would go with him. Or maybe even an officer would need your experience. Company CP was a better duty, always in the middle and hardly ever up front. These were serious benefits and not to be taken lightly. On the other hand, the radio was heavy, awkward, bulky, and something of a target. I really wanted to have more to say about my survival, and the awkwardness of the radio was the overpowering consideration. I wanted to be light and fast. Reed was a very proactive squad leader, always moving around and always going to where the action was. When the firing started, Reed got moving, and, of course, that meant that I was right behind him with this awkward load and a job that dealt primarily with the radio and not my rifle. I hated the job, even though it was a great learning experience.

I finally told Reed that I wanted out of the RTO position, and within a few days, he had me take over for Weber our grenadier who was going home to a dying father. I really wanted out of the RTO position, but I considered the M-79 a less than an ideal weapon, and one could easily see that the grenadier had a heavy load. Reluctantly, I went to the barge to find the gear of the outgoing grenadier. Weber was a big man, and his rucksack of M-79 rounds was in line with his stature. I didn't know how much it weighed, but I knew it was more than the previous radio gear I had just gotten used to. It was a metal-framed canvas pack that was as full as it could get with forty millimeter HE rounds making up the majority of the load. The HE round looks like a large, blown-up .22 caliber short round that had a grenade-like head, full of explosives and shrapnel. It traveled at about 250 meters a second, slowly enough that one could watch the round as it traveled through its trajectory. There was a total of sixty HE rounds, ten shotgun rounds, and ten white phosphorus (WP or Willy Peter) that had a parachute attached to the round. The WP round would shoot out, and then the parachute would employ at about two hundred feet. It was mainly used for night illumination. Also, a cloth bandolier of HE rounds would be tied around my waist for easy access, as the rounds in the pack were only accessible when off your back. HE grenades, my canteens, and smoke grenades were wrapped around the bottom tubing of the pack to top off the load.

I took down the single-shot M-79 and immediately became concerned that there was no sight attached. I began looking around in the conex for sights. No sights to be found.

The only time I had fired the M-79 was at Ft. Lewis, and that was with sights. I was impressed at the accuracy of the grenade launcher, and I wanted it with a sight. The sight was one that flipped up when needed for distance. You moved the sight up to the appropriate marks corresponding to the distance, and you were good to go.

I went back on the ship and found all the other grenadiers in hopes that one of them had an extra. To my amazement none of them used a sight and didn't know where any were.

They all told me that a sight wasn't necessary, but I just passed it off thinking, "What do they know—they're all probably city guys who don't know marksmanship from marbles."

So I went to the company clerk/supply sergeant and demanded one. I told them I was going to refuse the mission unless one was found and that was that.

To my disappointment, one was found in short order. I was now a grenadier and not really happy about it, but this was the army after all, and I knew I'd have to suck it up and do my best once again.

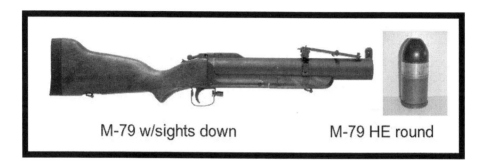

M-79 w/sights down   M-79 HE round

The next morning was my first as a grenadier. We were inserted by Hueys into a large paddy and immediately began moving toward the nearest wood line. I was then ordered by Reed to start prepping the wood line. As I guesstimated the distance and rolled my sight up, all the other grenadiers had already shot two rounds out apiece. I fired my first round out, which promptly hit the ground halfway to the wood line. I then made another adjustment while walking toward the objective and fired it; it was only three-fourths of the way to the wood line. I was now really embarrassed and pissed off about my inefficiency, the next round landed to hell and gone well into the wood line. I ripped the sight off my weapon and threw it into the wet paddy. This was going to take some practice, I thought.

The beauty of the slow round is that you could follow its trajectory like one would an arrow shot from a bow. Each time you shot and followed the trajectory, the computer between your ears took note for the next round and distance. In no time at all, one was reasonably accurate and much faster than with a movable sight. I would also learn to put the next few rounds within easy access. One would be in the band around my camouflage helmet covering and the other two in my two front pockets.

The M-79 round itself would not become armed until it had made a certain number of revolutions or traveled about twenty-five meters in distance. This was a gray area, as twenty-five meters could easily be too close and return shrapnel back to the grenadier or anyone else within close proximity. One grenadier in Third Platoon had wounded himself three or four times just since I had been there. I had also been told that someone before me had shot a VC straight in the chest at a close distance, and although the round didn't go off, the VC was dead from the damage of the penetration to his chest from the heavy round.

There was one great satisfaction about the M-79 in that it gave great pleasure to the eyes with its explosive hit. You could definitely tell where you hit, unlike a regular ball round from a rifle. I couldn't wait to hit my first VC with a round square in the chest; it was going to be a good show.

The grenadier would get in plenty of practice prepping wood lines and firing at bunker openings and any other possible ambush points throughout the day. The job of following the point man was the worst, however. Everything had to be checked out, which meant going inside the hooch's and the bunkers. Because of my limited range, I would have to pull off to the side and watch for longer-range danger while the others behind me came up and helped out the point man. Once clear, we went on our way, watching every step for booby traps and ambushes. I was unsettled to find out that the way you handled the possible booby trap locations was to walk around them, as stopping to check them out would be too time-consuming. This revelation meant that I had been subject to booby traps all the time before. Being back in the line, I had assumed that by the time I came through, all was clear. This practice would prove to give many a soldier back in the line his share of booby trap death and destruction. Time and demand of movement didn't allow for in-depth inspection. The more slowly you went, the easier it was for Charlie to ambush. Damned if you do and damned if you don't.

One of the advantages of having the grenadier up close was that the explosion of the round and its cloud of explosive power could be used as a marking round. This was especially useful for those further back that were not able to define the exact position of the enemy fire.

We had been humping hard all morning in what was your typical hot, humid Mekong day, so a lunch break was welcome. We sat along the edge of a coconut grove with a rice paddy to our front that had a graveyard in it just feet from the grove. After chowing down and taking a temporary horizontal position, the typical conversations came up: I'm gonna buy me a Corvette when I get home; I'm gonna marry my girlfriend; I'm gonna see the world; I'd give anything for a glass of ice water; God, a cold watermelon would be great, and so on.

While enjoying our shade and lack of movement, a Tiger Scout went into the graveyard, soon came back and went directly to the CO. The CO then ordered Second Platoon to investigate the Tiger Scout's claim that there were weapons buried in some of the graves. Two-six and I walked over with the Tiger Scout, and he pointed to a couple of graves and said, "There are buried weapons in these graves."

The decision was soon made by the powers that be to blow up some graves and check them out. Two-six didn't want to have more than one of us blowing the graves as miscommunications could be hazards between those throwing the grenades into the graves. The job was mine because he knew that I was the son of a funeral director. This didn't make me happy, and I didn't have any real idea as to how to do this. We hadn't had any classes on this subject.

I decided that I'd dig a hole in the corner of each grave at an inward angle and then throw in a grenade, and then a mud ball on top for backing. The graves had a foot of dirt on top above the water level. We only had an entrenching tool or two in the entire company because any hole you would dig would fill up with water in no time. Besides there was water to hide or lie in everywhere in the delta. This ground was wet and muddy, making the digging tough and useless. I dug my first hole, pulled the pin and threw the grenade in with a scoop of mud right behind it. I then ran like hell through the mud. I only got about ten to fifteen feet from the grave when it blew. I looked back only to see large mud clods flying up into the air and then falling as I dodged the ten-pound mud balls. I couldn't believe the power the little grenades had; they moved hundreds of pounds of mud, opening up the grave and its contents. As I peered into the grave, I could see that there were no weapons as the smell hit me in the face, making my eyes water and my nose pucker.

This rancid process was repeated time after time as the security slowly but surely began moving further away from the putrid smell. I was getting plummeted by the wet, muddy, smelly clods of mud and body parts. An army photographer took advantage of the scene and was right there clicking away at the sight of me running each time, with the mud flying. I was getting tired physically and was taking a short break as a Huey came overhead at treetop level. Just as I looked up at Colonel Pete's command chopper (CC), the pilot ran into the top of a coconut tree. The treetop wedged itself between the fuselage and the right side landing skid as the bird made an immediate uncontrolled 180 degree turn about the treetop, as the tree bent and then left the top leaves inside the bird and on top of Pistol Pete's lap. The pilot, having made a miraculous effort at saving the bird, then grabbed the collective and gained altitude as Pistol Pete threw the last of the coconut leaves out of his ship. He then circled around the scene with a hanging broken skid while talking to Captain Kincheloe (Bravo 6). He ordered the mission of excavation by grenade ceased. I was one happy, tired smelly mud ball.

When I reunited with the guys, my putrid scent was not appreciated. I was not the most popular guy in the platoon, and a fair distance was given to me.

Pistol Pete landed. The bird left and Pistol Pete remained behind. He was our new battalion commander, and he wanted to get to know each company in his command by spending some time walking with each man. This practice was totally foreign to us. We had never seen a field-grade officer in the bush. Rainville, our brigade CO. (brigade commander) flew so high that you couldn't hit him with an M-16 if you tried, just one of the many reasons we had no respect for the man. But Pistol Pete was obviously of a different cut and was going to prove it.

We soon headed out, walking parallel to the river on a nice, often used trail, what we called a hard ball. Second Platoon would pull drag with Pistol Pete armed only with his 1911 .45 caliber pistol started as the last man. He introduced himself to each soldier, asked his name, and maybe even started some small talk.

It wasn't long until he was with me. He had no more than said hi when all hell broke loose from across the river. We both took cover behind a dried mud pile (the remnants of a bunker) and started returning fire. Charlie's fire soon slowed, and I quit firing because I now carried only fifty rounds of HE for my

M-79 grenade launcher and the river kept the enemy from any serious attack. Pistol Pete immediately got on my ass, ordering me to keep returning fire. He said, "Keep firing! I'll get you more ammo if you need it." Soon the firefight was over, and we had artillery pounding their position. Pistol Pete said, "I'll get you guys all the ammo you will need—that's a promise." He then walked on to the next guy as he made his way up the line.

I was impressed. The man wasn't afraid to stick his head up during a firefight and return fire, and he made me feel much better about getting low on ammo. We all felt a little bit better; morale had never been this high.

Pistol Pete made his rounds, and we soon were configuring for a PZ for his departure. Pistol Pete was hanging with the company CP when he got a call from the brigade CO. The call was on the company CO's radio, which had a speaker attached to it. We all could hear his voice loud and clear as Colonel Rainville carried on: "What the fuck are you doing down there with those guys. You stupid bastard! Your job isn't down there, you fuckin' idiot! Get the fuck out of there and now!" He went on and on calling our beloved leader a fucking moron, and it was heard by all. We were all embarrassed for the lieutenant colonel and pretended not to hear. Our already low opinion of Colonel Rainville just took a dive to a new low. What a cocksucker, I thought. Here's this chickenshit calling a real man every name in the book. It pissed me off! Rainville was supposed to be a West Point grad but sure as hell didn't act like it. I now felt sorry for anyone under his command.

There were many instances that I remember as a "thumper man" (grenadier) but probably none as vivid as what happened on this evening:

We had just finished a day of humping our asses off with only a couple of short firefights with no particular pertinence. We had a fifteen-foot canal to cross before setting up for the resupply chopper and our RON (Remain Over Night) location. We were the last squad to cross the river, and I was dry, an unusual situation for the delta. While we watched the rest of the company cross, I was busy working a leaning coconut tree back and forth in hopes it would fall, giving me a bridge to cross, thus keeping me dry. All the others had crossed when the tree finally fell, giving me hopes of staying dry for a full night—a real treat and one that was a rarity.

We got our supplies from the resupply ship along with a sniper team and then moved to our RON, which was wooded on two opposing ends and open paddy on the other two sides. I was on a wooded side of the perimeter. Every night the cardboard from the C rats would be given to a different person. I needed the cardboard to make myself a bed off the damp ground so that I could enjoy my dryness. I haggled and begged, but it took $20 to get the cardboard; that worked for me, as money meant nothing anyhow. As I prepared my lair of cardboard and banana leaf, I was the only one in the company standing up when I noticed movement a few dikes away. It was two VC with AK-47s creeping into position for ambush at minimum M-79 range. As I reached down for the M-79, I was thinking, Should I shoot one or go for both? As I rose up ready to fire, I had made the decision to shoot between and go for both as the dike wall was only inches from their bodies. I launched the round perfectly between the two and watched it explode as I hit the dirt for whatever more was awaiting us. I had no more than hit the ground when all hell broke loose on the western ninety-degree open flank. I didn't have a good line of sight on the action but could tell that there was an intense firefight going on between First Platoon and some charging VC in the open. Soon the green tracers started to give way to red tracers as those still alive retreated to their wood line while leaving their dead and wounded to lie in the wet paddy. As the firefight started to wane, a female Vietnamese bolted from the only hooch within our perimeter. I heard the CO yell, "Stop her!" and then saw a burst of tracers tear through her body as she fell. I then heard the CO say, "Goddamn it! I didn't mean for you to kill her, only tackle her." She was too far gone to tackle, and no one was going to expose themselves running after her in the middle of a firefight anyhow. After all, women fought alongside the men in the VC ranks. There was no response, and no more about the subject was raised as the firefight slowed to a stop. I would, however, always remember that incident as she was the first female I'd seen shot. Not the last, but the first. We bedded down on full alert. The night was slow except for two rounds fired by the snipers at probing VC. The tide rose until all of us, including me, were sitting up with the water at armpit level. Another night in the beautiful countryside of the delta, soaking wet.

Ed on his C-Rat cardboard bed

Another day went by, and as evening set in, B-6 ordered a temporary defensive/ambush perimeter next to the river, which was flowing parallel to us and to the south. We were in the Kein Hoa Province, which we knew well in that it wasn't our favorite place. It was our usual false night perimeter, which gave all a chance to check out our equipment and grab a bite to eat before our next move to our RON location.

As darkness set in on the moonless, clear night, we were ordered to pack up and shift our positions a hundred meters or so further up the river. Our platoon was to secure the corner up and parallel to the river. Our main position was to be the corner where the river and the jungle trail met, a position manned by a machine gunner, radioman, grenadier, and the normal riflemen with Claymores set directed up the trail and parallel to the river.

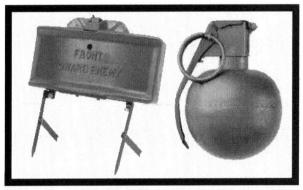

Claymore & Baseball Grenade

I would be setting up more inland, twenty meters from the corner position with two riflemen and me with my M-79. As the darkness set full on with the normal tension and awareness of all night positions, those not on guard duty pretended to get some sleep—a pretense that would not last long as the sounds of the "fuck-you lizards" gave way to the thumping sound of a one-hit engine in the distance. Before long Reed came over to my position and asked me to join the corner position. He was taking one man from each position and reinforcing the positions along the river, as were the other squad leaders and platoon sergeants.

As I joined the position, the engine thumps were getting closer as we began setting the ambush. All river travel in the area had a curfew after dark. So this one was free game. As the boat came closer and closer with each thump of the engine we all squirmed like piglets in the mud lining up in the same direction waiting for a tit. There was an air of excitement as we all knew that this should be a piece of cake and maybe even a little exiting with little possibility of repercussion. The thumping continued and became louder and louder as the boat slowly plied its way down the river. The tide was high, and the river itself was rising, along with the tension and the reality that something could go wrong, e.g., a contingency of VC could also be behind this boat or in another being towed. In fact, we really didn't know how many boats were coming or how big. The river was only twenty-five to thirty meters wide, and most boats on these rivers were only sampans with small engines at most. However, I knew that the sound of this engine was from a larger than normal sampan. I had not heard this sound for many a year. It was from my days as a child and the ending of the (Johnny Popper) John Deere, one-hit engine era.

The coming of the boat seemed to take an eternity, and then it rounded the corner above us as the thumping sound became dominate. We could only see its outline with the Starlight scope at first, and then a growing shadow loomed over the slivers of lighter shadows among the coconut tree outlines. This fucking thing was huge; I'd not seen a boat this size on such a small river. It was fifteen to twenty feet wide and forty feet long with an upper deck and no doubt a lower deck. It took up half of the river.

As it approached us on the other side of the river, our aim became focused and then the order to fire was given. I dumped an HE round into its side as the others unloaded full bore, as tracers dominated the scene. Because of the tracers' light and the flash of the M-79s, for an instant you could see the details of the craft and the inhabitants; it was loaded with live bodies and at this time of night--definitely VC. About then a secondary explosion engulfed the entire boat in fire as I reloaded. The fireball lit up the entire river as burning bodies and debris flew through the air. In amazement I never fired another round as it became apparent that that nobody was going to survive as the small ship sank rapidly and the fire spread to the water as it and the burning bodies floated by the rest of the company and disappeared down river. As suddenly as it had started, it ended as small snakes of fire dissipated into the downward flow and eddies of the river. The night became dark and still as we crawled back to our original positions and pretended to catch some sleep as though nothing had happened. The fuck you lizards continued their surreal fuckyou, fuckyou call as the night progressed.

M-60 Machine Gunner | Riv-Div deep into the Delta

Chapter **6**

W A L K I N G   P O I N T /
H U M A N   M I N E
D E T E C T O R

My time walking slack was perfect training for the job of walking point, a position I dreaded coming my way and prayed never would. While I was honored by Reed choosing me to take the job, I was also shaken, not visibly, but bothered at any rate. My actions from now on could cause dismemberment or death for those behind me and myself.

You're very alone in most of the decisions you make while walking point. Decisions came literally with every step. Every action, every movement, and every visual choice of every minute of every day could have major ramifications. My first few meters were at best slow while I tried to manage my senses to a new degree of acuteness. You must be able to juggle all senses at one time or your demise will come sooner than later. Once again the butterflies of inevitable death showed up when least needed. I'd long realized that I probably wasn't going to survive the war because of the way things had been going, and now that reality was making itself known once again in the form of a tight stomach.

Booby traps in the delta were abundant, and more than once I had heard that they accounted for close to 40 percent of all grunt casualties—a statistic I would not challenge. And now I was the one expected to first detect their existence or possible existence. Every step was chosen and every section of trail was reckoned by the eyes, as one approaches the next section of the puzzle. Any irregularity in the trail surface was acknowledged and noted of and then demanded a decision before taking the next step, all while scanning the surrounding area for possible ambush sites and irregularities that change with every step.

You don't have the time to check out every leaf, soil disturbance, or stick lying on the trail, so you plod on, stepping carefully around the possible dangerous areas while scanning quickly for any trip wires or pressure triggers. Every place the trail or dike has been mended is suspect, every overhanging limb is suspect, and every mislaid tuft of grass is suspect. In short you'll never in your life be so aware and acute of your senses for such a length of time. It must be like walking down to the OK Corral for hours upon hours, day in and day out.

Booby traps came in all shapes and sizes. Only the human mind limited the types of booby traps and the means of triggering them. The VC were very creative.

We had the "toe popper," a common one and almost impossible to detect. This booby trap was usually below the ground, and the most common one was an old casing with a live round inside. A soldier stepping on it would pressure the live round to a pin or pressure point within the larger (spent) outer casing.

Later when I was a platoon sergeant, Seamster's squad was checking out a hooch on our way. As I approached Seamster, a pop suddenly put Seamster's knee into his chest. Shaken up but still standing, Seamster turned around to see the new hole in the hard-packed ground. We all chose our steps back to the trail as Seamster sat down to check out the sole of his boot. I looked and couldn't find any obvious holes. However, Seamster knew there was now something wrong with his foot, as the aching pain came on. I searched the bottom of his foot along with Doc and once again saw nothing. As Doc pressed the foot with his thumb, searching for damage, a drop of blood oozed out of his sole from a tiny hole previously not seen. We got Seamster's boot back on. He was walking, but slowly. A Dustoff was called and was shortly on station as we set up the PZ for Seamster. I walked him to the chopper and said, "See you in a week or two" then grabbed a business card from the copilot's outstretched hand, which headlined, "Have Dustoff, will travel." We never saw Seamster again in Vietnam. He had received the million-dollar wound.

Medevac/Dustoff

Another favorite of the VC was the grenade. Sometimes it was deployed in a clump of mud. As the mud dried, the pin was pulled, allowing for the now dirt clod to keep it from exploding until a soldier, child, woman, or civilian clumsily knocked the dried dirt loose from the handle. Just as often the grenade was set with a trip wire stretched across the trail, which would pull the pin and activate the fuse. Oftentimes you could feel the trip wire as you tripped it. If it was a grenade, you could sometimes elude the blast and shrapnel as most grenades had a five-second fuse, giving you time for a lunge and a low profile. When not noticed by the tripper, it would be awaiting the guys five seconds behind. In this case, the damage could be horrific and deadly.

Another form of booby trap setting was the "daisy chain," a method of connecting multiple charges of various types (grenades, claymores, artillery shells, and handmade charges) to one another at specific distances, usually along the trail where it would do the most damage. The first victim would trip the wire, which in turn would trip the other mines behind that he had already passed.

As infantrymen, we felt very alone and separated from most of the support personnel in Vietnam. But we always got a lift when the dog teams showed up, as they were some of the few soldiers who understood what we went through, and, conversely, we were some of the few who knew what burdens they carried. We looked at them as brave men, as most of the time they would take over walking point (the worst job of being infantry), and the point man, of course, would welcome the break. The dog teams also made us feel a little safer from the deadly booby traps so prevalent in the Mekong Delta. One dog handler and his dog will remain in my memory forever—a hell of a nice guy we had worked with before as a tracker.

We were inserted onto the island known by all in the 9th ID9th as VC Island—an island of only a few hundred acres, no more than a mile long. It sat in the Song My Tho just south of the village of My Tho in the Kein Hoa province. It was also visible from the shore of our division base camp (Dong Tam). The island was known for its booby traps and as a place the VC set up mortar attacks against Dong Tam.

The dog was trained as both a tracker and a booby trap/explosive dog, and as such was a great asset to our company. As we proceeded down the trails through the coconut groves, dikes, and jungle, the dog was becoming a concern as he was balking and false pointing every few meters. The entire company would stop as we in the point element would get on our hands and knees and search the area to no avail. The handler was getting more and more upset with the dog as we slowly progressed. Finally, in an overgrown coconut grove, the dog stopped and pointed. The handler, frustrated by all the false alarms, kicked his dog in the butt. A chain of mines went off for thirty feet, probably three or four mines in all. But the most damaging was the lead charge most probably a 105 arty shell.

As luck would have it, I was back a ways and just missed the flying shrapnel on both sides of me. I was luckier than those in front of me and behind me. We all hit the ground as usual and then the moans could be heard. Doc Schuebel and I ran to the point to find the dog and handler shredded. The handler had both legs ripped so badly that for all practical purposes, he would be an amputee, but that was the least of his problems—his intestines were now on the outside. His multiple other wounds were now insignificant. As Doc bent down, the handler asked him how his dog was and then requested that his dog be treated first. I couldn't believe this guy was so lucid; shock didn't appear to be a factor with him.

Realizing that Doc had his hands full, I walked back along the trail, checking out all who were wounded. Everybody seemed to be taking care of one another, and most wounds seemed non-life threatening for the immediate future. However, there was one of the FNGs raising hell, the last one to get wounded in the daisy chain. He was a big kid, six feet four or so, and looked like a defensive end, but his actions were those of a lesser man, as he threw a whining fit, demanding Doc's attention. Doc and the Third Platoon medic weren't paying any attention to his lower-grade wounds. I tried to settle him down and get him to allow me to check his wounds. He finally took his hand from the side of his neck where a large gash showed itself. I knew this area of the neck well from my days living and working with my father in the funeral business. The muscle was torn badly from a slashing piece of shrapnel, but the carotid artery was not torn at all, a wound I knew not to be life threatening with minor medical care. However, my assurance of this observation was not consoling to him at all, as he continued to go into shock. I asked those around him to keep his mind busy and off the wound as I went back up to the point element where Doc and the dog handler were. I gave Doc a sit-rep (Situation Report) on those behind as he continued to comfort the still lucid dog handler who was still worried about his now dead dog.

I returned to the neck wound only to find the soldier being taken hard by shock. The efforts of those with him weren't working. I knew it was time to get physical with him with slaps to the face and loud, corrosive words. I didn't want to lower his head any more than possible due to the bleeding wound. The loud noise and slapping seemed to work, as he appeared to acknowledge me. We kept it up, bringing him back to an acceptable awareness. As I stood up and looked over to Doc, I couldn't help but acknowledge the situation: here were two wounded men, one critical and one slight, yet the effects of shock weren't where they were supposed to be. The human mind is a funny thing. Just goes to show you how mental shock is.

All were dusted off within a half hour, and all were alive when they left. The dog handler, as suspected, didn't make it to the other end of the flight. I couldn't help but think about his attitude and ability to fight off the effects of shock, even though he was around strangers. We were lucky; we would die among close friends!

Booby traps were responsible for over one-third of our casualties and became a part of our days and ways. Gruesome wounds kept reminding us that there were worse things than dying. And we knew that the point man had the best chance of all to be taken by this cowardly/indiscriminate manner of terrorism. I could understand the enemy trying in any way to kill us, but to subject their own to such atrocities on these public trails was beyond my American way of thinking.

A prisoner who was caught rigging a booby trap was lucky to make it to division interrogation and was often beaten to within an inch of his life.

My favorite booby trap story was about a time when a couple of us rounded a corner in heavy grass only to spot a couple of VC preparing a booby trap. We got low, which caught the attention of others, including Gaa, the Second Platoon Tiger Scout (A VC who defected to help the U.S.). As Gaa approached, he held his hand on my M-16 as if to say "hold it a minute." He started talking with the VC, as though they were old friends talking, but their attitude changed as Gaa purposefully said something to startle them. They looked up just in time to blow themselves up with their own booby trap. Not a shot was fired. I asked Gaa what he said to them. Gaa said, "What's going on?" They replied with eyes on their work, "Don't bother us—we're at a critical moment." Gaa replied, "I guess I'll have to kill you then." That's when they realized that Gaa wasn't a fellow VC; they broke their concentration, resulting in their deaths.

TIGER SCOUTS & ED

The whole idea of having to be the first to walk through an area, be it dense jungle, broken groves, or open rice paddies and then have to watch for booby traps and at the same time keep from walking into an ambush was daunting. Yet I had the luck of always seeing them first or at least before the trap was to be sprung. Many times I had the luck of being the ambusher instead of the ambushed. I got a wonderful feeling when I put one over on them. I had good people behind me in Ramos, the machine gunner, and especially in my friend JR, who was never far behind and was always in tune with my actions and reactions. He seemed always to be there within a second or two, even when he was three or four men back.

It got to the point that if I thought I could wait a second before acting, I would, just so that JR would have time to join me. With him by my side and the others close behind, including Reed, we were a terror to the hearts of the VC. Vicious were we, with no slack given. Many times I would charge a bunker with him by my side, firing on the run, reading each other's moves, instantly knowing each other's magazine load and position, and killing the bastards at our earliest chance. We grew to understand that to wait was to lose fire superiority and opportunity. With the old guys and Reed behind us, we knew that a mistake could be forgiven with their help.

As point man, I was the first one to walk through the hooch's and see the fear on the faces of the civilians. Many times they just froze with eyes wide open and with a begging fear on their faces as they clutched their children tightly. Some would hide in the bunker (all hooch's had one) with fear to come out and fear to stay. Some were VC, and some weren't. These were the worst of times. Without knowing who or what was in there, I couldn't talk them out or take them out with a grenade. My safety and the safety of the men behind me depended on me making the path safe. Only when I thought that there was a chance that the inhabitants were scared civilians would I enter the bunker on my own with pistol drawn—a God-fearing moment to say the least and one I did not relish. Nevertheless, I got a feeling of pride when I knew I had saved the woman and children.

Bunkers were everywhere in the delta, and the ones scattered outside the hooch's along the trail side gave special fear to all. Most were vacant, but all had to be acted upon as though they were occupied. My normal way of dealing with them was to circle behind the bunker with the weapons of others trained on the opening. I would throw a grenade in after counting three seconds off the fuse. However, after a couple of grenades broke the sides of the bunkers out and threatened to give me some of my own shrapnel back, I decided to stand on the top of the bunker, where the thickness was improved, and then throw in the grenade. While doing this often gave me a small boost in the air and might even collapse the roof, causing me to fall in, it became my choice of actions. Later, when concussion grenades became available, I started to use them constantly, especially after my first kill with one when I realized that the concussion alone would bring blood to the eyes, ears, nose, and mouth of the enemy in a paralyzing, deadly manner. While the concussion grenade gave me a little less fear of eating my own shrapnel, it was not a popular weapon because of its lack of versatility. After all, it didn't work well when the VC were in the open. Paper shrapnel doesn't do a good job of killing at a distance. So I went back to the baseball grenades, only to find out later that there was rash of these grenades going off within three seconds instead of at five seconds. Fuck, what a deal! Damned if you do, and damned if you don't.

Then there was the daily river crossing, where the point man would be the first to test the currents that would take many of us. Once on the other bank, you really felt naked and alone until the slack man showed up and then the others who then gave you the power to continue.

| It's difficult to make time in terrain like this! | Another canal to cross |

It was not uncommon to see VC appear through the foliage only to disappear, never to be seen again. I caught many running beside or ahead of us at a distance in an attempt to get ahead for an ambush or to get word to other VC elements. They seemed always to know when we were around. It's hard to be quiet when there are forty to eighty men behind you loaded down with gear. We didn't have the advantage that recon units such as the Long Range Recon Patrol (LRRPs) or the SEALs had in that they were few (harder to see and hear) and lightly loaded down, with no constant demands for making distance.

Why I would fire on certain VC and not others was usually because of the effect and or chances of having an effect. However, if I thought I had a chance of nailing one of the pricks, I'd take it. I didn't mind missing now and then, especially if I thought they had already noticed us anyhow.

Walking point on night movements was the worst because you couldn't see for shit, and you would just have to resign yourself to the fact that if there was a booby trap, you'd just have to eat it and that if you walked up on someone, he had the advantage. Once again, we weren't LRRPs. Besides, our job wasn't to recon; it was to hunt them down and kill them, and if you're going to have that job description, you'd better be of size.

There were some good times on point, such as when we came upon a hooch where a woman was ready to give birth. She thought hell had descended upon her at first and then realized that Doc was there to help. Captain Kincheloe decided to hold up and secure the area until the birth was complete, we all dug into our pockets and left a pile of C rats for the new baby. Then we all went on our way, leaving life instead of death. We were proud of ourselves for putting the mission on hold and for our generosity of C rats for the special moment even though we were now low on rations.

I can only think of one funny point man story: A point man was rounding a curve in the trail when he suddenly came upon a VC walking in the opposite direction. Both startled, they raised their rifles and unloaded their magazines at one another only twenty feet apart. Both still standing and untouched, they just looked at one another in amazement and instead of seeing who could reload the fastest, they both chose to turn and run. The point man's eyes were the size of half dollars as he rounded the corner looking for backup. After hearing the story, I laughed my ass off. Lucky men, they both were.

This time period, however, would be some of the hardest for me to recall specific events, probably because of the intensity of it all. I do remember the day I was taken off point and always will!

Elements of 5/16th VC Bn. Ben Tre

Chapter 7

SNIPER SCHOOL

In my third month in Vietnam, I was still trying to make sense of who and what I was, but mostly trying to figure out how I'm going to survive. Combat was so much more brutal and physically demanding than I ever imagined. The reality of my death became more evident every day that I walked the trails and paddies of the Mekong. I seriously thought of reenlisting for a safer job, but my pride just wouldn't allow me to go there. Then, out of the blue, the company clerk came into the berthing area and asked if anyone wanted to volunteer to go to the new Sniper School. He was greeted with mostly laughs and chuckles and a few "fuck you" remarks before heading back to his office. But the thought stayed with me for hours as I analyzed the difference between being a sniper and a line grunt. The Infantry Company plodded its way through the bush with increasing sounds of loose gear, footsteps, radio conversation, and the clanking of weapons. The more men, the more sound, I surmised. The movement made by eighty men made it eighty times likelier that you would be seen, as opposed to the movement of one or two. Besides, snipers were stationary, right? Sniper School also meant being out of the field for a period of time, thereby increasing my chances of survival, I further surmised. So within no time, I was in the company clerk's office asking Bucky to sign me up. I only had to get Captain Kincheloe's permission, and Bucky was ready to call the battalion with my name.

When I got back from my next mission, Bucky told me I had orders to be aboard the USS *Benewah* at 0330 hours the next day. He arranged a shuttle boat for me, and I was on my way as a lone passenger on a twenty-man boat. It was a very dark night with no wind, just the diesel smoke hugging and rolling on the river as we passed the other ships in silence.

I disembarked onto the *USS Benewah's* attached barge to a surreal setting of stationary shadows being contorted by the diesel exhaust coming from the side of the ship about head high. It was so dark I could barely make out where I was and then voices from the shadows came "You here for the shuttle to Dong Tam?" I walked over to three who were sitting with their backs to a conex. "I'm here to get a ride to Bear Cat," I said. They also were there for Sniper School and awaiting a ride to Dong Tam and then to the airport for the flight to Bear Cat. They were from the other companies of the 3/60th, and all like me had some time in the field. One in particular struck me as out of place. He was an older man in his late twenties by the name of Waldron who was rather opinionated. We were all in the same wonderment of what we were getting into, and so we presupposed as to what was going down as we awaited our boat.

The Sniper School was a creation of our commanding general, MG Julian J. Ewell. Prior to assuming command of the 9TH ID, Ewell persuaded the army to direct the US Army Marksmanship Training Unit (USAMTU) to create a sniper training course. The USAMTU was made up of the army's best competitive shooters. Once in Vietnam and with the 9th ID, Ewell convinced the army to start up the Sniper School within the 9th ID. The USAMTU, under the direction of Major Powell and his eight NCOs, moved fast to supply the school with the necessary equipment, men, and weapons. The National Match M-14 was the basis for the XM21 (their basic sniper rifle), of which the school had only fifty-four, meaning that there would be only fifty-four snipers maximum to begin with. The 9th ID was then in Bear Cat, east of Saigon, which was its divisional headquarters then. There, the engineers made a rifle range with target berms at three hundred meters, five hundred meters, seven hundred meters, and nine hundred meters, with a firing line to rival any in the United States. The NCOs themselves went out on sniper missions with great success to further fine tune the program before training the first class in October of 1968. Our group was to be in the third class.

As we arrived in Bear Cat, it was immediately obvious that the base camp had been taken over by the Black Panther Division of the Royal Thai Army. The 9th ID had moved to the delta, and Dong Tam was now its division headquarters. However, the Sniper School remained in Bear Cat until the new range in Dong

Tam could be built. The school was located in the corner of the camp close to the range, which was outside the protected perimeter of the base camp.

We were given a decent barracks (for Vietnam) to call home. There were about thirty of us billeted together. We each grabbed a bunk, slid our duffel bags under the beds, and were soon in a classroom for our orientation. Major Powell introduced the team to us and gave us a brief outline of what to expect. We were all very impressed by the caliber of these men. Most were designated as Distinguished Riflemen, were members of the President's 100, and had many medals and records in national and international competition. Our training was first and foremost all about shooting ability. We were to use only open sights for the first week, as good basic form and practices were the first goal. Shot groups, not bulls (Bulls- eyes), were the school's first goal for us as marksmen. We would shoot all day and have classes at night. At the end of the week, a shoot off in which only the best ten shots would be remain was a reminder that this was not a given. We were to be in the classroom bright and early from which we would immediately go to the range and start our training. My first pleasant observation was that we were treated as soldiers, not raw trainees. Discipline was not needed here. We were all combat soldiers with CIBs, and you either paid attention or you were asked to leave; this was the gist of things. There was no need for tight military structure as such, and the relaxed but demanding was to be the norm. We were there to learn.

After a short morning class, we walked to the range with our new weapons where we broke into two teams and cleared the range, as each team patrolled one side. My team was led by a Staff Sergeant Gapol, a wide-shouldered man of Hawaiian descent. As we walked past the three hundred-meter berm, a peacock jumped up in right to left flight. Gapol raised his open-sighted M-16 and dropped him with one shot. Dinner for the NCOs was to be interesting, I thought. We knew these guys could shoot, but this shot by Gapol was amazing. I was now really looking forward to my training!

Our only target all day and weeklong was the three-hundred-meter, eighteen-inch-wide torso silhouettes. Our instructors spent some time refining our prone position, and we were off and shooting. After each round, our instructors critiqued our techniques. We shot three rounds, and then the target would be pulled down and marked with three-inch black markers for each round. Then the target would be raised for just a few second, then pulled again and raised again, ready for the next three rounds. Our front sights covered about twenty-one inches at three hundred meters and at first the effort seemed daunting, probably never tried before by most of us in our previous years. Slowly but surely, the shot groups tightened, and most were on paper. We broke for lunch and returned to shoot the rest of the day until dinnertime. After dinner we had class. On the fourth day my target was pulled and raised with only one marker attached. My heart sank; I wondered how could I have missed with two of my rounds. My instructor radioed the target crew wanting to confirm the marker. The word came back that "All rounds were inside a three-inch group." The instructor announced to the rest of the cadre that he had a shooter here. I was the first of the group to have achieved this feat. I was jacked now that I knew I had a chance of getting through this course.

For six days this schedule repeated itself. On the seventh day as we sat in the bleachers at the range, we were told that today was to be a shoot off and that no more than ten of us would be staying for the remainder of the course. All were now nervous as we took our positions and began the contest. There were, however, a couple of the guys who were having second thoughts about being a sniper. They probably purposely threw their chances that day just to go back to where they came from.

We broke for lunch and were assembled afterward for the results. If your name was called out, you were staying; if not, you were headed back to the Mekong that afternoon. As the senior NCO called out our names one by one, I was counting with my fingers behind my back. When he got to seven or eight, my doubts about whether or not I was going started creeping in. Number nine came and went, and I was about to panic. And then the NCO announced that the top shooter of the day was Spc. Ed Eaton. My lungs filled with air as I smiled and turned to wish the others good-bye and good luck. We were given the afternoon off, and I floated back to the barracks to relax.

The evening class was all about our daytime scope. It was called the ART (Automatic Range Telescopic) scope. It was a three-by-nine-power Redfield with a cam that increased the holdover for the ballistics of the Match 7.62mm round;

as the power was increased, it kept the crosshairs on the target for point of aim/point of impact as long as the reticles were properly placed. It was made specifically for the program, and the ballistics of the National Match rounds that we used. It also had two stadia lines on the horizontal crosshair and the vertical crosshair. The vertical lines were meant to measure thirty inches, or the approximate distance from a Vietnamese crotch to the top of the head. The horizontal lines were meant to measure the distance of the average entrance of a grass hooch, or sixty inches. One would crowd the stadia lines to where they fit these measurements, and theoretically one would be ranged and on target as one increased the power. We used this scope the majority of the time for the remainder of our training. Our classes covered all that one could think of in the world of marksmanship, and as we progressed the instructors covered things such as calling in artillery, communications, camouflage, stealth, ballistics, navigation, and range estimation.

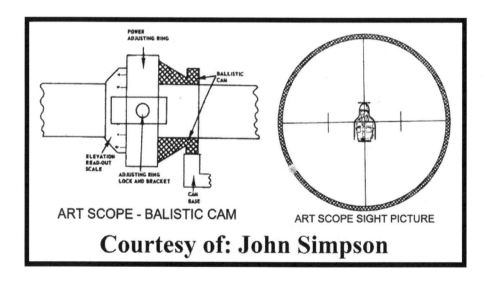

ART SCOPE - BALISTIC CAM   ART SCOPE SIGHT PICTURE

Courtesy of: John Simpson

Day after day, we shot all day long and had classes in the evening, giving us very little time for recreation. There was no EM club for us to get into trouble, so that left us with making friends with the Thai soldiers. The language barrier made communication a little difficult, but if one tried hard enough, he could acquire some kind of alcohol from the Thais. I was in one barracks of Thais and noticed a pot bong sitting out in plain sight, as though smoking marijuana was no big deal. A different army, for sure.

We started working on longer distances little by little, getting used to the effects of the wind. Our main distances practiced were at three hundred meters, five hundred meters, seven hundred meters, and nine hundred meters. Once in a while, the instructors put targets at varying distances between these berms. Most of our targets farther than three hundred meters were not physically manned and marked, but rather the instructors watched the vapor trail of the round as it went down range. One could see where the vapor trail ended when hitting the target, thus giving them a good idea of target impact. They would do this by backing off the focus of the spotting scope until there was a blur, they could then see heat waves rising from the ground. The direction and pattern of the waves would give them an indication of the wind intensity and direction. The instructors could then observe the sonic wake of the round as it flew down range, not unlike the wake of a speed boat.

About halfway through our training, our shooting was cut short because visitors started showing up. I looked back to see who was in the bleachers and saw all generals and colonels. Soon we were in the bleachers off to the side as Major Powell addressed the distinguished guests. It was an open house of sorts, as generals and field-grade officers came to see what the Sniper School was all about. Even though the program was young, it had made a name for itself fast. Major General Ewell had invited all who cared from all branches and corps of the Vietnam forces to visit and learn what we were all about. Choppers came in from all over Vietnam for the event. Soon we were excused, as the sniper cadre paid full attention to the officers. After the brief seminar, most left on their Hueys and were on their way to their respective base camps. However, a few stayed for a barbecue put on by the school, outside Major Powell's office. I happened by the area when Major Powell called me over to make an ice run—seems they didn't have enough ice for their beer and soft drinks. After I filled the cooler with ice, one of the generals from up north decided to ask me a few questions about what I thought of the school and inquired about my background. He was soon handing me a beer and asking me to sit on the old run-down couch next to him. At first I was nervous and tried to excuse myself after the first beer, but the general wouldn't have it. He demanded my time and a drinking partner. The room was filled with generals and conversations, but the uniqueness of having a Spc. 4 (Specialist 4—E-4 rank) in the conversation seemed intriguing to them, and I was allowed to remain. As the party wound down, the general made an amazing statement to the others and me: "This war is fucked up, and it's fucked up because of the politicians; these young men deserve better. I'm sick of telling the powers that be what they want to hear. I've thought of getting out and retiring, but all that would happen is for another with less experience to replace me. I still have something to offer the young men of my division, and for that reason I'll stay until they throw me out." It was as if he were saying to me, "I'm so sorry for what you and the other young men have to deal with; I wish I could be of more help." As I left for my barracks, I felt sad for the general and myself all at the same time. What the fuck have I gotten myself into? We had personally felt the deadly effects of Johnson stopping the bombing of the Ho Chi Minh Trail. We all prayed that President Nixon would start the bombing once in office and leave the war to those trained in war.

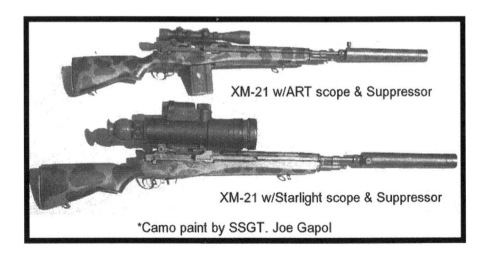

XM-21 w/ART scope & Suppressor

XM-21 w/Starlight scope & Suppressor

*Camo paint by SSGT. Joe Gapol

One night, instead of having the classes in the classroom, we were told to gather at the corner of the base camp's perimeter with our Starlight scopes. As we arrived, we sat in a semicircle facing the corner berm. We were told to focus our scopes on a bucket within the inside corner of the berm. Soon Staff Sergeant Ninoa lifted the bucket off the ground, only to expose a cobra immediately coiling and ready to strike. Boom! A rifle went off behind us as Staff Sergeant Gapol blew the cobra's head off! Holy fuck! I thought, Wow! What a way to introduce us to the effectiveness of the Starlight. This is some exciting shit! We were all excused to the classroom for our first Starlight class. It was the one class everyone paid attention to right down to the last detail. We all had used the scope in the field for night observation but had no idea it could be so effective. In fact, we had never had any training on the scope at all; it was all trial and error in the field. We were excited and could now see that we would have something to offer once we were snipers.

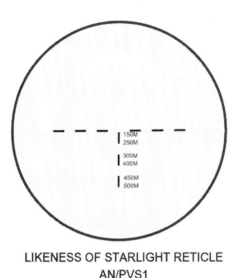

LIKENESS OF STARLIGHT RETICLE
AN/PVS1

S.Sgt. Aprail "Joe" Gapol was my favorite instructor by this time. His was smooth and to the point, with no arrogance associated with his stature. He had killed nineteen enemy soldiers in his short time learning the ropes as a sniper prior to becoming an instructor at the school. Joe won his Distinguished

Rifleman Badge in 1961. He won the prestigious Pershing Trophy in the National Championships in 1967. He shot high score in the 1967 President's Hundred Match and would again in 1973–74. Joe would go on to win two consecutive All-Army Championships in 1972–73 and later be inducted into the Service Rifleman's Hall of Fame.

Other than the occasional VC sniper throwing a round or two our way while at the range, the remainder of Sniper School was rather uneventful in that every day was; shoot, shoot, shoot. The instructors mixed up things once in a while with different instructors and ranges, but for the most part, it was all about making us better shots and preparing us for our final shoot-off.

The day of reckoning soon came as we all were a little nervous about passing the course. I wasn't worrying too much as I had beaten all in the earlier open-sight contest and felt as though I had progressed as well as anyone had. It was a beautiful day with a slight breeze. We were all assigned a coach/instructor who would call our shots and the wind for us with their spotting scopes. Our targets varied from 150 meters to 900 meters. We were given five shots at each target and required to hit each a minimum of three times, but we also needed a total score that required a much higher percent than the three of five. So no fewer than three hits per target or you failed, and no less than a high percentage of hits or you also failed. While I was slightly nervous, I felt as though I was doing well. At 900 meters I was asked to hold off (three and a half times the target width) to the right. I missed my first shot. I was corrected to three times to the right and my second shot hit. On my third shot, I missed. Now I was sweating it because I needed to ace the rest of my shots. My fourth shot was a hit. To my utter disappointment, my fifth shot was a miss. I'd only hit two out of five. I just stuck my face in the sand, unable to face my instructor or myself.

As the shoot ended, there were no cheers or hoopla as the final tallies for scores had not been made. We all returned to the barracks to await the results. Even though I knew I had failed on one target, I still had hopes that somehow my total score would negate the inevitable. We waited and waited, not understanding why the scoring was taking so long. Finally, one of the instructors showed up and asked me to go to Master Sergeant Falcon's office. I knew I had flunked and was prepared for the worst. He explained to me that there had been a lengthy discussion about my dilemma, but the need to keep the standards high and intact had won out. I had flunked out! In the two previous classes the instructors had also weeded out all but approximately ten students per class so they could concentrate on them for the remainder of the course. I was the first of those kept who had failed.

I returned to the barracks to pack up and head out for Dong Tam and say my good-byes to my newfound friends. I found them celebrating their passing grades along with their reward, a leave to Vung Tau for an in-country, three-day R&R, the general had rewarded each for passing the course.

I caught a ride to Saigon and got drunk for two days before catching another ride into Dong Tam, where I partied until I ran out of money.

As I took the shuttle boat back to the company, I decided not to look back but to use my newfound talent and start using the Starlight on my M-16 at night. While I realized I wouldn't be able to properly zero it, I could do some damage at short distances. It was what it was, and I might as well get over it and deal with it in a positive manner.

Sniper Range Dong Tam

Chapter **8**

S Q U A D   L E A D E R

The makeup of Bravo Company was four platoons and one command post (CP). The First, Second, and Third were of equal strength that varied in size from time to time, battle to battle. The Fourth Platoon was a much smaller platoon, originally the Mortar Platoon that now served mainly as CP security and of smaller size ran by a platoon sergeant. The CP was made up of the company commander (CO), the forward observer (FO), and their radio telephone operators (RTOs). The CO had two RTOs, one for the battalion network and one for the company, whereas the FO had his personal RTO for calling in army and air force air strikes and, of course, our main support, the artillery. Each platoon leader, platoon sergeant, and squad leader had his own RTO.

By early 1969, we had had lots of officers and platoon sergeants come and go since I came into the company. I had gone from a green FNG to squad leader. On my first day of being assigned to Bravo, our CO, Captain Poole, was on his last day of command. The new CO arrived on his chopper only to get killed while still aboard the landing Huey. Captain Pool was also wounded that day, so another captain who was slated to go to another company was diverted to Bravo Company while still in the air. We had three COs in one day. Captain Kincheloe would serve as CO until Captain DeEdwardo came in early January. That's four company commanders in as many months.

In the First Platoon, Lieutenant Wright was replaced by Lieutenant Ed Earnst. In Second Platoon, Lieutenant Wolfer was replaced by Lieutenant Frobinius. Sergeant Toth was replaced by Weicht. SSgt. John Sperry of Third Platoon was acting platoon leader after Lieutenant Kemp was wounded. Lieutenant Livermore took over Third Platoon, only to get killed soon thereafter. Shortly after that, Lieutenant Bradford took over the Third, and Leon Edmiston took over as platoon sergeant. All this in just over two months. We also went through two FOs, and Ed Ziek went from being the RTO to the FO soon thereafter.

We were lucky for the most part in that we had good officers. Some were better than others, but most learned quickly and knew how to trust their platoon sergeant and squad leaders. We could trust their intelligence and ability to keep us in contact with the right information when available. There was one CO, however, from earlier in '68 whom the men still moaned about. Seems as though nobody liked the SOB. We had one while I was there who was a little too concerned about his awards. We really didn't learn about his methods until later. He never put anybody in for anything unless it benefited him in some way. I found out later he told one of the men that he was interested only in attaining medals while with Bravo. Had the men in general found out this, he would have led a miserable existence.

Things weren't done the same in the field as they were in the rear. Attainment of rank was one of them. For enlisted men, it was usually nothing more than just being there for a longer time than the others below you. Most came to the line companies in Vietnam as private E-2s, and a few were sent to the NCO School, which afforded them the rank of sergeant E-5 upon graduation. We commonly referred to the school as Instant NCO or Shake 'n Bake. However, having the rank didn't necessarily mean that you were going to be put in a slot that was meant for an NCO. The rank still had to be earned, although to a lesser extent. In Bravo Company Second Platoon, it was by vote or a general consensus by the men, the platoon sergeant (B-25), and the platoon leader (B-2-6). Sometimes the men went to the platoon sergeant and platoon leader and asked if a specific person could be their next squad leader. These decisions were usually made based on one's specific performance while with the squad. This is how we chose most squad leaders.

I hadn't been back from Sniper School long when Reed was rewarded for his exceptional performance with a job in the rear with Brigade in Ben Tre. This change meant that one of the squad leaders was to be promoted to platoon sergeant and as such the new platoon leader elected to promote Ortiz, meaning that someone was also going to be promoted to squad leader. The men of the first squad decided that it was to be me, although it was a job I asked not to receive. They voted and went to Ortiz with their decision, and that was that; I was the new squad leader. This decision, however, created a dilemma because there was already a sergeant in the squad, and I was only an E-4 wearing E-3 stripes. Clark had gone to Shake 'n Bake (NCO School) and had been with the squad since before my arrival in October. At first he complained to no avail to Ortiz and 2-6, and then he just gave me the evil look and went on his merry way. He would be where and when he chose and carry what he chose, looking like a point man with a light load of just his bare necessities, carrying none of the extra grenades, machine gun ammo, claymores, smoke grenades, or any other gear.

I allowed Clark to go about his own way for some time until someone sarcastically mentioned his prima donna state. That's when it really hit me that he wasn't part of the squad, which was also the reason he was never chosen to lead. The next time we geared up for a mission, I grabbed three hundred rounds of M-60 ammo and handed it to him. He didn't like someone of a lesser rank telling him what to do, but he bucked up and took it anyhow. As we humped throughout the day, I noticed him wriggling and rearranging his load to accommodate the ammo. If looks could kill, I would have been dead. But what really happened this day is that I took charge, and it was now my squad, and these were my men. The load shared by all was my concern. I finally was actually doing my job instead of just answering the radio when called. You could see it on the men's faces now; they had someone who cared for and was there for them. I was a squad leader now and damn proud of it.

I had learned most from Reed, but I also learned from Ortiz. Ortz, as we called him, was a California boy and a Shake 'n Bake. But he did apply what he learned in NCO school in that he watched out for his men and their needs. While he didn't have the field experience that Reed had, he had something to offer just the same. I like to think that I learned from Ortz to watch out for my men. Their spacing, their ammo loads, among other things, were most important. Men have the tendency to "cluster fuck," as we called grouping together, a deadly habit around booby traps and enemy fire. It's only natural for the VC to want to take out a group. Even though all knew of the hazard, they constantly had to be reminded to spread out; misery and curiosity love company.

It was also my responsibility to inform the platoon sergeant as to my men's needs, whatever they may be, but on a daily basis I was to keep him informed about the amount of ammo; the number of grenades, smoke grenades, and claymores; the supply of water and C rations; and what was needed on the next resupply chopper.

My buddy JR Roniger was also now a squad leader, and from time to time, he would walk with me and my squad, especially when we were on point. Walking together gave me a lot of moral support. Because Roniger and I had worked together so many times, I always knew I could count on him. I always knew that when I charged a bunker, he was to my side and at an angle that needed to be covered. It got to the point where we would put our squads together and co-manage them as one. When mine was on point, there he'd be, and when his was on point, there I'd be.

While Roniger was one of the bravest men I knew, he also didn't really want to be in Vietnam. When he was in the field, he did his job and was an ass kicker at it. But he was always hoping for a million-dollar wound or a way to get out of the field. On one mission, I noticed that JR was soaking his feet in the canal water when we took a break. And when we actually had the time to take off our boots to try to dry things out, he would be soaking his feet instead. He then decided to soak his lower torso. His mission was to get ringworm so bad that he'd miss a mission or two, and maybe even have to go to the hospital. He soon got his wish and was covered with ringworm. Doc just shook his head in disbelief. Finally, JR couldn't take it anymore and asked for medical help. But all the medics did was put him in his bunk with a salve on the infected area. He lay there naked on a plastic sheet with this shit all over his lower body for all to see. It looked very painful, as the skin was cracking and bleeding from the acute infection. JR laid there in pain, wishing he'd taken Doc's advice. Ringworm was no picnic, and JR was paying for these days off. JR just said, "On to plan B." We all took notice of the pain and probably took better care of ourselves afterward when it came to ringworm.

We had good RTOs who stuck to us like stink on shit most of the time. We didn't expect them to follow us when charging or putting ourselves away from the squad, but they always seemed to be right there. I expected mine to be a rifleman first and then an RTO. I don't remember ever having to get on mine for not being there when I needed him.

I will always remember Stevens, an Oklahoma boy who looked fifteen; Doc called him The Kid. He was always there, even though his eyes would sometimes be open wider than one would think possible. You could tell he was scared as hell, but he never said a word.

On one mission, we had a lot of shammers (those who went on sick call, shirking their duty), and we were very short on men anyway. We had just come off a bad mission, having lost some men, and the morale was lower than whale shit. Stevens wasn't feeling good anyway but felt it was his duty to be there, especially after he overheard me calling some of the men pussies for not bucking up. We hadn't been out for more than an hour or two when he had to drop his drawers from diarrhea. Diarrhea was a common thing with us and wasn't necessarily anything to worry about, as it would usually go away after the poison was purged. But Randy's diarrhea persisted to the point that he was stopping every thirty minutes or so, and his color looked terrible. I told him to ask the CP for a Dustoff, but he refused, thinking he would get better. I finally had to order a Dustoff, as his condition was holding us up, and he wasn't getting any better. We never saw Randy again except on the front page of the *Stars and Stripes* newspaper months later. Randy had caught one of the worst forms of malaria and had been on a lung and kidney machine for a record length of time—so long that it was newsworthy. Fortunately, the article also told of his recovery.

***

The one thing I hated about being a squad leader was the petty bullshit between some men. "So-and-so isn't carrying his load" or "So and so is careless with his rifle." I'd just let it roll, but there were times when you needed to hear from your men when someone was putting others in harm's way. Sleeping while on watch and not carrying your assigned load were two actions I wouldn't put up with. The worst part of the job was having to tell someone he was now on point; I hated that decision every time.

While we were part of a platoon, which was part of a company of men, we were a squad first. We walked, ate, slept, flew, rode Tangos, and fought together. Sometimes one would be assigned to another squad for one reason or another, and, of course, there were the wounds and deaths, but the squad and the platoon's heritage went on.

John Beck, Willy Perez, Dan Hendricks,et al: 4th Plt.

It had been a long mission with many small firefights resulting in two dead from Third Platoon and one wounded. We also lost a man from drowning in a canal crossing and were more than ready to go home and clean up our ringworm and emersion foot, not to mention our jungle rot and morale. We were moving in position to secure the PZ for our extraction.

Roniger and I took our squads over to the north wood line next to a small river that was rising with the tide. As usual we stayed together and co-commanded both squads. We had no more than arrived in the area to be secured when the incoming Hueys radioed that they were coming in, meaning we needed to secure a landing zone (LZ) and fast. About that time, a VC jumped up, running like a rabbit for his hole. He then jumped into a parallel dry canal. Roniger and I were after him like smell on dung as he zigzagged through the grove. Roniger was on his left, and I was on his heels on the right. Firing on the run was ineffective and only spurred him on. He suddenly took a hard right and dived into a bunker. Roniger and I were on his doorstep faster than a rat up a rafter. There could be no time wasted as we needed to configure for the incoming birds. We had to take him out before he could throw a grenade or come out firing. Roniger covered me as I approached the bunker by continuously firing rounds into the bunker. I was now two feet from the opening. As I nodded to Roniger, he continued covering the opening with fire as I put in another magazine. I then shoved my 16 into the opening, working it from side to side. As my eyes followed my barrel the rounds were hitting their marks The VC writhed from the rounds entering his body. We took a small break as a good hunter would to let the animal bleed out. I then dragged his pitiful ass out of the bunker and searched him and the bunker. Nothing out of the ordinary! I would keep his cigarette lighter as a souvenir. Having taken the extra time, we now had to change the location of the PZ to a smaller paddy across a canal from the larger one. We completed our search of the north side of the PZ and then turned to the staging area for the extraction.

PZ in large Paddy: Courtesy of: Willy Perez

It was getting dark fast now, and we really wanted out of this area. We could hear the whop whop of the slicks'/Hueys' blades as they came closer. Soon we were popping smoke for identification while at the same time configuring for extraction. We loaded and began climbing out as the Heuys' blades pumped the air and two Loaches protected our left flank, which was over our original PZ area. At about 150 feet above ground level, a flash suddenly woke up the darkening, dusky skies to our left at about the same altitude as us. I turned to see what was happening; a Loach was falling from the sky in a ball of fire as tracers coming from the nearby wood line drove up and through the fiery ball. The other Loach turned to attack the wood line, and just as he started firing, its red tracers were met with returning green tracers that found their mark immediately. As the rounds penetrated the second Loach, it also blew up into a huge ball of fire, lighting up the sky even more. There were now two Loaches falling from the evening sky at the same time. One behind the other they made contact with the paddy below, and the ball of fire expanded on impact, it was obvious to all that there were no possibilities of anyone making it out of this three-ring circus alive.

Our hearts sank for the lives of our comrades and for the now obvious night location we would be dealing with.

We circled the fireballs at altitude, watching the whole time for any sign of life and/or enemy. The only thing happening was the reduction of the fires as the paddy slowly became part of the night once again.

Command had another company close by, and the decision for them to come in was made, giving us the break we needed as the Cobras on station stayed in the area.

***

It's another mission and a beautiful, hot, stinking day in the Mekong. We were somewhere east of Ben Tre and close to the infamous Crossroads. We came into a sparsely populated area where we evidently weren't noticed until the last moment when people started running like crazy in all directions. Our orders to halt (Dung Lai) went unheeded, and we were forced to fire at these unarmed young men, one of whom took us seriously and froze, hands held high. Second Platoon was on point and our Tiger Scout Gaa, with the help of First Platoon's scout, took it upon themselves to interrogate this young VC. It didn't take long for him to talk as they pretended to cut his stomach open as he lay painfully bent over a bamboo pole placed behind his knees. He soon spilled out all, including the fact that he was in charge of the setting and placement of the booby traps in the area. I was amazed; this guy actually thought we'd look upon him in a better light because he wasn't a gun-bearing soldier, as though setting booby traps was a more honorable, harmless job title. We hated these terrorist bastards in the worst way. We'd seen how they indiscriminately set them and the effects they had on their own. These guys were lower than whale shit in my book.

As we were ordered to head out, I had the prisoner put in the lead with his hands tied behind. This guy was going to be the first to blow up as long as he was under my command. Fuck the REMFs (Rear Echelon Mother Fuckers) of the Geneva Convention; my men were more important to me than any fucking bullshit rules of politicians. Within a few hundred yards, this decision paid off in spades. He knew right where the booby trap was and was more than happy to point it out to us. A few more yards and yet another one. This guy was a gold mine! No way did I want this guy to go into division for an interrogation.

I was hanging out behind point as I was breaking in a new point man and didn't want him to be too overburdened with the job at hand and also have to watch out for the prisoner. We were walking parallel to a large canal that was low from the tide being out when we broke into a small open area and then at the same time heard some talking from the foliaged area forty feet in front of us. About that time, I realized he was talking to six men who were swimming in the canal only fifty feet to my immediate right. Their weapons were all lined up on the canal's edge twenty feet from them. Assuming that the position in front of me was a lookout or guard I fired on his hidden position first and then turned to the swimmers who were now in a race for their AKs. As they struggled with the knee-deep mud, I fired on them and then back to the unknown position and then back and forth until I was out of ammo. To my amazement, I only shot one in the leg; I put in another magazine; they then disappeared into the Nipa palm and took up positions and started returning fire with others who were already in the wood line. I was totally disappointed in myself, the point man, and the slack man. While I was busy spinning my wheels, they just stood there and watched them get away. FNGs just can't be trusted.

Our FO had been killed a mission or two ago, but Ziek, who was now our FO had already been in contact with some F4 Phantoms that were nearby, and they were on their way. We popped smoke, and within just a minute or two of the incident, they were on station and diving with full loads of Napalm and HE (High Explosives). Incredible luck on our part. The first napalm was right on target, splashing across the canal to within feet of our position, heating up the already hundred-degree day. We cheered as they came in one after another burning and blowing up the entire area, leaving no doubt in our minds that all were in VC heaven. The only casualty we had was the prisoner, who caught a stray round from his brothers, my marksmanship ego, my point man, and my slack man got an earful of me chewing their ass. Their actions were not acceptable. They very well could have allowed enemy soldiers to live another day to kill more American and ARVN forces. We, however, lucked out because Ziek was on the ball.

***

As we descended into a final approach readying ourselves for our fifth chopper insertion of the day, the choppers took a sudden hard right as the door gunners opened up on the hooch's below, and the VC fired their green tracers back. Red smokes were thrown overboard to mark the location of the returning fire as the gunships flowed in behind us with a non-varying attitude bearing down on the hooch's with certainty. As we circled around, I could see the area take a beating as the UH-1 gunships and Cobras fired their rockets while simultaneously firing their 7.62mm minigun into the area. As the hooch's burned, we circled around for a new heading into the same rice paddy as the gunships hooked up on our flanks. The landing was surprisingly quiet as we offloaded and disappeared into the wood line awaiting and looking for Charlie.

My squad was linked up with Ronigers, and Roniger and I were, as usual, breaking all the rules by walking together, co-managing our squads. The gunships hung around for a while as we searched the area, and then, as always, they left us alone with Charlie. Feeling pretty good and presupposing that maybe

Charlie had left, we opened up our step and proceeded on our heading when sniper fire immediately dropped us all in the mud and canals. It became evident that it was just a couple of snipers, and because we were behind the lead element, we had the dubious job of just waiting it out. Roniger and I lay in a muddy canal together with our RTOs in the next canal. The snipers persisted as though they were effective, as Roniger stuck his right foot up on the dike as to give them a target or maybe hoping to catch a lucky round. I thought this to be pretty funny as I did the same and yelled out "Here, VC! Here, VC!" as though I was calling in the hogs. Pretty soon Third Platoon started getting in some good shots as the incoming rounds lost their persistence. Roniger then asked me if I'd shoot him in his foot. I couldn't believe it, and then I caught myself asking him to do the same. We may have been warriors, but we also wanted desperately to live. We argued as to who would go first, and then the CO broke up the conversation with an order to move out.

We circled around the snipers and then headed right for them. As we approached the area, I could see that the snipers' lair was on a peninsula of coconut groves between two paddies. I knew then that First or Third Platoon would get the little fuckers, as there was no place for them to go. As we held up covering First and Third Platoon's rear and flanks, they proceeded to the end of the peninsula. But no Charlie!

Confused and now worried that the VC were somehow behind them, they turned back, scratching their heads in wonderment. Then, all of a sudden, a rifleman turned to the flanking paddy with his weapon aimed at what seemed to be nothing but a pile of rice straw; then a squad leader joined him, and they pursued with live fire. The small straw piles in the paddy exploded with writhing bodies of surprised VC as the whole platoon opened up, eliminating all in a matter of just a handful of seconds.

As the platoon returned, the story was a joyous one and one that made us all jealous for not being a part of it, and all without harm.

We continued on our way as the day became shorter, all the while feeling as though Charlie was near. One klick and then another were put between us as the sun lowered. As we rounded the corner of a rice paddy inside the wood line, all hell broke loose with the point element and a VC ambush. The firing went on at a brisk rate, and then the M-16 firing subsided under an ever-increasing blanket of green tracers. Even from my rear position, I could tell by sound alone that Charlie had won the battle of fire superiority. He was the one making the most noise, and the green tracers proved it! We all closed up our ranks. Members of each platoon positioned themselves behind the lead platoon's positions. I could only listen to the screaming on the radio as the firing continued and then silence followed by another exchange of fire.

The point element had walked into an ambush and had two dead and two wounded. The wounded men came back to the rear element for Dustoff as we proceeded to secure an LZ for the Dustoff. It was then that I heard the details.

The lead platoon had two dead in front, and they were separated from them. They were currently trying to probe a way to recover the two men who were now behind the VC lines. My heart sank. There is no feeling like leaving a grunt behind, even if he is dead. We would not leave until we recovered the bodies.

As night set in, the firing ceased as we all awaited an assault on our positions that would never come. The CO kept the perimeter intact and soon came the duty of recovering the bodies in the early a.m. hours of light.

The platoon moved up with no resistance to find their friends' bodies nude and mutilated. We once again prepared for a lone incoming chopper as our hatred for the enemy marinated in our minds.

We got back to the ship, and all were settled in, having eaten and showered. A few men were down on the barge cleaning equipment and weapons when soldier from another company started yelling, "I'm not going to let those fuckin' VC kill me!" He shot himself, committing suicide there and then with little else said. Everyone was stunned and little was said of the incident or mentioned again. You just suck it up and go on with a little more of your heart ripped away.

Soon we were back out. This time we inserted at night via Tangos. We rarely inserted or were extracted by Tangos at night. However, this was an exception to the rule. We inserted off the Song (river) Ham Luong east of Ben Tre well after the sun had set. We were barely off the Tangos—they hadn't even closed their ramps yet—when a short automatic burst pierced the night. The call of "medic" soon thereafter answered the shots. We could hardly tell where the shots came from or how far away they were, and not knowing the exact location of the other offloaded troops, there was no reply by our weapons. That was it—short and brief. Two men were wounded in what were lucky shots of harassment. Chief had been shot in the jaw. He was from another platoon and one great guy, a large-boned American Indian over six feet, who loved being called Chief by his Bravo Brothers. With our Tango boats right there, the decision was to retreat to the Tangos and take care of the evacuation of the wounded. Besides, our surprise insertion was no longer a surprise.

Huey Cobra Gunship

Loading Tango Boats in Mud

My mind can't help but go back to my time in Madigan Hospital at Ft. Lewis. I was in there for a hernia operation during my basic training cycle. Most there were wounded from Vietnam. One in particular was seared in my mind. He had been shot in the jaw, just like Chief. The round went in one side and through the other side, disengaging his entire lower mandible. The damage was so bad to the jaw that the entire disengaged portion had to be removed, bone, teeth and all. My guess was that infection prompted the removal. He was two bunks from me looking like a monster with his lower lip hung down with the remaining skin sagging down onto his Adam's apple. He tried to talk but just made frustrated sounds with his fluttering, hanging, uncoordinated tongue. Being a mortician's son made me a little tougher than most for the unsightly. However, I just couldn't bring myself to an introduction, and I would just try not to go his way when it wasn't necessary. After a couple days of acting like this, I was ashamed of myself and finally went over to talk with him. He was one hell of a man. He felt good about his chances of looking reasonably well and had no sympathy for himself. He was embarrassed for others from time to time about his looks. Before I was released for duty, the surgeons had taken a rib from him and bent it into the shape of his jaw and then attached it to the remaining mandible. They wrapped his loose tissue around it, giving him a rough-looking jaw. It was still ugly, but it was wonderful to him. The next steps were to promote tissue and bone adhesion and then add artificial teeth. I was so happy for him but so disappointed that I never got to see the final results.

I was wondering as I looked at Chief if he had what it takes to deal with this type of wound, and for the first time, I seriously looked deep inside and wondered if I had what it takes. I had been in denial for some time about the possibility of being hideously wounded. Getting killed or having legs shot off or an arm blown off didn't seem to bother me. In fact, there were times I would have given a leg for a pass from the Delta Sewer. But fighting facial disfigurement was going to be a hard one at best to accept. It's a quiet ride down the dark river.

A time came when it seemed all hope of surviving had diminished to a point that I really didn't give a fuck anymore. If I was to go down, I may as well go down fighting. In fact, I was almost itching for a fight some days. Time would go by with only snipers firing at us or halfhearted ambushes that would end at the first sign of fire superiority. Today was one of those days; I was looking for a fight. We were walking through a beaten up, shredded by artillery coconut grove when we came upon two VC with AKs. We made eye contact at the same time. Instead of taking cover and firing upon them, I decided to run them into the ground. I charged, firing as they took ran and cover in a bunker. I threw in another magazine and continued charging an enemy who had the advantage of cover. I was now at the point of no return, as there was no cover for me, and my actions took my men by surprise to the point that they stayed behind. If I failed to keep up the pressure and allowed them the opportunity to return fire, my ass was grass. As my second magazine ran low, I hooked around the side of the bunker and put in another magazine, jumped on the bunker, bent over, sticking my 16 in the opening, and emptied it. I then grabbed a grenade, pulled the pin and counted to three before putting it in. The roof rose with me on it and then collapsed inward. I had killed these fucks, and it felt wonderful. As I looked in to see the damage, I was mortified; there wasn't a soul in the bunker. They had run in and then out of the rear of the bunker, escaping the madman charging them. Fuck! All that for nothing!

After action and alive---4th Plt.

We were at the firebase as the sun broke, bringing its treacherous heat and humidity to the Mekong. Pistol Pete had blade hours up the ying yang and had the heat of the division to use them. We'd been averaging five to seven helo insertions a day, and this day was to be no different. In fact, I can remember one day we had ten insertions. It was crazy; you never knew where you were and seldom had the maps on you, which delayed artillery strikes even more. We called this type of strategy "Recon by Blood." The division called them search-and-destroy missions via a checkerboarding stratagem. The reality was that the first sortie or two would be based on intelligence, and the rest would be based on using the blade hours given you. If we found Charlie and were in contact, then we could stay. If Charlie wasn't there, then we secured a PZ and flew on to the next LZ. No Charlie, more flights. More blood and guts meant fewer flights. They were nerve-racking, to say the least. Charlie loved to fire at the choppers when they were landing and taking off, as it was the one time they were an easy target. More LZs and PZs meant more booby traps, more ambushes, more paddy mud, and more of being in the open. There was nothing worse than having Charlie in the wood line firing at you when you had nothing but a few inches of paddy water and blades of rice as protection.

At times you thought of certain birds as your own private Huey. You got to know the gunners and the back of each pilot's helmet. We had one Huey with a Mexican American door gunner who kept a stash of Tobasco sauce. Whenever a flight came in around lunchtime, the men of Mexican descent would almost fight to see who got on that bird. About the only good thing that came with the sorties was the air flow on your hot, wet, sweaty body. The cooling effect was fantastic, and it made keeping food down a lot easier. Thus, lunch on the Hueys was common.

After a few flights, we all returned to the open paddy alongside of a firebase. Only this time all the birds shut off their engines as another joined us from the north. We were all ordered to go to the new bird in the group, and we found it full of brand-new gas masks. They were passed out to all, including the crews of the Hueys. We all took them out of their bags, fitted them to our faces, and returned them to the bags on our thighs. We were back on our birds in no time. No one even gave us a hint of what was to come down. Of course, common sense said you're going to use them—and soon.

After about a fifteen-minute flight, we began a descent from the two thousand feet altitude, and we were all ordered to don our gas masks. What a sight, I thought as I looked at the two pilots flying with them on. I wondered if they had the same gas training as we did. We were descending to an open rice paddy flanked by a wood line in a coconut grove, but there was no sign of gas yet. Then, as we broke the five hundred-foot level, white, spherical clouds of gas rose just above the tops of the trees of the wood line to our right flank. First we saw five air bursts of gas, then five more just adjacent to the others, then fifteen, then twenty. In no time the wood line filled up with the thick, white clouds that settled to the deck and began moving horizontally. As the birds started to settle into their landing zones, you could see the gas being sucked in by the blades as they created vortices off the blade tips. It was a surreal sight; I had never seen this sight before, but I knew I liked it immediately. There was no way Charlie had any gas masks, and the gas provided a smoky wall of protection from our open exit to the wood line. This was going to be a cake walk, I thought to myself.

As we got on line, the thick, white gas met us as we entered the grove. The immediate contact to our skin in the boiling midday sun told us that it was a kickass CS gas of some sort. The skin irritation was immediate, but our masks were doing the job.

Our only previous experience with the gas was in Bear Cat during our in-country orientation. The instructors had set up a small, rectangular building of about fifteen feet by twenty-five feet, and they ordered us to walk through the building and exit out the other side. The cadre donned their gas masks and then popped the gas grenades inside. As the white gas rolled out of the building, they were on our shit immediately to get inside and get going. The entrance was a door all the way to the left of the long side of the building. We all had experienced CS and tear gas in training and weren't too overly worried about just having to walk through such a small building, thinking that the exit must be just on the other side and we could hold our breath long enough to get through. But to our dismay the cadre was blocking the obvious route, and the exit was all the way to the right on the opposite side. Their blocking move and the lack of light forced us to open our eyes and then take a breath prior to exiting. This shit hit us immediately and hard. Our eyes were burning beyond belief and the throwing up commenced within feet of taking a breath. We couldn't breathe, so we were forced to the ground within a couple steps. Just beyond the exit was a pile of bodies writhing and rolling in the paddy water. Everyone was upchucking and just trying to find his own private wallow of despair and pain. This CS gas had a vomiting agent added to it, no doubt. It was much worse than the gases we had experienced previously.

We weren't in the wood line for fifty feet before seeing right in front of us a VC with AK and a homemade gas mask throwing up, disorientated, and incapable of defending himself. I kicked the AK a little further away and reached down and removed his mask, only to find it filled with his fishy rice puke. He just lay there convulsing; it was a beautiful sight. As the guys searched the area, we found a few more in the same situation—all incapacitated. Of all the VC prisoners we had taken and the dead we had previously searched, we had never seen any with these homemade gas masks. They were light-green plastic with an elastic band sewn in, a clear plastic front for vision and a Kotex-like pad sewn in for filtering the gas. They obviously didn't work worth a damn, but the real question was why did these guys have masks? The first time we had gassed or even heard of it in Vietnam, and these guys had masks?

Soon the gas dissipated, and we were able to take the masks off. The VC slowly were able to rise and see once again; God, they were a pitiful mess. I loved it. This was the way to fight these guys; no doubt gassing was going to save many lives—Charlie's and ours! We were elated; we had captured a handful of VC and their weapons, which was a big deal because in the delta, they always seemed to hide their weapons in the canals, rivers, or paddies by the time we got to them.

Our morale was high. Was this the way fighting was to be in the future? Then someone said, "I think this is against the Geneva Convention." We never used gas again—how sad!

CP group in canal

Chapter 9

MEDICS

Medics were gods to the infantryman, even if you didn't like them personally, you wanted (in the worst way) for the medic to like you. You don't start thinking about your medic until you come to grips with the fact that you will be in true combat. You start running combat scenarios through your head with all the possibilities that you've learned in training or heard of or saw on TV or the movies. Over and over again, you visualized how you would react and whether or not you would be a man who is accepted by his peers or would you instead be a coward. Even before being in combat, you knew this to be true: cowards were the non-players, the bench sitters, the ugliest of all because they represented what you were most afraid of. And in your mind, you knew that Doc was going to go after the hero before he went for the coward. The mere thought of being looked down upon by your fellow infantrymen was bone chilling, but the thought that Doc might not come for you was even worse. It was a nightmare to think of dying in a foreign country and nobody caring enough to help.

I originally went into active duty wanting to be a combat medic. I thought that my background as an ambulance attendant and as a son of a mortician would help the army see my usefulness as a medic. The thought of saving lives as opposed to taking them was paramount in this decision. Even though I had a Seventh-day Adventist side to my family, I didn't feel good about declaring myself as a conscientious objector, as my churchgoing practices were less than stellar, and there seemed to be a stigma attached to the classification. Nonetheless, a good percentage of medics were conscience objectors to war, but they still felt a duty to their fellow countrymen to serve. The medics of the Seventh-day Adventist church were an example that the church was proud of. Many medics

91

would come to the company without a weapon. Most who were not objectors to war would come with a .45 on their sides. All would within minutes of their first firefight reconsider their choices. Most would arm themselves as soon as they could. Those rearming and arming themselves would reconsider the amount of ammo or choice of weapons carried. The reality of death without one's own ability to have a say was bone chilling, to say the least. Some would find themselves changing and acting more like infantrymen, carrying more and more bullets and fewer and fewer bandages, to the point the platoon sergeant would often have to say something.

Not all medics were of the same mold, however. Some (just like infantrymen) had to deal with their demons of fear. However, all found a way to do their job and usually in a meritorious manner. While Bravo Company had its share of great medics, we in Second Platoon were especially proud of our Doc Schuebel. Doc was a proud man from Wisconsin who had a large-boned frame and was a wrestler in high school with ape arms able to drag the largest of us to safety. He was truly a team player who got to know each and every one of his men, and make no mistake about it, we were his men and nobody fucked with Doc Schuebel's men. Doc had the balls to walk with every man, even if it meant walking up front and behind the point man. He was always cruising through the file as we made our way through the obstacles of the Mekong. Doc was able to carry a large ruck and, therefore, carried large amounts of ammo for his M-16 without cutting back on his medical needs. He was first a team player in an infantry platoon and second a medic. Doc would lay down the fire and maneuver with the best of us. But once someone was wounded, he morphed into the consummate combat medic. The morale of an infantry unit is directly tied to the way it views its medics. While the army and navy did a wonderful job of training these men, these organizations fell short in the way they chose them. Physical makeup was and is not usually a part of the consideration of selection, yet it should be. The ability to physically drag or carry a wounded soldier to safety prior to performing his duties in first aid should be part and parcel of what a combat medic is—not only for the safety of the wounded, but for the medic himself. Don't get me wrong. There were plenty of great combat medics that were of slight stature. But the reality is strength is power, and power in combat is life!

Beside the physical strength needed, a medic had to have the stomach for the proverbial blood and guts. No matter how much training one had, the reality of the hot fluids, agony, torn tissue, shock, filth, and smells of the wounded and dead are an awakening to anyone the first time. These guys had to get it together and now. Anything less was not an option. I've seen these guys shaking like a leaf but performing nonetheless. They knew what their job was. Triage must have been the hardest of all for them, deciding who was going to receive attention first and on down the line. The making of life and death decisions will shake the best of men, yet they kept on going and never complaining. Having more first-aid training and experience in torn bodies than the average guy, I tried when possible to be Doc's right hand. It may have been in the form of triage or just attending to one of the lighter wounded, but it was a good feeling to be of help when the medics were overwhelmed. To this day I would have given my left one to have been a combat medic.

One time we had been out for about a week as Colonel Rainville pushed Pistol Pete and his battalion to the limit. Because of this push, the ringworm and especially the emersion foot were at critical stages. For two days the medics had been warning the CO that there was an issue with the men's feet. And for two days they were told that they were going home soon, but it never happened. There is a reason we had been going in at least every three or four days max—and that reason has been to control the ringworm, emersion foot, and various kinds of jungle rot. It's a pyramid effect that reaches a point where the value of being out is outweighed by the expense of the time lost healing. Even though we usually went in (back to the ships) only for fourteen to sixteen hours or less, it was long enough to get your feet dry, put on some flip-flops, and squirt some Tinactin all over your body, and you were usually ready to go.

This day, Doc and the other medics got their heads together and determined that over half of us needed medical attention to our feet. Some of us had been bleeding for two days. The medics decided to push the CO and ask for over twenty-five men to be medevac'd. No one knew where this was going to go, but the CO went ahead and told battalion that we needed medevac's for one-third of the company. This plea finally got the attention needed to get us the fuck out of the soggy-ass delta paddies and rivers. The brigade paid for it because it took us three days to muster enough men for another mission with any strength at all. Another lesson relearned by Rainville.

The most devastating event to the morale in Bravo Company concerning a medic played itself out not on the battlefield but in the rear, aboard ship. We had a medic whom I will not name as he preferred to be called "Doc Soul," and, in fact, he had a personalized name tag on his uniform that said "Doc Soul." He was a strongly built man and as brave as any. As we ended a mission and were unloading from the Tango boats, our company clerk came out on the barges to meet us and proudly announced to all that Doc Soul had fulfilled his combat obligation and had orders to report to the rear. All medics we served with split their tour of duty between being on line and in the rear hospitals and/or infirmaries. We all cheered, knowing Doc had made it and was one of us who was going to live through this shit hole called the Mekong. Maybe we too would make it to that day. It was a wonderful sight to see someone make it out on their own two feet.

We determined that there should be a celebration and started working the ship's crew for any alcohol that may have been illegally stored aboard. After putting our gear away and retiring to our berthing area, whiskey bottle in hand, we awaited Doc for the party to begin, but Doc was nowhere to be found. He was working the powers that be (Captain Perkins) to not be taken away from his beloved men. He did not want to go to the rear and was visibly upset about it. Finding no answers to his liking, he made it to the berthing area where we awaited him. Doc started pulling on the bottle hard as he told us of his dilemma. Bravo was where he wanted to be. He hated the REMFs, and going to the rear was not on his agenda. To say the least, we were all taken aback, having never heard anything akin to this espousal. Not knowing how to deal with it, we just kept trying to calm him down and tell him that it was all going to be OK. We tried to talk only about the good things about the rear: the cold beer, massages, and USO shows among them. After the bottle was finally emptied and our exhausted, overworked bodies crashed, we went to our separate bunks as we contemplated Doc's dilemma.

The next morning, before heading out again, the usual yawning and ass scratching began as we dressed to make our way to the ship's galley. Doc's bunk wasn't moving, and his blanket covered his head—surely a sign of a hangover, we all thought. But soon someone tried to awaken Doc so that he could make it to the galley before the cooks wrapped up breakfast. There was no response! Doc had died in the middle of the night. There were numerous used Morphine Syrettes under his blanket. The rumors were varied as to the cause of death, but we all knew it was from a broken heart.

Doc Schubel & Ed

| Tending to the wounded. | Dustoff on Tango W/helo pad. |

Chapter 10

TIME OFF

Most of our time off was just for a few hours—time enough to dry out, get a good night's sleep, and eat a good meal before going out. Once in a while we would get a couple of days off for one reason or another. Being young men and having the ability to recover from the exhaustion of the field, we would soon find ways to entertain ourselves.

Just thinking about using our time wisely started even before going aboard ship. It was always a dogfight trying to offload the Tango boats when arriving back at ship. We would scramble to get in line for the wash down by the navy with the fire hose. We would put away our gear in the conex and make our way to the berthing area, leaving a brown trail like a slug behind us, only to get first in line for either the shower or the ship's galley. One way to get ahead of the line for the fire hose was to get rid of your fragmentation grenades prior to offloading, as the navy would not allow you to get hosed off with them still attached to your gear, this would required extra time and put you further back at the hose line. Apparently, one time the fire hose tore a grenade from one of the guys' web belts, which activated the grenade. He lucked out as it was washed overboard prior to detonation. So in order to get rid of the grenades, we threw them overboard as we traveled down the river on the Tango boats. It was great sport pulling the pin, throwing the grenade overboard, and waiting to see what the concussion would bring up. The rivers of the Mekong have some ugly, prehistoric-looking bottom fish.

Our missions were so physically demanding that it sometimes was all we could do to put our gear away and board ship. Regular bowel movements were difficult in the field because of the extreme physical demands. However, once on board and with a meal in our guts, we would head to the berthing areas for showers and a change of clothing. At about this time, Mother Nature would call, and we would line up for the toilets. There, for the first time, many would relax, and many would fall asleep on the shitter. It was a sight to behold a man completely passed out, his pants around his ankles, totally asleep, and unaware of his surroundings. Many times we literally had to drag them off the stools, lay them on the floor, and then take our turn. Many a picture was taken unbeknown to the poor slobs passed out.

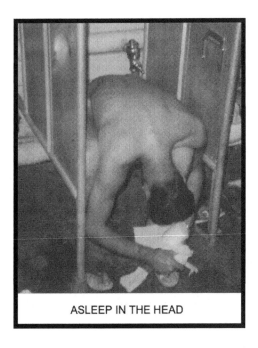

ASLEEP IN THE HEAD

Mail call would be called after most had gotten fed and settled in the berthing area. It was something all looked forward to. One was always aware of who was getting mail and who wasn't. Dear John letters, while not all that rampant, were still a significant problem. I loathed the women who wrote them. My opinion was that they could have at least waited until the end of his tour until they put a man's morale in the cesspool.

Three days before leaving for Vietnam, I went hunting for deer and shot a nice buck. I took it to the local butcher and had him make the entire dear into jerky. My mother was to send three-pound packages of the jerky to me on a weekly basis. The guys loved the jerky and knew when my package was in. I didn't mind sharing, but it became so popular that there really wasn't anything left to share. One time when my package came in, the guys got to it before I could; they left me one piece. Nevertheless, it was a real treat.

Our loved ones sent us all kinds of treats and goodies. My mother was sending me half-gallon containers of powdered orange drink, a gift always appreciated. One day we were ordered to pack up our duffel bags and move to a new ship. I packed everything in the bag but the orange drink. I then put it on the top of my clothing, closed the bag, and off we went. It was a typical hot, humid day in the Mekong Delta, and although we didn't have far to go, we were all sweating by the time we made it to the new ship. We chose new bunks, reserving them by throwing our duffel bags on them. Later that day I examined my duffel bag only to find everything in an orange glaze. The dry powder had sifted all through the bag and then set up in the humidity to a gooey, sticky glaze. I had no underwear, socks, or uniforms other than the orange-glazed ones. So into the dirty clothes pile went my entire duffel bag, and I was relegated to smelling like a swamp rat for the next few days.

KLOPH, DOC SCHUBEL, ED, RONIGER, REED, SEAMSTER

The first time I observed this, it blew me away: after a mission from which we all came back and did some damage to Charlie, we'd usually be feeling pretty good, and many times the atmosphere would be akin to that of a football locker room after kicking some ass. Those who did the scoring and were the players would go over the action play by play, while those on the bench and the non-players would look on and listen to their after-action recollections.

Once in a while we would be treated to a beer call on the barges. The beer was always warm and usually Carling Black Label. (The REMFs always got the good beers like Bud and Miller.) Usually only two beers were allowed, and they were 3.2 percent at that. But, hey, it was better than nothing.

One day as we came in and put our equipment away in the conex, the navy was setting up for a beer call, and I could see that they had some Bud and—most important—some ice. There were two troughs made of fifty-gallon drum barrel halves welded together end to end. In one barrel was the Bud and the ice, and in the other was brown river water and the Black Label.

Soon the ship's loudspeakers announced a beer call on the barge, and we were ready and waiting with wet lips. But as we approached the iced-down Bud, we were told that it was navy rations not meant for army slobs. Dejected, we grabbed our warm Black Label and huddled around the conex, bitching and complaining. Finally someone said, "Fuck those Swab Jocks! We've got all the guns, and I'm not drinking anymore of this warm piss as long as there is iced-down Bud!" And that's all it took. When we went for our second beer, we went for the iced beer and plainly told them to fuck off when they tried to stop us. And that was that—mission accomplished! However, the navy seldom ever had another beer call with us. They always had theirs from then on when we were out on a mission. Chicken shit fuckers!

The navy never did like us rampaging through their ship, and at times there would be confrontations. One day one of my grenadiers found one:

Harrington was a raw-boned boy we put on the M-79, so he soon had the nickname of Thumper. The M-79 had a sound similar to a thump when fired, thus the name; it was one he was proud of. He was a good soldier and carried a heavy load of M-79 ammo. He was one of those guys you didn't want to fuck with; he had a short fuse and just had that look that said, "Don't fuck with me!" For some reason he got into an argument with one of the ensigns aboard ship. Thumper snapped and turned on the ensign, giving him a right cross that knocked him down the stairs. Thumper's ass was wanted by the navy brass in the worst way. He spent a couple of days in the ship's brig and was released to the army for court martial. It didn't happen. They just sent him back to Bravo as though nothing had ever happened. We loved it!

The only good thing about losing a brother is that you would be given time away from the bush to honor the ones you lost. We would gather on the ship's deck, where the helmets, rifles, and boots of those lost would be set up front and center; the Chaplin would say a few words, and then a recording of taps would be played. Many times, in conjunction with this ceremony, there would be an awards ceremony. We weren't into medals that much because we had more important things to worry about. Besides, it seemed to be only an officer's duty to award, as most of us enlisted men didn't have any idea how to go about recommending anyone anyhow. I, for one, never knew how, and it pains me all these years later that I had not awarded even one of my men so much as an Army Commendation Medal; they all deserved so much more!

Cpt. Perkins & Bravo Co.

When the ceremony was over, the guys scrambled to the barges to catch the shuttle boat into Dong Tam. I was one of the slow guys, having some things to catch up on, and before I knew it, I had missed the shuttle into Dong Tam. Totally dejected and bummed out, I sat with four other guys in the berthing area trying to figure out our next move. During our conversation, one of the guys mentioned that the navy would have such things as ice cream and steak on the menu when we army guys weren't around. The thought of having ice cream was almost overwhelming. It was hot in the berthing area, with no air-conditioning, and before you knew it, we had come up with the idea to raid the ship's freezer. The majority of the swabbies had also taken leave into Dong Tam, leaving the ship almost unattended, with the exception of sparse security. We moved up into the ship's galley and started casing the joint. It didn't take long before we found the freezer and stuck our heads in. Lo and behold, there was the ice cream— gallons and gallons of it, five-gallon containers stacked on top of one another. We all grabbed a five-gallon container and ran like hell to the berthing area; the mission was successful. We made sure we all grabbed a different flavor. We soon decided that twenty-five gallons of ice cream was a little too much for the five of us to eat. So we took turns tasting one another's ice cream. About the time we were getting brain freeze, we heard an announcement that there would be one more shuttle into Dong Tam. We all scurried down to the barges, jumped on the shuttle, and away to the land of cold beer we went.

We made it to our respective NCO and Enlisted Men's clubs, consumed mass quantities of beer, had many a laugh, flipped the REMFs some shit, and then took the shuttles back to the ship. That afternoon the sun continued to heat the berthing area, melting the ice cream, which then oozed its way out of the paper containers. There was a twenty-gallon Neapolitan mess that everybody disregarded and walked right through as though it wasn't even there, tracking the gooey mess throughout the ship.

We awoke at 0430 hours and were on our way for another mission. The whole time we chuckled and fantasized about what the swabbies were thinking and calling us as they cleaned the gooey, sticky mess from the ship.

***

Sometimes, although rare, we would fly into Dong Tam. We had just landed in Dong Tam coming in from a long, hot mission, and a rest was much needed. We were given a vacated area inside Dong Tam with barracks to call our own for one day. We stacked our weapons and were then treated to a barbecue and cold soft drinks. There was a basketball court of sorts and plenty of benches and seats for everyone. Some took advantage of the cots inside the barracks and took much-needed naps. We were in heaven, enjoying our break from the mud and Charlie. Soon we got our hands on some beer, and the party became real. Life was great!

Just as all were settled down and slowed down by the barbecue and beer, machine-gun fire broke out from one of our barracks. I looked up to see a steady stream of tracers arcing their way across the parade field and into the MP head-quarters about a thousand yards away. I couldn't believe my eyes. One of us was taking on the 9th ID, MP headquarters all by his lonesome.

We all had a dislike for the MPs; they seemed to have it in for us off-base grunts. We were seldom in proper uniform, giving them that reason alone to screw with us. One time as we unloaded from the shuttle boats for a couple of hours of time in Dong Tam, the MPs herded all of us to the seamstress shop, de-manding we all complete our uniforms before proceeding. The lone seamstress was overwhelmed, and it soon became evident that if you weren't in the front of the line, you weren't going to enjoy a beer or a massage at Ahn's Steam Bath. Many just went back to the harbor and awaited a ride back to the ship. This kind of disrespect of the grunts was enough to piss off anyone.

They invented police brutality and had their own good ol' boy ways of deal-ing with things. One time while I was traveling, I stopped in an NCO club in Long Binh. I found a friend I had known in infantry training at Ft. Lewis. We soon invited a couple of Aussies to share our table. The club rules were when you finished your beer, you put the can in a garbage can. The Aussies thought they would instead start a beer-can pyramid in the middle of the table. Soon my friends and I were adding to it. The bar M.A. (Master of Arms) came over and instructed us in a rather rude way to clear the table—a reaction that started the guys at the next table adding to the growing stack. Soon there were close to one hundred cans in the stack. Our way of thinking was that the Aussies had been mistreated by the M.A., and this was our way of showing solidarity. Other than the beer cans, we were not being out of line. However, within minutes, the two doors to the NCO club broke open with unhinging velocity as a dozen or so MPs rushed in, blowing their whistles and demanding that all take the prone position with hands on their heads. Those who hesitated were promptly clubbed about the head with full force. I couldn't believe my eyes. There were no questions, just demands, and I soon realized that I too needed to take the position before my skull was cracked. We, the rule breakers, were all kicked out, and the MPs went on their way as though nothing had happened. I learned a lesson there: don't fuck with the MPs.

Another time I went to one of the whore houses between Dong Tam and My Tho only to find an SFC (sergeant first class) going crazy with his pants half on and drunk on his ass. He was calling the girls every name in the book as he tore down the bamboo walls. This was no place for me, I ascertained, and promptly left. A month or so later I went back there to a pleasant atmosphere. I ordered a cold beer and began flirting with the girls, only to be suddenly surrounded by MPs. They rounded us up, and as I was being taken to the paddy wagon, I noticed that the NCO in charge was none other than the SFC who was there tearing the place apart the last time I was there. As I walked by him, I let him know that I was witness to his bullshit last time he was there. He promptly ordered me to be taken to his jeep. As the MPs and their prisoners entered the main gate of Dong Tam, he stopped his jeep and said, "Get the fuck out of here!" I promptly accommodated. I had missed another Article 15 (non-judicial punishment).

So it wasn't any great surprise to see someone strafing the MP headquarters because we all hated their friggin' guts for one reason or another. Soon you could see the MPs scattering; it was just a matter of time before they would be here ready to blow the machine gunner's ass out of the barracks. Immediately a couple of the machine gunner's friends from his platoon went running into the barracks, and just as the MPs showed up, they managed to talk some sense into him. They soon came out of the barracks, but there was no doubt where he was going. The MPs would have their way with him and the company or battalion COs weren't going to get his ass out of this bind.

One time when we came into Dong Tam after a hard four days out in the boonies and having lost more men, we were in no mood to be fucked with as we flew into Dong Tam for a night off and aboard ship. The Dong Tam chopper pad was at the opposite end of the base camp from the harbor. As we departed, the airport dump trucks awaited us for the short trip to the harbor, and while transportation was greatly appreciated, the dirty dump trucks weren't. We all loaded up and proceeded to the south end of Dong Tam. We were now feeling a little surly and like a bunch of animals being transported by trucks. For amusement we made barnyard animal sounds. While we were mooing and baa baaing, someone threw a smoke grenade overboard as we passed through a rear echelon's company area. That was all it took, and the fun began as we all joined in and started smoking up the east side of Dong Tam with our smoke grenades, as if to say "Fuck you, REMFs."

As our small convoy approached the harbor area, we were met by two jeep loads of MPs blocking the road. We all thought this was very funny as we thought: What the fuck can these guys do? We then all pretended to ready arms, knowing full well that this was not worth deadly force but, at the same time, worth the fun of fucking with the MPs.

The CO/B-6 had stayed behind at the boarding area and left 2-6 in charge. Two Six unloaded and was met by hostile MPs. As he tried to reason with them, you could see the movement of their heads in disagreement by both sides. An MP officer soon was on the scene, and the argument seemed to go even worse for 2-6 as he returned to the truck, grabbed a radio, and called Pistol Pete. Within minutes Pete's Huey was overhead, stirring up dust for a close-by landing in the streets of Dong Tam; the dust was flying everywhere as the MPs held onto their helmet liners. The lieutenant colonel jumped out of the chopper as though he was heading to a fist fight and went directly to the MPs in a confrontational manner while waving the trucks on. He laid some finger-pointing shit on the MPs and then boarded his chopper; it was a quick, direct, one-sided conversation. The MPs left the scene as though nothing had happened at all. All the while whistles and middle fingers saluted the MPs' as they evacuated the area.

Pistol Pete couldn't have done anything more to bring our morale to peak. We knew our leader was our man and wouldn't take any shit from the fucking REMF MPs. His support made our day as we boarded boats for our short ride to the Mobile Riverine ships and a cold shower followed by real food and a real night's sleep with a smile on our faces for a change.

Many times when we had time in Dong Tam, guys would go their own way looking for some kind of action—maybe just a massage or some gambling or maybe they would go outside the base camp perimeter and explore the whore houses. Sometimes the brave would even go into My Tho, and so it was with one man. He never came back, and we just thought he'd gone AWOL for a day or two. Then the rumor came back that he'd been found alongside the banks of the Song My Tho. He was dead with wire wrapped around his hands and neck. No one ever knew the details.

Bravo Company having its share of characters is an understatement. We all came from different walks of life and the four corners of America. Every platoon had its cards and comics. Just as every platoon had its own con man and its honest Abe, it had its genius, and it had its dimwit, the underachiever and the overachiever, the Yankee and the Redneck. Some were from Podunk, USA; others were from big-city, USA. I was from small town, USA, and as such I received a little ribbing from the big-city boys when my local newspaper would arrive on a weekly basis. When the *Valley Herald* newspaper came in from my little home-town of Milton-Freewater, Oregon, the Gammer (as we called Gambino) from the big city of Buffalo, New York, would grab the paper, demand everybody's attention, and start reading selected articles from the newspaper. He was totally amused that farmer John's cattle being loose or Mary Jane's trip to Portland would make the news or that the school cafeteria menu would make the front page. I was so naïve at first that I didn't understand what there was to be amused about. But the big-city boys loved it, and it was a weekly attraction right behind my weekly package of mule-deer jerky. One of the guys from New York City would always asked when we came in whether or not my *Valley Herald* was in. We were easily amused.

One evening before an operation, 2-6 asked me to make up a list of the men in the platoon, and in that list he wanted me to describe each person's job and what he was expected to carry for the next morning's mission. I had a problem defining some of the guys' job descriptions, as one fellow was overweight and out of shape (I couldn't believe he made it through infantry training). His every step through the rice paddy seemed to be a strain, combat terrified him, and when the bullets started flying, he planted his face in the mud and never fired a shot. But he still showed up for each and every mission, which was more than I could say for some. He had value in that he carried a heavy load, so I called his position "Pack Mule" in the list. We had another who couldn't walk across a bamboo or coconut tree bridge to save his life. He got to where he didn't even try and would just jump in the water or mud and get it over with. We had many a laugh, and he was good for the platoon's morale. So I put him down as Super Private, our nickname for him.

When we were lucky enough to be aboard ship, the navy would provide us with meals. The sailors, however, had a propensity to favor their own and would at times literally look up to see if you were navy or army and then make the decision as to which cut of meat you were to receive. I've actually seen times when the army would get an entirely different main course. There was no love lost between the ship's crews and the army. Their choice of menu would drastically change when we were out on missions, as they would save the good stuff for themselves, such as steak and ice cream. The wounded left behind and the company clerk were witness to these tactics.

We were aboard the USS *Benewah* from time to time, a barracks ship that also served as the headquarters for our battalion and sometimes the brigade commanders. The brigade commander demanded his own cook, so the army had a cook who would help the navy when not attending to the brigade commander (the hated Colonel Rainville). He was a large-built man about 240 lb. with rippling muscularity. I first remember him as the guy who could not get enough of Ernie Banks when he came aboard for a visit. He knew every statistics of Ernie's Major League Baseball career to the point Ernie himself was astounded. I never knew his name, although he was a likeable guy and frequently came down to our berthing areas hoping to find conversation with someone other than the sailors. I felt sorry for him because he was an outcast and not very assertive in his willingness to converse. Mostly, he just wasn't one of us, and we just couldn't relate to him. He'd just stand there alone sometimes, watching us and then move on.

One day shortly after we got back from a mission and all were in the berthing area, he came down, cleared his voice in an attention-getting way and announced,

"I know how you all hate the colonel, and I'm no different. The SOB demanded that I have breakfast awaiting him at 0330 hours this morning. I went down to the galley in my underwear, opened it up, turned on the grill, and cracked the eggs on the cold grill as I always do when he wants an early breakfast. I usually return to my area, get dressed, and then return to the galley just in time for the eggs to be cooking and to be scrambled. But this morning as I cracked the eggs with my early morning hard on, I noticed the roster sperm within and couldn't help but think about the colonel eating enlisted man's sperm. Well, he says with pride and his chest puffed out, I just wanted you to know that the colonel ate enlisted man's sperm this morning." We all cheered, and he was as proud as a peacock. He'd finally gotten the attention and respect he was looking for.

Weeks later, the army cook got into a beef with the navy cooks. As the story goes, he locked the doors to the galley and commenced knocking them out, one by one. Those not knocked out pretended to be so. Nobody wanted this animal on them. He was quickly apprehended and put into the ship's brig. It took Pistol Pete some wrangling to get him out, and that was the last we saw of the burley cook.

Chapter 11

I S L A N D   S E C U R I T Y

Although island security was a necessary function, in that we provided protection for the artillery barges, it was truly looked upon by us as a break from the action, almost a mini R&R.

Our mission was to clear the river islands of any VC and then form a secure semicircle perimeter for the artillery barges. They would tie up to the beach and prepare for fire missions. It was quite the sight as each 105 mm Howitzer and its ammo would take up one barge. The battery would be spread out on these barges up against the beach with the CP (Command Post) barge in the middle. There was usually at least one navy boat attached with supplies at hand. The navy, for practical reasons, didn't want us around their barges, but it was mostly to keep us out of their rations. They knew that we had a hunger for the little things that made their life tolerable, like Tang, PX candies, and soft drinks.

On the other hand, we were allowed to order an SP (Sundry Pack) of rations with our resupply for the mission. The SP pack would contain a large quantity of candies, cigarettes, toiletries, and writing paper. We would also have the navy supply boat pick up a load of soft drinks and beer. We always paid an exorbitant price for this service, but it was almost always worth it.

One time we ordered five cases of pop and twenty cases of beer only to have a different boat show up with the five cases of pop and no beer—and no refund. The crew's excuse was that the other boat had a change of orders so this boat was to deliver the supplies to the arty barges and us, and thus didn't know anything else about our order or money.

We were pissed and wanted the bastards bad. Their asses were ours if we could of ever found them. I'm still looking for the squid ass fucks.

ISLAND SECURITY

We only got this mission about once a month at best, but it was received well and needed by the men. Most of the time it was just a relaxing time as though we were on a tropical island with no cares. We always made sure that a certain percentage of us were sober and keeping an eye on anything suspicious. A little bullshit, sun tanning, eating better food, and a lot of sleeping on a banana leaf bed was the usual.

During these days of working island security, I always enjoyed listening to the stories from the old-timers and their experiences from before my time in Bravo. One that sticks in my mind was from Middendorf when he was an FNG. Middendorf was a short but stocky Texas boy. One night they sat up on a canal in ambush, one platoon on each side of the canal. A sampan came down the river, and the platoon on the opposite side opened up. A survivor swam to the opposite side and started running down the trail toward Middendorf. It was dark as hell, and Middendorf was just standing there squinting when the VC ran directly into him, knocking him down. Both were surprised as hell and found each other lying there face to face. Middendorf no doubt surprised and in fear immediately broke the VC's neck—a night I'm sure he'll never forget.

There are two other stories that will always stick in my mind: while on an island on the Mekong River near Ben Tre: One day we noticed a sampan headed our way with purpose. As it got closer, we could tell that it was a lone woman. She soon ran her sampan onto the opposite beach of the arty barges as a couple of others and I grabbed a weapon and met her at the beach. We searched her, and it was obvious her sampan was empty. She didn't speak English, but we tried to ask her what she was up to. She began clapping one hand over the open end of her cupped other hand, sign language for "boom boom" or "wanna fuck?" This gal was uglier than shit, I mean one of the ugliest Vietnamese women I had ever seen. Her face looked like she was hit by a Chinese Claymore mine. Thinking this situation to be rather humorous in that she thought we would have anything to do with her, we took her over to 2-6 to see what he thought. After all, she was at least good enough for a laugh. None of us had been to Dong Tam or a whore house in over a month, but I still didn't think she would be successful making any money here. In fact, we were all broke, spending our last MPC (military payment currency) on beer and pop.

Two-six didn't want anything to do with her, as she went through the motions of clapping her right hand on top of her left fist and saying, "boom boom?" Then Barnes offered her some C rats for payment. At first she refused; then he offered more. Realizing we had no MPC, she motioned to the seclusion of the foliage. All of a sudden Turse jumped up and made mention that rank had its privileges, as he pulled out some C rats for payment and took her to the bushes. He also mentioned it was his duty to check her out for the men. Ya, right. This was way too funny. I couldn't believe that he was screwing this gal. Soon all the guys were laying out C rats as if to say, "It's my turn next." I started giving 2-6 a bad time about being our leader and not showing us how it was done. He said he was low on C rats. We all offered to pitch in, but he still refused. Soon Turse returned with the little Boom-Boom girl and arguments started about who was next. She had a cute little body. Her face, however, gave her away as an older woman. She would lead the guys across a couple of muddy coconut canals where she laid her rice mat on the grass and then take care of the men. She would then jump into the canal and wash her crotch in the muddy canal, put her pants on, button up her shirt and back she went for next guy.

I didn't know whether to be grossed out or amused. I watched with amusement as the men jockeyed for position. Soon the line was gone, and to my amazement Turse wanted more of this Mekong Mud Sex as he begged for C rats and cigarettes from the guys.

Soon the Boom Boom girl was on her way, having taken on all but one or two from the entire platoon. With her sampan loaded with C rats and riding low in the water, she stroked back up the river from where she came. The power of youth's hormones once again showed its ugly head. It wasn't long until we realized that we needed to be resupplied, as our stomachs were now growling for food. This was one of the few times we could eat and enjoy real food in the field but we had none to be found. We weren't going to get a chopper resupply and could only await the navy Tango boat that was serving as a resupply boat. Just another day in paradise as we begged the artillerymen for C rats with minimum results.

The battalions with base camps had the advantage of having their own whore houses that were managed by their medics. Battalions were always trying to improve their whore houses with new talent and would stoop to the low of stealing whores from other battalions when the opportunity arose. Some would make trips to Saigon, recruiting them with promises of riches and stability. The competition could be fierce.

Another time we received notice that we would soon be on island security, but we still had some miles to go before our pick up by the Tango boats. As we were clearing an abandoned hooch, we flushed out a nice, plump chicken. I grabbed him up thinking that once we got on the island and cooled down, we'd be ready for some solid food, which we hadn't been able to keep down in days. I tied him to my web belt and away we went. I soon realized that the chicken wasn't going to go peacefully. I had to tie his wings up and somehow shut him up. I wrapped some trip wire around him. This did the trick, and he quit flapping around and making noise. I was on my way.

We caught our Tango ride to the small island in the river, disembarked, and got online as we swept the island, clearing it of any possible VC. We then set up our perimeter just inside a wood line, with the paddy between us and the artillery barges. Because I was a platoon sergeant, I chose a large hooch as my CP, as Doc and my RTO made themselves at home. I gave the chicken to the Mamasan of the hooch and in my lame Vietnamese got it across that I wanted her to cook it. I left and made my rounds, checking out my men's positions, making adjustments as needed, and taking the time to shoot the shit with the guys. They were busy making banana-leaf beds, stripping down to allow the air to dry their clothes and feet, and in general, just loafing around, which is what island security was all about. Two-six had made his CP out of the other hooch in the area and was enjoying the break also. There were about four families on the entire island but, to our disappointment, no young children to play and joke around with, not to mention to hire for the little things we didn't want to do. One island we frequented had a little six- to eight-year-old who could tear your rifle down and clean it in no time at all. He loved hanging with us.

Local boys hanging with the GI's   Willy Perez enjoying the children

I returned to my hooch to see how Mamasan was doing with the chicken, only to find it cooked and in a large aluminum pot with rice and lemongrass. She was waiting for us to sit down and enjoy. I yelled at Doc to come and eat. He showed up only to say that he wasn't having anything to do with it. "Hell, it's cooked. What can be wrong with it?" I asked.

He said, "You should have seen the way she cooked it. She wrung its neck then stomped on it time and time again and squeezed as much shit out of it as she could. Then she plucked the feathers and put the whole thing in the pot and commenced cooking. Threw in some rice and grass and called it good."

I didn't believe him. I thought he was just trying to screw with me. I sat down at the table with Mamasan and Papasan and commenced to fill my bowl. The very first ladle came up with intestines wrapped around it. I stirred around only to find the head and a foot also in there. That was it for me. The meal was all theirs after that nauseating experience.

I went outside to take off my boots and enjoy a meal of C rats, when all of a sudden I saw a fight going on as one of the men tackled another. I ran over to see what was going on. Apparently Big Red had found some Vietnamese rice whiskey and gotten all fucked up, grabbed a sixteen, and was going to kill 2-6 when he was tackled on the way. He looked like a wild man, and it took three guys to keep him down. He was shouting, spitting, and writhing like a maniac. I had him tied to a coconut tree, which he didn't like and then he threatened to kill me and anyone else who got in his way. So I ordered him to be gagged also. Besides, it was getting dark, and we didn't need any noise out here. It may have been an island, but that didn't ensure that Charlie wouldn't make a visit.

Big Red was a transfer from another company who probably had spent some time in the stockade prior to being sent to us. This wasn't the first time I had a run-in with him. But he was riding a completely different horse this time.

As morning broke I could see some of the guys heating water with some C4 explosive, getting it ready for some coffee, a rare treat and one I was also looking forward to, even though I wasn't much of a coffee drinker. I walked over to where Big Red was tied up, and what a pitiful sight he was! He had puked through his gag, and the vomit had run down his chin onto his chest and belly. He was passed out now. We all ate a nice meal for breakfast, as our appetites had returned from all the exhausting humping and heat of the last few days. I told one of the guys to untie Big Red, figuring he'd learned his lesson and had sobered up.

As the gag was released, Red came to and with a vengeance. He was still in a crazed mode, still wanting to kill 2-6. We gagged him again. We couldn't deal with his shit any longer. Red was going to have to go. We had a resupply ship coming in later, and he was going out with it. As I called in my resupply list, I informed Battalion that we had a problem child who would be returning on the Huey. All this time 2-6 pretended as though nothing was wrong and just left the problem to me.

Making new friends

As the Huey came in, I had Big Red hung from a bamboo pole as you would a dead deer. As soon as the men had unloaded the chopper, here we came with Big Red hanging under the pole, writhing like a pissed-off banshee.

We dropped one end of the pole in the middle of the chopper floor and were about to skew him off when the entire crew came unglued as the pilot came out of his seat, immediately getting into my face. "What the hell are we going to do with this?" he says. We argued for a bit, and then I agreed to tie him to the cargo rings on the floor, securing him from the crew. The pilot didn't like it, but it was better than just leaving him on the deck to his own rampage. We got him tied down, and away went Big Red, never to be seen again. We went back to our happy, little family and lay around the rest of the day as though we we're at a tropical island. Life was good this day.

ED TAKING A BREAK/ ISLAND SECURITY   BREAK TIME: COURTESY OF WILLY PEREZ

Assorted photos:

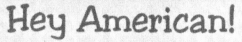

Hey American!

Join the winning side and be paid!

You do not have to fight!

$10,000 Cash Reward

Hey American!
$40,000 Cash Reward!

You do not need to fight your own people! We just need your cooperation in learning your training!

You can earn extra cash if you choose to assist in our training or intelligence programs!

Live in comfort and safety in Europe or Asia!

Enemy propaganda pamplets

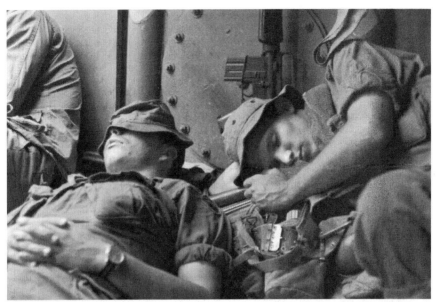

Catching a nap on a Tango Boat

Bull riding in Vietnam!

Doc Schuebel & Gaa

Break time!

Ed cleaning rifle with Shaming

Stauffer

On the move and vunerable in the opoen

Crossing the river with Papason

Proud ARVN's with captured flags

VC PRISONER

Chapter 12

PLATOON SERGEANT

Bravo Company had been having lots of contact with Charlie for the last couple weeks and I had my share of them personally. I had killed six VC in the last ten days. One here, two there, and so on. Mostly I had been lucky in that I had been in the right place at the right time. I caught one sneaking up on us in the middle of the night and took him out just three coconut dikes away. Another time my squad was running point, and I was breaking in a new grenadier who was pulling slack. We were transitioning from a rather open area into an area of thick foliage. I walked up to the grenadier to ensure that he was changing his chambered round from an HE (High Explosive) round to a shotgun round, which was more appropriate for the surrounding area. As I approached him, he quickly turned to our left, pointing his M-79 at some thick foliage only a couple yards away and said, "Halt." Being new he hadn't gotten down the Vietnamese word for *halt* (dung Lai), and I was fairly sure he only had an HE round chambered, which was nothing more than a single shot without an activated round at that distance. I immediately knocked him into the ditch to our right and unloaded my magazine into the unknown target to our left. As the bush came alive with writhing bodies, I also took cover in the ditch, reloaded, and fired another magazine into the bush. As we dragged the bodies out, I could see that two of them had nothing on but black shorts. Worst of all, they were both young boys—maybe ten to twelve years old. My heart sank to an all-time low. We searched the area but found no weapons. We then searched the bodies only to find booby trap trip wire and a two-bit VC identity card rolled up in their waistbands. Thank God, I thought. At least they were VC. But what kind of low-down motherfuckers would send their kids out to, of all things, set booby traps? I was now even more furious at my enemy; they had stooped to a low that I had not even thought possible. Having immature kids take on the job of being indiscriminate terrorists was in my mind the worst.

Around this time, one of the other platoons had found a large cache of weapons and ammo. As our situation was reported to HQ, we were asked to bring the cache and the bodies to an open rice paddy and to secure a LZ for an incoming news team. I had a couple of guys drag the boys along to our objective. I heard from one of them—Big George who was a large man, so I figured he could handle the extra weight. He let me know in no uncertain terms he didn't appreciate being given the job because he thought it was racism for me to give it to him. I disagreed and called it sizeism. I didn't appreciate Big George calling me a racist, and I let him know in no uncertain terms that he was the racist for even thinking that way. I pointed out that there were other black men in the company who would probably kick the shit out of him for even talking that way. There was no racism here that I had detected. We as a group had many problems to overcome, and the last one I gave a fuck about was somebody's skin color. Racism in an infantry company is a rare thing and usually culled out. The racists either found a way out or we put them out.

So the TV crew came as I was busy making sure my men had good positions to keep the area secure. The CO then called to tell me to come to the landing site so I could be part of the filming. I just pretended that I didn't hear him and stayed away from having my picture taken with dead children. The fact that they had VC ID cards didn't diminish my sadness all that much.

Once in from the mission, the CO (DeEdwardo) informed me that he had enrolled me in the division's NCO school as a reward for being such a good little killer of a sergeant. I didn't look this gift horse in the mouth. I knew this meant a week to ten days away from combat and a fast track for E-6. I was off and in Dong Tam early, as I didn't want to take any chances that he'd change his mind.

The NCO school was nothing more than a boring class in a stuffy, hot room. Nothing in the class had anything to do with being a better NCO in the field. Every night was spent at the NCO club hanging with the other infantrymen in the class as we drank our way to a better sleep. The biggest obstacle was keeping awake in class and avoiding the wrath of the instructor.

I had only a couple of days of this torture left when I was summoned to the entrance of the barracks. Awaiting me there were three men from Second Platoon who had a box with them. As I looked inside, I could see Roniger's .357 magnum and holster as part of the contents. My heart dropped. I knew what this meant—my best friend had been severely wounded or at worst killed. It was the latter. They explained to me their nightmare of February 20. Another good friend and our machine gunner, Stauffer, had also been killed among others from Bravo. I said very little as they looked for words of encouragement and offered me their words of sympathy.

As they left me with the box of Roniger's belongings (less his personal items sent home), I knew what this meant. Roniger had recently been promoted to platoon sergeant, so I was the new platoon sergeant now—a job I really didn't want, especially this way.

I went to the NCO club to be alone with my thoughts and a cold one. To my surprise, I felt as cold as they get. I had just lost my best friend and had shaken it off like it never happened after a couple drinks. I had hardened beyond comprehension unbeknown to myself. My survival instinct wasn't going to allow me to mourn. I also knew that since Roniger got it, I would have been right in there with him. The NCO school saved my life!

I made my way back to the ship after milking my last day in Dong Tam. There I would get more details about February 20. Apparently one of the other companies in the battalion had been hit hard by a battalion-sized VC unit. They were called VC units but the reality was that they were made up of just as many NVA as VC. The company had suffered many casualties well into the double-digit figure and were in need of help. As Bravo choppered in, it received casualties while still in the air, one being the first sergeant, who got it in the lower torso. The platoons got separated and the Second found themselves online trying to fight their way into the wood line. They met hard resistance and were forced to take up positions behind the thin paddy dikes in the open. The other platoons were unable to reach them, and soon the enemy fire became deadly, wounding many and killing Roniger and Stauffer in the Second Platoon. The other platoons had their share of casualties and death, as did the helicopter crews, who lost five or six birds. It was a day they all will never forget.

There was a look on my men's faces that I shall never forget. It was as if they were looking for some magical words of wisdom from this twenty-year-old. What they really wanted was to see me as their platoon sergeant and with strength and conviction. We had also lost Doc Schuebel, as he had fulfilled his combat tour as a medic. Doc would be sent to brigade in Ben Tre, where he would finish his tour in the rear. I would do my best to try to fill some of these major losses to the platoon!

Plt. Sgt. Ed Eaton taking a break

My first mission as platoon sergeant (Bravo 2-5) I wore Roniger's shoulder holster and its .357 magnum as a tribute to him, but it never felt right for some reason, and I soon gave it to one of my point men for bunker clearing.

We got a new medic. Doc Harneck, a kid from my old stomping grounds in central Washington, showed up with enthusiasm and conviction. He was no Doc Schuebel, but he had what it took.

Tangos following Monitor down a narrow river.

On the next mission, we got orders to board the Tango boats for a mission on the infamous South Bank of the Song My Tho. Rumor had it that the mission was going to be watched from the air by the secretary of defense. We went further up the river than normal for a South Bank insertion. It was an open area with limited Nipa palm on the banks and a klick from the wood line. As we approached the landing zone, the boats were ordered to open fire with all they had. This is when I knew for sure that something was going on as we would have never wasted that amount of ammo on such an open area prior to landing unless we had received fire. But, hey, it was a good display of firepower, that was for sure. The ramps were dropped, and we made it into the wood line, which was really more of an open agricultural area sprinkled with hooch's here and there with the small open rice paddies between. The trails were lined with coconut trees. This was a cake walk and we knew it, but the gunships continued circling overhead, not for us, but for the secretary of defense's security, as he also circled above with our general. This mission was a joke, but it was what we needed—a walk in the countryside. We covered some territory and finally took a break. I chose a small hooch to hide from the sun. The Mamasan inside was a little nervous while rolling herself a Beatle Nut chew (a mild stimulant), she kept looking in the direction of the small bunker inside the hooch. I had my point man check it out; sure enough, there was one lonely VC hiding in it. We now had a detainee and at least felt like we did some good. We were soon told to return to the river, and we proudly strolled back with our prize while looking over our shoulders, wondering if our general and the secretary could see us. That was the closest we came to the enemy that day. It was like having a day off, and we hoped that the secretary of defense would come visit us more often.

Being a platoon sergeant in combat is more about being a part of a team than being a heavy-handed controller of men. There were times, however, when I had to make decisions that I expected my men to obey. There were also times when my men just didn't want to volunteer for a nasty job, and asking for volunteers was a waste of time. There were also times when I had to be the one showing the way: We had been on a nasty mission with many firefights and numerous sorties. The men were tired, and we were in desperate need of resupply. We sat up inside a wood line with a small paddy beside us as we put together our resupply list. The resupply chopper was soon on its way when a mortar round landed on the other side of the paddy, lighting up the night sky ever so briefly. Everyone hunkered down awaiting the next rounds, but they didn't come. We were sure that the enemy had at least registered their mortar tubes and that the next rounds would be walked in on us rather expeditiously when they saw fit. Second Platoon was given the job of bringing in the resupply chopper. It was night, and smoke wasn't going to work for identification, so a strobe light would need to be taken to the middle of the paddy for the identification of the resupply bird's LZ. I asked for volunteers to go out and call the bird in and gather the resupplies. I met stiff resistance to any suggestion: "You want me to go out into the middle of a paddy that has just been registered and stand there with a strobe light in hand, awaiting the inevitable from Charlie?" "No way, man—you wouldn't do it." "Yes, I would," I told them, but my words had no effect. I either had to order someone or do it myself. I grabbed a PRC 25 radio, a strobe light and soon heard the chopper blades from afar. I went out into the small paddy and finally the call came in to identify. I nervously put the strobe into my helmet and held it on top of my head to lower the chances of my body being an AK target. The pilot came back with, "Which one of the strobes do you want me to come in on?" Oh fuck, Charlie has our radio frequency and is trying to call these guys into a trap. I turned mine off and on a few times to help them identify the LZ. I informed them that they needed to start dumping the supplies within feet of the landing and get the hell out of the area ASAP, as I had no help unloading the ship. As the pilot came in and turned on his landing lights, I awaited the inevitable as my sphincter muscles contracted, and I got ready to kiss my ass good-bye. As the Huey started to hover, the supplies came flying out of the bird, and it was soon off into the dark Mekong sky. To the amazement of all, no mortar rounds and not a shot was fired—I'd dodged another one!

The next morning as we swept into the wood line, the point element came upon the site where the mortar had exploded. The mortar had exploded inside the tube, killing the two VC manning it—a lovely sight, bringing smiles to our faces.

We were on our second day of another mission and across the river, west of Ben Tre, when we came upon what could only be interpreted as a VC training camp. Seamster was trying to be funny and said it looked like a Vietnamese boy scout camp to him. We dug around for a while but found no weapons or cache. The enemy had split the scene, leaving it like a ghost town. We circled around the area and came back around dark to set up ambushes. Second Platoon had a nice "hard ball" trail with which to set up an ambush with claymores, a machine gun, a grenadier, and riflemen. Around midnight, two VC came into view on the Starlight scope with AKs slung. As they approached and came within range of the claymores, the striker was depressed, blowing the shit out of those guys.

The one who took the brunt of the blast lay dead in the middle of the trail; the other one was blown to the side and into some dry sugar cane. Soon he started moaning, keeping all of us up. The poor bastard was in terrible shape if the noises he made had anything to do with it. The guys couldn't take any more of it and wanted to throw grenades out to put him out of his misery. I asked Doc if he wanted to go out and see if there was anything he could do. He wasn't having anything to do with it. "You don't expect me to go out there and get my head blown off for one of those fucks, do ya? Besides, I'd need to use a flashlight to find the fucker and to treat him—no way!" I didn't blame him. In fact, I may have done whatever needed to stop him. Doc was more important to us than what was out there. Besides, these fuckers had never shown any mercy to us or their own. The moaning continued until I couldn't take it anymore. I crawled out either to blow this fucker's head off or to bring him back. I didn't know which, but I knew I couldn't take it anymore. We had no pity for him, as we had heard our own moan all night more than once. As I got closer, he quit his moaning. I lay there five feet from him, waiting for any signs of life with my pistol on him, still not knowing what I was going to do. Five minutes went by, and there were no more sounds. He chose to die silently. I chose to consider him dead and go back to my position. I didn't know whether he chose to keep quiet because of me or whether he had, in fact, died. It didn't matter as his wounds were such that no medic was going to save his life anyhow. War is so fucked! As morning crept in, we went out and checked the bodies for anything significant. They were both dead.

We had been checkerboarding for a couple days now and were getting tired of this recon by blood method that the Butcher of the Delta (M.G. Ewell) was so high on. Although we had killed a half dozen VC, we had lost two to booby traps who probably weren't going to make it, and if they did, they were going to have big problems as life went along for them. We had also lost another to the deceptive rivers of the delta. It was just a simple fall off the bamboo bridge into the canal and then no sign of life again. He just said, "Oh, fuck," and those were his last words. He was a new guy who couldn't swim, and it probably wouldn't have mattered if he could as the swirling current swallowed him like a monster from the deep.

As we cruised along in a Huey at 1500 feet AGL (above ground level), we were met by another Huey off our flank. As it moved in closer, I could see a cameraman hanging out the side, filming us as we flew along. The pilot would come in and out, side to side, and as we started our descent, he fell behind and above.

As we landed and started toward the wood line, we received orders to hold up and stay in the paddy while the other platoons continued in to secure the area for the landing of a news team. As soon as the wood line was secured by the other platoons, we headed into the wood line ourselves with this three-person group from CBS. This CBS team consisted of a cameraman, a human mule, and the best-looking American woman I'd seen since leaving the states. She was the leader of this group, and everybody was googley-eyed immediately, paying her homage as though she were the president. Sex is a powerful distraction for a young man full of hormones.

We also had a young sergeant get off the bird who was assigned to us as a pathfinder, whatever that was, I thought. I'd never heard of the school myself. As far as I could, tell he was just another guy who was not carrying his load and couldn't be counted on to be anywhere in particular. Nobody knew why he was here, and nobody, including the CO, knew what to do with him. He was just this guy who had gone to pathfinder school who was along for the ride, as far as we knew.

As Second Platoon continued into a stand of high elephant grass, it was obvious this scenario was going to be a problem. None of my men were paying any attention to their job, only to the gal with the film crew. They found any reason to fall back for a look. I also found myself smiling for the camera and looking at her with lust in my loins. The female presence along with the camera was overpowering. I didn't know which was worse, her or the camera. But I knew one thing for sure—the combination was deadly. We were in Indian country, and my men were walking around like smitten kids in a park. I hoped she wasn't going to stay long.

There was also a Cobra that didn't go off station and was hovering above—I was sure it was there for extra security for the news team and to help Charlie know our position. I was pissed; this bird could have been used by someone in the delta who was in bigger trouble than us. We were even in an area that we ordinarily wouldn't be in because of its relative safety and lack of VC.

Soon the going got tough as the mud became a problem in the form of sporadic wallows, and the mosquitos were rising for blood. The heat was in the ninety-degree-plus range as we sucked our feet from the peanut butter mud one at a time. Then all of a sudden, the point element stopped, and I went up to see what the matter was. Seamster had come onto to a trail that crossed our path and had fresh footprints in it. Our orders were to head in a westerly direction, which meant continuing on our way. We were concerned, however, with this evidence that we weren't alone in the area. But I never thought we were alone anyhow, so why worry? As I headed back to my position, the news team came wanting to know what was up. I was as brief as possible. What the fuck is this, I thought? Do these people have carte blanche to just run around and go anywhere, or do they just have no common sense?

Firing from the Cobra's minigun brought attention to the tracers coming down to within fifty meters of our position. Ten seconds and the firing was over. B-6 Oscar told us that the Cobra just shot a VC following us in the grass. I didn't know whether to believe the pilot or not. Something just wasn't right—maybe he was just trying to get on camera, as my men were. I couldn't trust anything now.

About then the pathfinder came up front and took point. At first I didn't have any problem with that. Hell, maybe he'd actually save someone by being the first to a booby trap. We soon came to a large, open rice paddy about eight hundred meters wide. There was a VC close to the wood line across the paddy. He was too far for any of us to shoot at with any certainty. Besides, firing would just further give away our position. And then as the camera crew came up, the pathfinder took it upon himself to order my men to open up on the lone VC across the paddy. My guys, with one eye on the camera and the other on Charlie, began firing like wild men. It was a waste of good ammo, and I ordered my men to cease fire only to have the pathfinder order them to continue firing. I was outraged, and my men were confused. They didn't know whether to perform for the camera or the pathfinder or me. With rising anger in my voice, I finally got them to cease fire. As I was admonishing one of my machine gunners for disobeying my orders, the pathfinder took off with one of my squads to check out an area to our flank. I was really fucking pissed off now. Who the hell do these people think they are anyhow! When my squad returned, I had some words with the pathfinder and then my squad leader. My squad leader apologized, but the arrogant pathfinder thought he was above us. I flat out told him to just go elsewhere and torture some other platoon. He went whining to the CO to no avail. However, our time with Hollywood and John Wayne was soon ended by their Huey returning to pick them up, once again unnecessarily exposing good men to Charlie.

Life returned to normal soon, but I shook my head in amazement about what a camera and a good-looking woman could do to disrupt our common sense. They weren't a news crew; they were opportunists who offered nothing to our survival.

Frustrations came in many packages, and one of them was Waldron. While we loved to have the snipers join our RON locations, it wasn't so with Waldron. He always seemed to have a kill every time he showed up that was suspicious. But we rarely had time to prove it until one night he and Brewer showed up and took up positions on my platoon's flank. Just after midnight I heard a shot coming from their position. I took up my Starlight and viewed the wood line before us. I couldn't see any movement at all, then another shot was fired from his position as I watched. I watched for another half hour before lying down. When morning came, so did the resupply chopper. Waldron and Brewer left on it. Waldron claimed two kills, according to the CP. I took the opportunity to take Second Platoon and patrol the wood line. As I walked the muddy edge, I found nothing resembling drag marks or tracks of any sort, not even a water buffalo track. I was pissed! Waldron had given away our position over his need to be somebody and rack up a body count. Fuck this guy is now my attitude! I had run into Brewer in Dong Tam a while back and asked him how Waldron was getting so many kills. He replied, "I let him do all the shooting." That would explain it, I thought at the time. However, the very next time Waldron came out to Bravo, I took him aside and told him if he ever gave our position away again for a fucking lie, I'd make him wish he was dead! Bravo never saw Waldron again.

High Tide in the Nippapalm

Canal crossing: Courtesy of: Willy Perez

We were lucky in Bravo when it came to our tiger scouts. They were, for the most part, good soldiers who weren't afraid of sticking their noses in bunkers, disarming booby traps, walking point, or whatever we asked of them. There was always something to learn from them.

One night after we had set up for our RON, Gaa and the other scouts went to the CO and asked to go out on their own. We could see a hooch across the paddy in the wood line that had its lights on, and they wanted to go and check it out. Permission was given, and passwords were agreed upon. It wasn't long before we heard some shooting across the way—not much, but firing nonetheless. An hour went by and they returned with a pocketful of ears. Seems as though they came up on a hooch where a handful of VC had taken over and were taking their turns with the farmer's wife. They crept to within a few feet of them before opening up on the careless soldiers who had their weapons at a distance. They, however, couldn't explain what took them another hour to get back. There was something fishy about their story, but ears don't lie. Gaa offered me an ear, which I politely refused. It wasn't the kind of present I wanted. They were an amazing bunch!

***

River drowning's were way too common. We crossed numerous bamboo and coconut tree bridges over the course of a mission, not to mention the crossings without any bridges. The bridges were narrow and flimsy and not meant for the overloaded, heavier American soldier and were best crossed with bare feet instead of combat boots. It took watching only one person drown and you were arranging your gear to come off as fast as possible, which meant using bow-tie knots instead of square knots. The canals and rivers were sleepers in that there were no rapids or churning waterfalls. They were slow but full of eddies that could suck a man to the bottom and keep him there for what seemed to be an eternity. The only chance a soldier had was to immediately get rid of his gear and swim to the river's shore away from the eddy.

I watched one day as one of us fell off a bridge and into the river, immediately sinking. The man ahead of him tore off his gear and jumped in, immediately sinking. The man after him got to shore, and he tore off his gear and joined the other two, immediately sinking also. I watched as guys were running along the river's edge hoping for any sign of life. Finally, the last one to jump in bobbed up and was helped to the shore. Still no sign of the other two, not even a bob or a desperate hand showed itself. We scoured the banks for what seemed to be an hour. It was a frustrating time. No one wanted to leave them there, but the river was faster than our clumsy progress down it's banks. We soon had to admit our losses and go on as though nothing had happened.

Another time when one of the guys fell off a bridge, we checked our watches as always, and he was not found for almost six minutes. We dragged him face down to the shore, and Doc Schuebel began respiration immediately. When one would go in, we would time his lack of oxygen, knowing that after four or five minutes, he didn't have much of a chance, and if he did survive, he would prob-ably have major brain damage. This was especially true because of the warm water and the hot Mekong sun. Doc worked on him for a couple of minutes with no response. The guys begged Doc to let go; it had been eight minutes since he had taken a breath on his own. We were sure that at best he would be brain dead if Doc were to succeed. Doc wouldn't listen to us and kept his rhythm up as though he had just fallen in. But miracles do happen, and on this day, the Lord was looking down upon us in favor, as he started to spit and sputter to life. With eyes wide open, he slowly rose and rolled over, spitting and coughing to his feet. We were astonished at this gift. I couldn't look him in the eye for some time, as I had been in favor of giving up. I would never give up on life again!

The sun was going down, and we were setting up our RON in a coconut grove. Guys were downing a C rat or two, and others were just lying around resting, as I was when it hit me. Mother Nature was calling for a number two. I went three dikes away from our position to take care of the duty. I had just about finished when I heard and then saw two VC running full bore and parallel to our position with AKs pointing right at me and the rest of the company. I had no more than seen them and they opened up full auto, right at me. I jumped from the squatting position backward into the dike behind me. They unloaded their banana clips and kept running, disappearing before anybody could get an accurate shot at them. It was over just that fast.

A few seconds later, after realizing that it wasn't a full bore attack and possibly a recon by fire, I got up and pulled my trousers up, grabbed my weapon, and returned to my position. I had just settled in when it hit the guys in my position—I stank, and they weren't going to share a position with me in that condition. I realized that they were right. I checked my pants, and they were full of shit. Totally grossed out, I left the position, took my pants off, and washed my body down with mud and water. I started to wash my trousers and realized that it was useless, as all I was doing was smearing it around. I threw them away, washed my hands as best I could, and returned to my position and to laughs from the guys. I must have looked pretty ridiculous with a muddy cock and balls hanging below my bandoliers. I then gave them a bad time about not respecting my rank. Doc then said, "OK, Sergeant Mud Cock," as he laughed his ass off.

It was going to be a lonely night, and I wasn't looking forward to getting up in the morning and having the rest of the company take a humorous shot at me. I then realized that because we hadn't been resupplied tonight, that we probably would be in the morning. I had my RTO call the CP and add a pair of trousers to the Second Platoon resupply wish list.

Morning came, and Captain De Edwardo called me on the radio. He informed me that Pistol Pete would be coming in at the same time as the resupply chopper and that he intended to award me the Bronze Star for Valor for my actions a couple days earlier when I busted two ambushes and killed five VC. Because of my actions, he wanted me to be present when the chopper landed. He also ordered Second Platoon to patrol the area prior to the landing. I roger wilcoed him, and then my mind started to panic. I needed pants before the chopper landed! I started asking around for volunteers to give me their trousers. No one was interested. I begged, still no respect for my rank. Everybody thought this was funny shit, and I couldn't blame them. Fuck, what was I going to do? It just wasn't right for me to order someone to give me his trousers and for him then to go buck naked.

I decided to just ignore the problem for a while and went out on the patrol. Instead of staying back, I tried on purpose to make the patrol longer than necessary, but soon the captain was asking about my whereabouts. I put him off, telling him I would be in shortly.

Soon I could hear the chopper blades chopping through the air as we hooked up with the rest of the company. Captain De Edwardo called again, and to my relief he informed me that Pistol Pete had another company in contact with Charlie and that he had more important problems and couldn't make it. I lay back and awaited my trousers. With trousers finally on, the end came to this shitty tale. I never did get that Bronze Star. Shitty luck, I guess! We soon loaded on Tangos for our next insertion.

Making way to rivers edge.

***

It was another one of those beautiful, sunny days in the Mekong. Not a cloud in the sky, temperatures in the low nineties, and smooth air. It was to be the last mission for our CO, Captain De Edwardo, and the first for the incoming CO, Captain Perkins. Captain Perkins was a short but wide, tough-looking soldier on his second or third tour. This tour would be his first in the Mekong, as the first tour was in I Corps with the Green Berets, where he built the Lang Vei Special Forces camp. The Green Berets had lost their mission in Vietnam, and many of the infantry trained special forces soldiers were being assigned to regular infantry companies.

We had been checkerboarding around the Mekong from rice paddy to rice paddy, in one wood line and out another, LZ, PZ, LZ, PZ, and on and on. We ran into small groups of VC, killing a small number throughout the day. Then, while leaving one PZ, the chopper carrying the CP was shot down. With a new bird under B-6, we finally got on our way. This flight would probably be our last today, as the sun was starting to lower into the evening sky.

As we descended to our LZ, the area looked good. It was a collage of paddies, groves of coconut and banana trees, with a parcel here and there of overgrowth and few rivers. We were well covered on our flanks by a couple of gunships as we landed without incident. We watched the choppers fly off into the evening air, leaving us to the quiet of the surroundings.

Third Platoon took the lead as we headed into the groves and then an area of overgrowth. As we entered the thickets, Second Platoon assumed point. There was an air force (FO) Bird Dog above as we began plying our way into what looked like a surreal deathtrap. The foliage was high, dry, and noisy, with dead vines, and we couldn't see more than a few feet into the darkening tunnel of foliage, which smelled of mold and fungus.

Then, out of nowhere, a marking round (a rocket with smoke) exploded behind us near the CP. We stopped to take in what had happened and suddenly heard an F4 above that was obviously in a dive. As we turned to see the plane behind us, a most terrifying sight was upon us. The F4 was heading directly at us and had just released a napalm bomb that was getting ever closer, looking like it was going to land right on top of us. As we hit the dirt, we could see the bomb hit fifty meters directly behind us, where we had just been and in the vicinity of the CP—an unbelievable sight. What was even worse was the sight of his buddy (another F4) also turning on us. We could hear the yells and see the flaming bodies running as the reality of friendly casualties hit us. All were running for water to wallow in—except one. The sight of one lone man became obvious. Ziek (our FO) was standing with burning clothing and his radio in his hand as all the others tried to make time out of the area. Then the other F4 soon turned away at the very last moment. Ziek had somehow managed to keep his senses while denying his body relief from the napalm by jumping into the nearby paddy as the others had done. He kept his wits and changed frequencies to the Bird Dog's frequency, stopping the attack at the last moment, relieving us all from an attack of the five hundred-pound high-explosive bombs slung under the F4s.

We discontinued our approach into the foliage and ran back to the sight of the bombing. The CP and Fourth Platoon had been hit, but thankfully the pilot was off target, wounding only four or five men, including Ziek. The medics attended to all as we set up security for an incoming Dustoff and thanked our lucky stars that a Cool Hand Luke like Ziek existed. I will always remember his bravery. Soon the Dustoff was calling for identifying smoke as the night started to set in. The chopper landed without incident, loading all but Ziek aboard. Ziek was our only FO and was maybe the most important single person we had. He forwent medical treatment for the good of the company.

As the Dustoff began his slow climb to altitude, out of nowhere green tracer rounds began piercing the aluminum skin on the Huey. The Dustoff went down in a semi controlled but nonetheless hard landing close to where he took off.

We all moved out in the area where the Huey had landed and immediately set up a perimeter around the downed chopper. Amazingly, no one was seriously injured in the ordeal, although a crewmember had been shot. We then prepared for another attempt at evacuating our buddies.

It was getting dark, and soon we heard the whop whop of the Huey in the distance as he asked for a strobe light for identification and descended into the LZ. At about two hundred feet above ground level, the action start-ed all over again from another area. The pilot decreased his blade pitch and came in hot, evading his time in the kill zone. We loaded up the bird and off he went in a different direction, managing to evade any heavy fire from Charlie this time.

A sigh of relief came over all of us as we realized we still had a downed bird to deal with.

The decision was made by command to airlift the downed Dustoff out im-mediately so as not to give the VC any more time to gain force in the area and to give us a safer place to defend ourselves that night.

Once again we could hear a chopper in the distance, only this time it had a different sound—that of a Shithook (Chinook CH-47). He landed, amazingly without any rounds being fired at him. A crewmember ran out, threw a strap around the shaft of the downed Dustoff, and away they went, Huey in tow, wob-bling in the wind.

Just when we thought they were going to get out without a scratch, the firing began in force. AK rounds were hitting their mark while the slow-mov-ing Shithook gained altitude at an agonizing rate. This time there was a large group of VC taking aim—one with a fifty caliber machine gun. The tracer rounds were on target as they tore through the thin skin, hitting harder mate-rial and then flying out at a different angles than they had entered. The chop-per kept pumping its blades into the thin warm air as the VC kept pumping out the rounds. It seemed as though there was going to be no end to the pounding the bird was receiving, and we expected it to go down any second now. Finally, however, the distance was too much even for the fifty caliber as the bird con-tinued on its course. I still didn't believe it was going to make it back to Dong Tam. The helicopter must have received hundreds of rounds. I watched as long as the moonlight would allow but saw no smoke or fire. I couldn't believe that the pilot didn't order the Heuy released when he was getting pummeled by AK fire.

We shifted our RON position and set up for the night, one with little sleep as usual.

To our surprise we had no attacks throughout the night and rose at dawn for a breakfast of C rats. Soon we were on the march, looking for the bad guys, heading in their presumed location. At first it looked like we weren't going to find them, and we hoped they weren't going to find us. Then, as we entered a coconut grove, all hell broke loose from a wood line across a small paddy that separated us. I was in direct line of their fire as I hit the dirt behind a coconut tree that was less wide than I. The rounds didn't stop as dirt kicked up on both sides of me and the coconut tree splinters became part of my view. I couldn't get any lower, so I decided to return fire as best I could. I could see the muzzle flash of the weapons from behind the leaves as I zeroed in on one of the positions. As I rolled over to put in another magazine, I felt a tug and was then pulled into a depression by 2-6. We continued our firing as the M-79 and AK rounds kept coming our way. An M-79 round flew directly over my head and hit the CP group fifteen feet behind us, with sounds of agony being the result of the hit. Soon the firing dwindled to nothing, and we were able to tend to the wounded. I asked 2-6 why he had pulled me into the depression. His answer was "to save my life." I remarked that I had cover. He then pointed to the tree, which was halfway cut into by the AK rounds. I took a closer look and found wasted hot rounds lying where I had just been. My canteen and butt stock had also been hit. Well, maybe it was marginal cover? It worked however, and while I didn't appreciate him dragging me through an open area, I didn't say a thing because I knew he may have been right. Anyway, his heart was in the right place.

Ziek, with his red back, was again on the radio, and the artillery was now coming down on the VCs' previous position as we went back to the CP to check out the damage. The CP Tiger Scout had been hit along with one of the RTOs and a member of Fourth Platoon. None of the injuries was life threatening, the worst was the tiger scout. We had a large paddy just a short distance away and set up for the extraction of the wounded. The Dustoff came in with not a round fired at it, but he was not as lucky leaving. Those firing on the Dustoff were at a great distance and appeared to do no harm as it flew into the northern sky.

We headed back into the wood line in a direction that was probably meant to circle around the VC we had just had it out with. We had no more than started our move when First Platoon was hit with heavy fire from across a small clearing. There was no way to maneuver on the VC, so we backtracked to our previous position, and Ziek called in more artillery. The artillery had no more than ceased when we came under attack from another flank. Once again we experienced heavy fire, only this time, we could not see the muzzle flashes, so returning fire seemed to be of waste as we kept our heads down and waited for the firing to subside before trying to gain fire superiority. Then suddenly there was silence, as though nothing had happened at all. At that moment, we got our first sense of being surrounded on three sides, with the fourth side being a large, open paddy, offering no cover for them or us.

We lay low for a while before probing with patrol, only to be turned back again by enemy fire. The realization of our situation was now open conversation. It was getting late and we needed resupply for just about everything as we had not been resupplied the night before. Now the worries of how to get a chopper in and out became real once again.

Doc. Harneck & Tinkel

As the sun dropped, we could hear the whop whop of choppers. The supply chopper was coming in with his gunship buddies. We weren't going to get all of our resupplies, but we would be getting a heavy load of ammunition, the most-needed commodity. I was down to only two magazines, and my machine gunner had only one strand of fifty rounds. As the choppers came closer, the artillery started coming in on the two flanks of the paddy and then the artillery ceased as the choppers came closer and the gunships broke off to each flank of the wood lines, strafing as they came in. The bird landed briefly as First Platoon unloaded the chopper in record time. Then off they went in the same direction as they came in from, and to everybody's surprise, no rounds were heard and no tracers seen. The supplies were distributed to each platoon in a pile. I had a couple of guys grab what was ours and return to Second Platoon's position. To my bewilderment, there were no claymores. We were low, and it would have really been nice to have a shitload of them for this place.

We settled down for what was expected to be a bloody night.

It was another sleepless night, and to everyone's surprise, there were no attacks, not even a mortar round. Maybe they had left, or maybe they were waiting for us to go on the move again, awaiting us in ambush.

Our position was actually a good one in that we had good access to LZs for choppers; we were in a coconut grove that had dikes and canals running ninety degrees to the main threat of enemy fire. However, this configuration was also to the benefit of Charlie, which meant nobody really wanted to go out on patrol again, at least not in this neighborhood. VC usually leave as soon as they have done their damage or the artillery moves them on. When they stay, they usually are in force, and there was no doubt that these guys were in force. They may not have been bunkered up or staying in stationary positions, but they were there and in numbers nonetheless, just waiting for us to make a mistake, and we all knew that that mistake would be to walk into an ambush.

Nonetheless, we were infantrymen and the order to patrol was inevitable. Soon after breakfast the CO ordered each flank patrolled in close. One platoon would be out at a time and then the next. Third Platoon came back unscathed, a relief for all. Then it was our turn to go. The area immediately ahead, and where most of all the firing had been from, was our area to patrol. This was one time I wanted to pull rank and fall back from the point element, but that was not to be as all it took was one look from the guys, and I was right there once again. Each step became more difficult as we put distance between ourselves and the rest of the company. As we moved through the area, we could see where the enemy had taken cover and attacked. The mounds of spent casings gave away their positions; some were only twenty feet from our earlier positions. As we moved further, we came into the area that had some artillery damage. A hooch was there with a large pig wandering around that had broken free from its pen. I became fixed on this pig as my men searched the surrounding area. I wanted this pig dead; he was not to be fresh meat for the VC. I didn't want to shoot it for fear I would give away our position. So I took out my hunting knife my brother had sent me from home. I was going to cut its throat, but how was the question.

This was a huge hog; I was going to have to hold on to it with one hand and cut with the other, and then I imagined myself riding it while slicing and dicing. It all sounded so therapeutic. I wanted to go crazy on this pig. Doc then touched me and I realized I was in a trance. It all seemed so insane as we continued on our way.

The area became open due to the artillery, with obvious craters ahead that could be used as ambush points. Having fulfilled the CO's orders, we turned to return to the company perimeter with our assholes puckered and with a sense of relief. Maybe they had moved out? Maybe!

VC attacking from the left!

As we got back to our positions in the perimeter, all hell broke out again. It was coming from where we had just been. We laid into them with all we had, as it was obvious that they were hugging our belt only twenty to thirty feet away. I could hear the call of "Doc!" from one of Second Platoon's squads. I could do nothing because we were in perimeter, and I had to make sure that my section was solid. I moved from man to man, checking on them and trying to get a fix on the VC. They were close, very close as I sporadically threw a grenade in their direction. As I came up on my machine gun position, the VC laid in another fierce volley of fire. To my amazement Mark was not firing his machine gun. I was in fear of a total run over by these slime bags, tracers were flying back and forth with sonic cracks overhead, dirt was kicking up to our front, and the foliage was shredding in front of us, enhancing the visual portion of the ordeal. I ordered Mark to fire, but he just sat there hunkered down. I yelled again—nothing. I then took my rifle butt and slammed it into his helmet while unnecessarily exposing myself to the enemy. Mark began firing and firing like I'd never seen him before. He was grinding on the little fuckers, and I loved it. The battle ended after a while just as fast as it had begun, as the artillery walked in closer and closer to our positions and finally so close that the leaves from the coconut trees behind us were falling from the artillery shells' trajectory, as they dropped to the deck in front of us. It was then that I realized I had burn blisters on my hand from grabbing onto my gun barrel when I hit Mark. We then got our shit in order and were ready for the next attack in no time. I went over to the area where I heard the cry for Doc earlier. The wounded had already been moved to the back of the perimeter. One of the Second Platoon guys had taken an AK round in the neck. He was a good guy, quiet but likeable. I was told he would be OK. Someone else from First or Third Platoon had also been hit hard enough to warrant evacuation. Here we go again!

Once again we managed to get the wounded off with little hassle from Charlie. And once again the gunships helped make it a little safer for them. This time, however, they stayed on station, working over the area with their miniguns and rockets while their partners hovered above in reserve. To all of our amazement, one of the Cobras had an automatic M-79 grenade launcher in his nose instead of a minigun. It was way cool, and we immediately liked this guy as he pounded suspected enemy locations. The Gunships had no more than ran out of ammo when Zieks 105 Howitzer's began pounding again, working its way back and forth in front of us. It all seemed a good show, but we knew these guys weren't staying in one position, and it would take pure luck to get these wily fucks. Then the fly-boys showed up in their F-4 Phantoms with loads of 250 and 500 pound bombs—always an awesome sight watching these guys work. Any explosive help was welcome. We wanted the whole area blown up if we had our way.

Once again Pistol Pete was above circling and trying to make sense of his Bravo Company's situation. Pistol Pete had three other companies to look after, but it was obvious that we were taking up more and more of his attention, which was good as long as he didn't want us to charge into the wood line after the bastards. As the artillery subsided, the gunships came back aboard, leaving us to think that maybe we were going to go on the move again, but the sun continually lowered as the chances of moving out lowered. Soon dusk was upon us as the choppers left us alone once again. Minutes later a short but heavy volley of automatic fire came from the dark of the foliage, seeming to say, "We're still here, Americans."

I couldn't believe I was spending another night in the same position—our third night of not moving more than a hundred meters. This had never happened before. We hadn't gained an inch in over a day.

As night came upon us, a C-47 gunship (Spooky) came on board and began circling. He shot out short bursts from his miniguns to register his coming actions. Once we were satisfied that he knew where we wanted his rounds, he began firing a constant stream of tracers at five thousand rounds per minute, per gun. It looked like someone was pissing tracers as their trajectory arched toward his targets. We had only heard of Snoopy, and never saw him in close-up action before. We loved it!

Having Snoopy above made it difficult for those not pulling guard to find sleep (as though we could). Most hadn't had any sleep for three days now, and we were at our wits' end with this frustrating situation as the tides brought in the water to our canals, making sure that emersion foot, ringworm, and leeches were our bedfellows as the mosquitos chewed on us.

Being held to one defensive position for days was not our idea of a picnic. We were not a strong force anyhow. We probably had only seventy to eighty men to start with, and now with all the casualties, we were closer to the size of only one full-strength platoon. We didn't know the strength of Charlie, but by the amount of fire he could put out at one time suggested he could easily be of stronger force than us. The thoughts of what was to come of this situation were becoming stronger now for everyone. This was no game, and no jokes were being cracked. No radio air time was being used for anything other than direct business. Small shit just didn't matter right now, and, therefore, no small shit was being brought up by anybody.

We all took positions front and center. No one was lying on the canal behind our position sleeping and awaiting his turn for guard as usual. We weren't taking turns on guard; we were on guard. I went around to all my men, checking out their positions and fields of fire. All seemed to be doing pretty well and ready for some more action. Grenades and extra magazines were laid out to the sides of each position as if to say, "I'm not leaving here; you're going to have to move me, Mr. Charlie, you fuck, you!"

As the night wore on and Snoopy became a normal part of our evening, some of us lay down to try to get some rest before he went off station. We didn't know how long he could last in the air, but we assumed it wasn't going to be all night. We were also not too impressed with the way he was working the area, in a continuous, large circle. In my mind, the best he was doing was keeping the VC from being resupplied. At worst, he was keeping them in the area and close to us. We just knew that as soon as Snoopy left Charlie was going to hit us.

As the tide filled the canals, Snoopy left, and there was a silence in the air. We lay there with our ears turned on, pretending to get a nap, our 16s in hand as the dewy, chilly morning air with a crossbreed smell of lush green foliage and gunpowder flowed through our nostrils.

At about three in the morning, I heard the rustling of leaves and the sound of splashing water close by, not the sound of footsteps but of water movement created by humans in deep water. I was close to the only canal that ran perpendicular to our position. It ran straight out to the front of us, offering Charlie access to our positions without having to cross the dikes in front of us and thus exposing himself to the background of the sky. The sound kept getting closer and closer and I was convinced that someone was in the water behind me. I was in an awkward position, lying on my back with this noise behind my head only four to six feet from me. If I rolled over with my 16, I'd be way too slow and give my position away. In fact, if I rolled over, I'd fall into the canal parallel to me. I took a grenade within finger reach and pulled the pin and tossed it from my waist with wrist action, over my head to the area behind me. To my shock it didn't hit water. It hit the dike only two to three feet from my head. I'm dead, I thought, as I braced for the explosion. I didn't want to chance rolling around to find a grenade in the dark and get blasted in an exposed position. I was going to let my helmet and shoulders take it. And then to my relief, I heard the grenade dribble off the dike and plunk into the water, where it exploded immediately.

Frozen still, I listened for more noise. A few minutes later, I heard more, but this time it was from the front of our position. We readied for attack. All night we were ready as Charlie probed our positions. Infrequent grenades and a claymore or two are thrown and triggered to the sounds and shadows throughout the night. The Starlight scopes were rendered useless because of the closeness of the foliage and the overcast night sky.

To our amazement Charlie didn't hit us, and the morning sun started to light the eastern sky. As light came so did some rustling of the troops as they opened a can of fruit cocktail or some pound cake for breakfast. The radios of the CP start to squawk as communications to the rear took place. Soon there were rumors of a pullout. Some thought Pistol Pete was going to blow up the whole area and needed us away in order for the fireworks to begin. Regardless of the reason, we wanted out. So far we had been lucky. But how we were going to leave was the next thought. How were we going to get that many choppers in this paddy without major losses? Charlie was still there—we could bet on that. Who was going to secure the wood line as we left and keep the little bastards from laying into us? Soon the answer came; we would patrol outside the perimeter with heavy air above. Then as we retreated to our perimeter and the area for staging the PZ, the artillery would follow us back as the Cobras, gunships, and Loaches moved to the far flanks as the Slicks came in. Then they would follow us out as we gained altitude. As we left, the artillery would follow until we had sufficient altitude and distance from this shit hole. Sounded like a plan to me—one I was all for.

Captain De Edwardo sent out two platoons and kept the others in for CP security. My job was to take my men to the north side of our position along the edge of the wood line close to the proposed PZ. We saddled up and slowly made our way out. I liked this area, as the dikes ran perpendicular and into our old position, an area that offered the VC little natural cover and also was an area we received little fire from before. However, the area offered great cover from which to fire upon the Slicks as they came in or egressed. The platoon penetrated the area with no opposition, and we headed back toward the company perimeter. We then held up to give the perimeter a larger face until the time was right to configure into the PZ.

I was standing on the edge of the wood line watching the Cobras and Loaches work the outer flanks with their minigun's and rockets, when I noticed a VC sniper's tracer round headed directly for the rear of one of the gunships. I was able to see him fire again and again at the birds from a heavily foliaged area. The muzzle blasts were all I could see now as he discontinued the use of tracers. He must have been at least a thousand meters away and too far for me to be of any real effectiveness. It's very difficult for a chopper crew to identify where they are being fired on from, unless they happen to see a tracer coming from his front or sides. I called B-6-Oscar and asked to be patched through to the gunship's frequency. Soon I was talking to a team of Loaches and trying to direct them to the area of the sniper. After getting them close, I fired a tracer round at the position and directed them from there. "Red Devil Two this is Bravo Two-five, over."

"Go Two-five."

"Did you see my round, over?"

"Affirmative, Two-five."

"Roger, from the impact of my round; add five zero mikes, left zero five mikes."

"Roger, Two-five. Thanks, buddy."

End of transmission. We all watched the show as one Loach was high for backup and the other worked his way close to the ground, fanning the grasses and leaves aside at twenty to thirty feet above the ground. As they worked their way to the clump of foliage where the sniper was hiding, the gunner hung halfway out of the chopper, M-60 at the ready. We were all wondering out loud why they didn't just send a Cobra over to destroy the position. As the pilot approached the position, I grabbed my PRC-25 handset from Stevens and called the Loach again, saying, "Red Devil Two, you're on top of him." These would be the last words the pilot would ever hear, as from under the belly of the bird, a stream of green tracers boiled up from the ground, through the belly and out of the top of the bird at varied ricocheting angles. A second later the Loach exploded, falling to the ground and on top of the sniper's position, killing all involved immediately and with no possibility of survival for friend or foe. I was sick and had nothing to say to his buddy above, as he circled the fire looking for any possible sign of hope. Nearby Cobras quickly came to the area asking the remaining Loach for any directions or hope. There was just silence as he continued to circle his friend. After a few minutes, the others returned to their AO and resumed their harassment of the wood lines on each flank of the proposed PZ as though nothing had happened. I felt somehow responsible for the deaths and the gruesome work the incoming company of infantry would have to deal with.

Soon it was time to return to the perimeter and get ready for configuration in the PZ. As the lead platoon and then the CP exposed themselves to the paddy, the artillery started pounding the area we had just left and then followed us to the edge of the wood line. We then ran into the paddy to meet the low, fast-running, incoming Hueys. We all climbed in as the gunships started seriously pounding the wood line with their varied weapons. The Cobra with the automatic M-79 was letting it go as he ran alongside of us. I looked back in time to see the arty come all the way to the paddy behind us where we had just been. Whoever designed this extraction had there shit in order. If we were receiving rounds, you could bet they were from far away or with little concentration. Charlie had bigger problems to worry about than us right now.

As the chopper blades pumped through the hot, dense air and gave us distance and altitude from small arms fire, a sense of relief came over us as we knew we had just dodged a situation that could have easily been much more damaging than the 15 to 20 percent casualties we had received. I was ready for a meal, a shower, some ringworm medicine, and some sleep.

MORNING AFTER NAPALM

It was late afternoon when we got orders to rendezvous with one of the navy flotillas on a nearby river. As we settled down in the hulls of the Tango boats for a ride to coordinates unknown, we were informed that we were on a mission to locate and rescue POWs. Nothing more was known about the mission that was relayed to us. After an hour ride down a narrow canal that wouldn't allow for a U-turn, the ramps were lowered, and we were on our way. Our morale was unusually high as we disappeared in the wood line, working our way to grid coordinates that were to put us near the POWs.

As nightfall worked its way upon the delta paddies, we took a break, setting up a defensive position while we waited for nightfall to hide our move to our RON. This break increased the awareness that we had not been resupplied for a day now. Our water was low and our C rations expended. Hunger was starting to set in, but the high of actually being on a mission where POW rescue was a possibility stifled our hunger pains and our thirst. We were jacked! If and when we found the POWs, the VC were going to pay dearly, and there was to be no stopping us, come hell or high water.

We moved to the edge of the coconut grove where we could observe the paddies before us with our Starlight scopes and started setting up our positions. Having just made my rounds with my men and assuring myself that they had correct fields of fire, I returned to the CP where my RTO informed me that Captain Perkins wanted me at the company CP. The CO informed me that he wanted me to go with him on a recon into the paddy and the gathering of hooch's within. Being the only one with a sniper rifle and mounted Starlight I was chosen for this mission. Recently, the armorer at the Sniper School had put together a match-grade rifle for me, even though I hadn't passed the sniper program; it was an undercover thing of which Major Powell wasn't to be aware. A captain and a sergeant alone as a recon team, leaving behind capable men of lower rank. Oh, well!

The night was dark, ensuring our ability not to be seen, and the paddies had little water, making for stealthy, silent movement as we walked into the open portion of the paddy directly in front of the company. Seventy-five meters into the paddy we silently crept through a group of hooch's, stopping to listen and look every few steps. As we left the first couple of hooch's Cpt. Perkins asked me to set up behind a paddy dike and to observe the area around us, in particular a group of hooch's with foliage to our right. Captain Perkins continued further another fifty yards as I watched him carefully, also. Just as he started back toward my position, I again focused on the area to my right and found that a VC with an AK-47 was squatting and directing his hand-cupped ears directly at me. As he concentrated more on my direction, I began my concentration on his chest with my Starlight scope. He was only twenty meters from me as I squeezed my XM21 trigger. As often happens with national match rounds, its burn was so clean that the muzzle flash was nonexistent, allowing my scope to not burn out from excessive light and stay on. This allowed me to observe him being knocked back on his butt, where he lay still.

Captain Perkins was directly by my side as I told him the scenario. Then all hell broke loose behind us. Tracers were flying from a hooch in all directions but then concentrating on another hooch close to us. The fire was returned, and a full-scale firefight was on between the occupants of the two hooch's. Fearing being caught in the crossfire, and Captain Perkins needing to get back to his company, we crawled back to the perimeter just in time to watch the firing slow to a halt.

The night was dark enough that my Starlight scope was limited, so we could only wonder what that activity was all about. But my view was good enough that I felt whoever they were, they would be detected should they try to move from the area.

Minutes later we could hear chains rattling and the cry of "Chu Hoi" (the common Vietnamese word for "I surrender" but actually meaning "open arms"). As the sounds came closer, we realized that these were not Americans. Our Tiger Scouts gave them orders in Vietnamese to stay put until the morning light.

The situation was confusing, to say the least, as we all stayed alert—another night of no sleep for all.

As morning came, we ordered the chain-rattling shadows to show themselves and proceed in our direction. To our amazement we saw five men chained together as they came into the night perimeter. Our tiger scouts relayed the story as they interrogated them. It seems that when I shot the one VC, this distracted the prisoners' guards enough that one of the prisoners was able to grab an AK-47 and do away with the guards in one swift spray of rounds. They then started firing on the other hooch where the other VCs were as they made their escape toward our location. All were VC prisoners: One was chained because he had indulged in sex with his commander's wife. Another was AWOL. We were pissed. This is the division's idea of POWs? We were expecting Americans. Back on the boats and on to other hunting grounds.

Just north of Ben Tre was a large collage of rice paddies sprinkled with the occasional hooch. It appeared to be one large series of paddies that went for miles west to east, bordered by a wood line to the north, which was made up of unattended land, coconut groves, and the occasional tangerine grove or pineapple plot. Through this area, canals meandered their way through to the larger rivers and eventually to the Song My Tho. There were few hooch's and even fewer farmers in them when we arrived. This was Charlie's land, and it had constantly changing shadows flowing within the groves, bamboo, and the riverbanks of Nipa palm. It had that musty smell of fungus growing, the occasional snake, and plenty of rats and ants. There was also the occasional strip of Agent Orange land with its eerie lack of foliage, as though a fire had come through, leaving the trees bare and the hooch's to their own ghostly future. We hated this area as our hair stood up on the back of our necks twenty-four seven. Charlie was there, and they knew we were there. They were watching and waiting for us to make a mistake.

We had made it through a day of zigzagging through the area and worked our way to the edge of the wood line for our RON, where we would set up ambushes on the main trail paralleling the paddies and watching for any activity coming and going. As night set in, we made our shift to our final positions. Second Platoon set up on the trail, watching for activity to our west. I had a machine gun, ammo bearers, grenadier, a couple of riflemen, my RTO, and me making up my position. We were ready for Charlie!

I chose to take an early morning watch and found a depression filled with bamboo shoots that felt like it would make a good bed for the night and tried to get some sleep. The depression had something hard in it below the leaves, which I casually swept to the side and proceeded to pretend to sleep. I had almost dozed off when I was awakened by one of the new guys snoring, something we didn't tolerate. I poked him with my rifle a couple of times, and to my amazement he just continued snoring. To actually attain deep sleep in the field was rare, let alone to snore. So I stuck the flash suppressor of my barrel in his mouth and kept it in there for a few seconds. Nothing was said as I crawled back to my position. He would never snore in the field again!

I took my watch as Seamster took his turn to pretend to sleep. The Starlight scope on my rifle was working well with the star-filled night. The typical green shadows stirred and floated through the foliage, constantly keeping me alert. I also had a good view down the trail to any incoming traffic and soon saw a large, black, snakelike formation coming directly at us. Soon I could make out the weapons being carried; they were coming and would soon be flanking us for an early morning ambush, I surmised. I alerted the company, and all were awakened to full alert as some were shifted to beef up the flank. Captain Perkins was demanding a picture of the event as I tried to keep him verbally updated. Ziek was busy contacting artillery and gunships for the upcoming inevitable confrontation. First there were ten, then twenty, and then thirty and more. We were in for the fight of our lives, I thought, as I braced myself for the attack. Then, just as they would have taken a left into the wood line to flank us, they did just the opposite and took a right into the open paddy. Captain Perkins and I agreed that we wanted all of them and that meant letting them go into the open for the gunships and artillery where we could flank them and stop their escape into the wood line. This was going to be a massacre, I hoped. There was no way these guys were going to get away.

As they filed one behind the other into the paddy, I could finally get a good look at them. They were heavily loaded with RPGs and what looked like one crew-served weapon and a mortar crew. There were over fifty to sixty of these guys, and I was now thanking my lucky stars they broke when they did. These guys had us outgunned big time. As the last one broke into the paddy, I was starting to lose their point element in my scope. Anytime now I thought the artillery was going to start dropping, and I also should be hearing the whop whop of the gunships. But nothing. I called the captain and let him know that we needed to be doing something fast or they were going to get away. He informed me that they were having a hard time getting assets because another company was in contact and had priority to the assets. But he was assured us that they were on their way. Even so, you could sense the frustration of Captain Perkins. We didn't want these guys to get away to fight another day. By now I was thinking that maybe I should dog these guys. Someone needed to keep them in sight. But I couldn't bring myself to volunteer even the idea; these guys were loaded. However, deep down inside I was hoping that I would be ordered to do exactly that.

Soon I could hear the blades beating in the distant night air. The gunships were coming. But still no arty. By the time the choppers came and we directed them to where we thought they would be, it was too late. They circled with their lights, trying to pick up any sign, but to no avail. They had made it to the other wood line; they would live to kill more Americans, maybe us.

We awoke to a low-lying convection fog inside the wood line and got ready for another day of humping in the Mekong. As I looked to the left of my bed, I saw the hard object that was lying below me earlier in the night. It was a booby trap made from an old beer bottle filled with explosives, assorted nails, and metal. The pin was still in the striker. I had dodged another one and lived to tell about it!

Chapter 13

A P R I L   3

We had just came in from three days of humping the Mekong and were beat on our asses. I had no more than eaten and showered when word came out that there was to be a night raid and that volunteers were needed. Why I went on these is beyond me now. But I had a belief that I wasn't going to make it out of the delta alive anyhow. With my sense of doom, I just wanted to take as many VC out as I could before dying; this was my mentality then. Top that off with the confidence I had in Captain Perkins, and I was good to go. While we had a few good men with good experience, such as Bernie Beinwald, we also had a high percentage of relatively new guys on the team, and that worried me, as most of these missions were usually manned by seasoned vets. The exhaustion of the last mission was just too much for some of the guys, so many of the regular raid volunteers decided to stay onboard. Besides, the uniqueness of the night raids was wearing off for some.

We were soon gearing up as the night ensued and were on three Hueys flying south to an area unknown to most of us. Captain Perkins was with his team on one bird, and I was in another with my team. Pistol Pete was in the CC ship, which was a relief to me, knowing he was there overseeing the mission. This man had huge balls, and he actually cared about us lowly grunts.

Bravo loading aboard LST: Willy Perez

It was late night as we crossed the Song Hau (Bassac River) and began our late-night descent to our destination as two Cobra gunships came up on our flanks to accompany our sortie. We could see the artillery illumination flares pop at altitude before us, and soon we landed, one behind the other, with Captain Perkins in the lead as each of us took our teams to the nearest edge of the hooch line. The hooch's were in an *L*-shaped formation in the corner of a rice paddy. B-6 took his men to the right side, and I took mine to the left side. It was immediately tough going as the paddy was extraordinarily sticky and deep. There was about a foot of water on top of a foot of gooey mud. Walking in peanut butter would be a good analogy for this shit hole. As we headed for a paddy dike for easier walking, an old Vietnamese woman arose from the end of the dike out of a hole in the ground. I had never seen anything like this, as water usually filled all holes in the delta. This one had a lid to it, and I just thought of it as a makeshift shelter. But as I ordered the old woman back into her hole, I noticed that it was lined with concrete, also something I had never seen before. I should have checked it out more closely. We were soon on the dike and made it to the left edge of the hooch line, where we began searching each hooch. We came in behind the hooch's. They all had a small canal between them and the trail in the wood-line, with a board for a bridge to each hooch. All had extra-large bunkers in them that had to be cleared. The difficulty of maneuvering around each hooch and clearing them was taking way too much time, but it had to be done before going on to the next one. There was no sign of life until about the fourth hooch, which had a bunker in it as large as I had ever seen inside a hooch. It took up one-third of the entire square footage of the interior. Voices could be heard from inside the bunker as we ordered the inhabitants out of the bunker. Then we heard a baby cry. But still no one was heeding our orders to come out. My point man had just crossed the board bridge to facilitate the exodus of the bunker when we were ordered to configure for extraction by the Hueys. My point man suggested throwing a grenade in the bunker, but the sound of a baby crying ended that thought. We had a VC make crying baby sounds once before, and after digging him out of the bunker, we found no baby. This crossed my mind, but my order was to let them go as we began the time-consuming trudge through the sticky peanut butter paddy. Not being able to clear all hooch's and link up with B-6 and his team was not a good deal, and we all knew it. But it was what it was.

This time we weren't able to use the dike for travel, as we slowly pulled our feet out of the sucking mud one at a time in a painfully slow manner. As we got far enough out into the paddy for the extraction, I walked over to Captain Perkins's position, leaving my group behind. We had some small talk going on behind us, and as such our concern of voices and movement within the wood line became real. Then, suddenly, the birds came in, giving me no time to return to my team. So I decided to fly out with Captain Perkins. After all, the mission was over, and the team had no need for me anymore.

We laid out some minimal suppressive fire into the wood line as we boarded the Hueys, but soon the hooch's came alive with green tracers. The Cobras were right on top of them squelching the fire with mass quantities of rockets and minigun fire as the Hueys slowly pumped the air into submission for altitude. As I looked back I could see the Cobras still hammering the hooch's with all they had. I wondered what effect the small rockets would have on the large bunkers. Crying baby, my ass, I thought. I had noticed that the majority of the firing came from that same hooch.

As we attained some altitude, the Cobras went their own way, and Pistol Pete also broke off for his own azimuth. We soon took a body count and realized that one was missing from the other Heuy. Cpt. Perkins then ordered the Hueys to return as they made a 180 degree turn. Soon Cpt. Perkins sighted the lone soldier in the paddy. We descended to run cover for the other Huey, as it was to pick up the lone soldier. The Huey picked up the team member, but as he did so, another got off the other side in the confusion as the ship left him behind. We then circled to pick up the other soldier when all hell broke loose in the now non-illuminated paddy—once again the fourth hooch was a main player. This time the enemy was right on target, and there were no Cobras to stifle their accuracy. The tracers literally broke before my face as they riddled the Huey with holes and made their mark, hitting the pilot and others. As the chopper rolled to its right, I continued firing, but I soon realized that the floorboards were impeding my ability to stay on target because we were now at a ninety-degree angle to the ground. Soon I was flying backward as the chopper hit the ground, beating all within inches of their lives. It was a brutal crash that threw me out. I landed on my stomach with the Heuy landing on my back, pinning me almost under the water and into the mud. I managed to get my arms before me and raise my head out of the water, but I was stuck. I panicked, and with a push up, I manage to wriggle out a little each time I pushed. Finally free, I realized that tracers and rounds were still hitting the bird as the smell of fuel emanated from the fuselage. Fearing fire aboard, I climbed up and into the bird that was now lying on its side and started helping with the evacuation. The pilots managed to climb out the broken windows as the rest scrambled to the open left side facing up. Finally, there was only one man left. I yelled at Swanson to get his ass out of the chopper, but he didn't seem to hear me, so I grabbed ahold of his arm to help him as he screamed in pain. His arm was broken to hell; I felt terrible for yanking on it. I helped him up to the top and then went straight for the chopper's M-60 machine gun. It wouldn't fire, I proceeded to clear the weapon, but to no avail.

I then got off the chopper, fearing fire and wanting to hide from the firing directed at us from the hooch's. I checked on all, giving them some encouragement and demanding a defensive perimeter of sorts. I looked for weapons, only to realize they were all probably hidden in the water and mud. I returned to the smoking chopper and the M-60, determined to get it working as the firing continued from the hooch's and now the adjacent wood line. I then realized that most all the ammo had been ripped away from the gun during the rolling of the Huey and that, even if I did get it working, I'd be out of ammo in two seconds anyhow. I yelled for a rifle, hoping someone had found one. Soon one of the door gunners threw me an M-16. The use of tracers was now reduced by the VC, probably because they were now maneuvering on us and not wanting us to know their intentions. I fired in the general direction of their assumed whereabouts and yelled for more ammo and/or weapons. Soon the door gunner showed up again, but this time he had found my M-14 with Starlight scope, so I traded him weapons for reloading. I now had the ability to pinpoint their locations, and to my dismay it wasn't good. They had split up into groups, and it was evident they were trying to maneuver on us for a takeover as their firing continued. A rocket or M-79 round landed just short of the Huey, as shrapnel hit my chin. I fired a couple of shots at them only to realize that my scope had been knocked off zero and that my stock was also split open from the butt toward the grip. The door gunner again threw up the M-16, and I again I unloaded it on the now-known positions. I went back to my M-14 between him reloading the rifle and throwing it back up. Each time I would fire off a round or two while perusing the area with the scope. The next time I fired a round, the splash from the round was reflected by the moonlight and into the Starlight scope, showing me where I was off my mark. I was way low and to the side, so I corrected by using Kentucky Windage; firing high and to the right. I fired another round, and to my amazement, the VC dropped. I whipped the rifle over to the other side and dropped another one. Now needing to change M-14 magazines, I went back to the reloaded M-16 and fired off the magazine in no time at all. The enemy had completely quit using tracers at this point as they realized I was figuring out their locations. The group to the left disappeared for a while, so I concentrated on the group to the right, keeping them pinned down and forgetting about the others to my almost downfall. When I finally got back to the left, to my amazement, they had gained ground, and I now had to put pressure on them. This scenario went on for some time, and then, finally, they seemed to be lying low after I had put the hurt on them, I then had time to assess the situation further. Since most all the weapons had been lost in the deep, muddy paddy water, I wasn't getting any help returning fire. I jumped down, all the men were behind the Huey, taking care of one another and taking cover as Cpt. Perkins lay pinned under the Heuy. I returned to the top of the Huey with the fear of fire still with me, the protection of the tree line to the rear was looking good. However, it was an alternative that I could never live with. While the top of the Huey was a dangerous place to put oneself with no cover and the danger of the next tracer igniting a fire, it gave me a great field of fire and a vantage point that enabled me to see the VC hiding behind paddy dikes. I was really worried now as I didn't know if anyone knew of our dilemma other than the guys in the other Iuey. I assumed they had to refuel, and were using a different radio frequency, and that they probably had difficulty contacting Pistol Pete or someone who gave a shit. I would keep up the harassment, killing a VC once in a while, giving the rest something to think about.

However, Pistol Pete had made a 180 turn himself as soon as he knew of the crash. He had the pilot - Gary Green pushing his bird to the point of excessive vibration. Soon I heard choppers! They were coming in, and the VC disappeared again. It was the other Huey and the Cobras. And although the Cobras were low on ammo, they gave some suppressive fire until they ran out of ammo and rockets, as I jumped off the downed chopper to help get the guys onboard the incoming Huey. Not much room was available, but we loaded the bird to the hilt as they took off in all the confusion. I went over to Captain Perkins as Swanson followed me. I checked on him and let him know that I wasn't going anywhere until we could get him out. It looked like it was just the three of us in this shit hole of a rice paddy. Things did not look good, as I knew the VC would try to overtake us again. Once again I fired a round or two at them, trying to keep them at bay. But soon two more showed up, I knocked them down immediately. I now was running short on ammo as I realized I only had my M-14, and it was down to the last half of the last magazine.

Just when things looked the bleakest, Pistol Pete's chopper swept in. It landed close by as Pete got off his bird with his 1911 .45 pistol in hand, firing at the VC as he rushed to the downed bird and Cpt. Perkins. All hell continued to break out as Pistol Pete noticed two sets of green tracers coming from a close by hooch to which he engaged with his .45, firing his red tracers as the green ones came toward him. He fired three clips silencing the position confirming his nick name of Pistol Pete as few have or ever will. With help he then dragged Cpt. Perkins to his bird. Then to our surprise, others who were behind the tail of the downed Huey came out. There was now no room for me as Pete ordered his tiger scout to stay behind with me, as they took off into the night sky. My heart dropped to the bottom of my stomach, thinking I was once again in deep shit. But soon out of the sky came a Cobra to pick us up. We loaded on the outside of the bird and off we went, flying at treetop level heading north.

I was loving it, as I had a great view of the cockpit, and my ass was now saved. I knew the theory of flight of helicopters, so I was fixated on the cockpit gauges while the skin on my chin flapped in the air. After a good distance the relative wind slowed, and it was evident that we were going to land. But where was the question. There were no lights, no basecamp below. We were now hovering as the pilot knocked on the canopy and motioned for me to get off. I couldn't even see the horizon as I had lost my night vision due to looking at the instruments, and the bird was obviously not on the ground. Fuck this guy! I was not getting off! He persisted and even raised the canopy to say, "Get the fuck off!" I guessed that there must be a company of men close by, but I had stiffened up, and my legs weren't working at all. This guy was asking for a lot. I could only push myself away and off as I fell four to five feet to the ground, and the Cobra immediately left. The tiger scout crawled over to me and was as confused as I was. We waited and nothing happened. No one called out, not a sound. Then we heard some talking, but it was Vietnamese. Holy shit, I thought. I'm really dead this time because I can't even walk, and I'm out of ammo. We continued to listen and soon the Tiger Scout said with excitement that it was ARVNs (Army of the Republic of Vietnam) doing the talking. Soon my eyes got used to the dark, and I could see the outline of an ARVN base camp a couple of hundred yards to our front. Now it made some sense that we had landed there, but why there and not Dong Tam or an American base camp? After a time, an army Dustoff arrived and took us into Dong Tam. I was elated; I was alive! And what was even better was that Captain Perkins was lying next to me in the emergency room and looked as though he was going to make it. You couldn't wipe the smile off my face as I made jokes with the nurse about de-clothing me!

My right Gluteus Maximus was 100 percent contused. My right bicep was 90 percent contused. My right shoulder was hyperextended, and there were numerous other bruises, abrasions and the shrapnel in my chin. While getting my chin sewn up, I held my trigger finger up with its new concave burn mark and commented to the doctor, "I don't know what hell this burn is about." He reached up on the window sill and grabbed a spent AK round, which he placed in the depression on my finger and said, "Perfect match for a tracer." (The doctors never caught the breaks in my vertebrae until 1972, even though it was shown on an X-ray of my hip taken in Dong Tam). All and all, I was one lucky grunt this day.

While the backseat generals can point fingers and find many excuses about why the night was such a three-ring circus, one must realize that in war, the need for execution in an expedient manner is omni-important, not giving one the luxury of training for specific missions, and that if anything can go wrong, it's going to go wrong in war.

***You can watch both the History Ch. and LifeOfDuty.TV
films made on this event @ www.EdTheSniper.com**

Chapter **14**

R E C O V E R Y

I would lie in the hospital bed for a week before trying to walk. After all, I thought it was only a massive contusion of my butt keeping me from walking, and the injury needed to be worked out, as with any big bruise. After a week of hobbling around with crutches, I was starting to get tired of the hospital in Dong Tam, as there was little to do, and I wasn't allowed to go anywhere else as long as I was a patient.

I asked my doctor one day if I could be transferred to the USS *Colleton*, as it had a small ten-bed hospital on it, and Bravo was calling it home. He gave me my ninety-day profile of limited duty, and off I went. The ship's hospital was almost empty, with the exception of two sailors who were recuperating. One had a large gash from shrapnel (that was his story), and the other was walking wounded from an infection. It was great duty as I could pretty much go anywhere aboard and visit my friends from Bravo when they were there for their few hours' of rest between missions.

I hadn't been there for more than a few days when some corpsmen brought in a few seriously wounded, which maxed out the hospital's functional ability. The doctor and his two corpsmen went to work on them immediately, taking one into the surgical room where the doctor kept busy for an hour. He had no more than finished and was just beginning to sew him up when Sam, one of our Tiger Scouts from 3rd Plt. came in on a stretcher. Sam was a favorite of John Sperry, Leon Edmiston and their men. A onetime VC, he had defected to our side after his father the Mayor of My Tho was murdered by them. Sam was in bad shape, with multiple shrapnel wounds and was unconscious. There was no open place to work on him but the floor. The doctor immediately decided that because of his low blood pressure and wounds to his chest he needed to be opened up right then and there. The medical team put in an IV and commenced to opening up his chest, cutting through the sternum and clipping some ribs. The ribs were not completely cut, so the doctor grabbed the right side of the ribs with his hands and put his foot on the other side, forcing them open. I couldn't believe what I was seeing; blood flowed all over from the internal bleeding. The doctor sloshed some sterile water into the cavity, trying to get a better look at what was going on. I could see Sam's heart squirting blood from the left ventricle. The doctor squeezed the heart, forcing shrapnel out, and then sewed his heart up. He pulled some more shrapnel from the cavity and then started putting him back together. I was friggin' amazed at what I was watching; this entire surgery took only about ten minutes. They threw him on a bunk, put another IV in him and called it good. If this had been an American soldier, there was no way a military doctor would have done this, as he would have risked court martial, no doubt. I'm told that I had watched medical history, the first successful open-heart surgery without all the bells and whistles.

The chaos settled down, and Sam was still alive, to my amazement. That night he awoke from being unconscious. He didn't look good, but he was alive as the medical team had stopped all the leaks in his circulatory system. Within the week, Sam was up and walking around as though he merely had the shit kicked out of him. This fucker is one hard-core dude; he just shook it off and wanted out of the hospital as soon as possible. Most of the others were transferred to Dong Tam for recuperation. Sam would go back out into the field in three weeks.

The brown-water sailor from Galveston, Texas, who had the gash in his leg was starting to get to us, as he would play the tape of "Galveston" by Glen Campbell all friggin' day long. As he was still bedridden, we allowed it. That is until one day: a boat mate of his came in and apologized for stabbing him in a knife fight they had been in. He had no more than left when one of the guys went over and took his tape from him and threw it in the garbage. There was no more catering to this liar—he was now on our shit list. Shrapnel wound my ass!

Things again got pretty quiet around the hospital, so the surgeon announced one day over the ship's loud speakers that anyone wanting a circumcision should report to the ship's doctor. Within minutes there were enough to fill up the hospital beds, as it was a way to get some time away from the field. The surgeon started immediately whacking off the unwanted skin. He took each into the surgery room and then gave them a bed with an aerosol can that spewed out a freezing fog to keep any unwanted erection away. My roommate and I decided that it was time to hang up some *Playboy* foldouts for all to view. We then made sure the conversation of the day was about sex—sex stories, sex jokes, and all things sex. It was like when I had my hernia surgery; the last thing I wanted to do was think of something funny or hear a joke, and, of course, that was then all I was thinking of. The laughing would kill me, but I couldn't help it, no matter how much it hurt. It was the same thing here as the cans were emptied in no time. These guys were spraying coolant on their dicks all day and night. I never laughed so hard at someone's expense. I'm surprised one of them didn't kick the shit out of me.

I was finally walking pretty well and was released from the confines of the hospital. I returned to the company's berthing area on the *Colleton*, where I was asked by another platoon sergeant to go on an R&R with him to Taipei. His previous traveling mate was recently killed, so the slot was available. I really didn't want to waste an R&R while on light-duty profile. I was hoping to use it when back in the field. But he convinced me to go, as he had been there twice already from previous tours and knew the ropes. In fact, he was friends of the owner of the famous OK Bar in downtown Taipei, which was reported to have the largest selection of the most beautiful girls in all Taiwan. I was ready for this even though my right gluteus was black and still stuck out a couple inches further than my left one.

We went into Long Binh, where we were given khaki uniforms and processed for our flight to Taipei. The flight itself was wonderful in that there were no chances of us being shot down. We were given meals that were better than anything we had eaten since arriving in Nam. I was in heaven, and as the plane got closer, the conversations became more excited. I'm gonna do this; I'm gonna do that; I'm gonna eat this, and sleep for this long; I'm gonna have a different girl each day. It was almost too much to think of and sleep was out of the question for me as the excitement flowed through my veins like a new drug.

My sidekick, John, had it all together as we went directly to the hotel, changed clothes, got a Cadillac limousine with driver, and away we went to the OK Bar. It had a long, narrow room with a bar to the right and nothing but girls sitting on the left, maybe fifty of them. You would have thought by the way the bar was built that we were in Montana. We went directly to the bar and asked for the owner, who showed up within minutes. We were greeted as though we were royalty and went to an upstairs private room, complete with a small bar, juke box, and a large, pillowy, horseshoe seating area with table. We were accompanied by a bartender and waitress. The owner noticed that I still had my combat boots on and ordered one of the girls to get me a pair of shoes. She soon showed up with a large box full of shoes evidently left behind by previous visitors. He then had the girls show up two at a time. We were invited to spend as much time with them as needed. John whispered in my ear not to take any of the first ones and to be picky as they will get better as time goes by. Each time I refuse one, the owner asked me for details about what I wanted. Finally, the Asian beauty of my dreams showed up—tall, long hair, beautiful face, large breasts, and spoke English very well. We signed a $75.00 contract for 24/7 girls for the week. We soon had our girls in our limo and were on our way to the motel rooms. We took care of business and then began to party in downtown Taipei, looking for the finest restaurant in town. Life was good: we have 24/7 girls, a wonderful hotel, and an English-speaking driver 24/7, with a 1957 Cadillac limo in immaculate condition. I couldn't spend my money fast enough; I now knew what it was like to party like a rich man. The seven days went by way too fast. As we returned the girls to the OK Bar and I put my boots and uniform back on, the gut-wrenching knowledge of going back hit me. A solemn bunch boarded the plane, with some out of uniform and some passed out, being carried to the plane by their buddies. We slept on this flight, trying to make up for the damage done to our bodies.

Ed: Ready for R&R

Once back in Vietnam and with Bravo I was walking pretty well and was soon asked to go out on the next mission. I mentioned I still had sixty days of my profile left. But 2-6 said, "Man, we need you. You have no idea how we're hurting for experience." I was guilt-tripped into going. We had only two officers left—Frobenius/2-6 and Ernst/1-6 who was acting CO. Frobenius would manage the other platoons, and I would manage the Second. I didn't pay much attention while aboard ship to who was still in the platoon and who the new guys were until I was in the field. I was shocked; I hardly knew who my own men were in the Platoon because so many new guys had come in since April 3—it was scary. I had no idea who one squad leader even was! My empathy for Second Platoon was diminishing. Hell, I didn't even know some of these guys!

So here I was with Sixty days of a light-duty profile left, and I was back in the fucking field. I felt for these guys and the lack of experienced soldiers. Wounds and deaths had taken their toll with Bravo Company. But my cup was getting full, and these guys worried me. Why? Probably because I didn't know many of them. I'd never seen them fight. I didn't know what to expect from them, and I was now so jumpy and cautious that I didn't even trust myself.

We were short of officers often, and this day was no different. Two-six was in the rear on battalion pay detail, and 1-6, (Lieutenant Ernst), was now the acting CO as we went from LZ to LZ, our typical recon by blood method. Pistol Pete had the day off, and Colonel Rainville was managing his companies while he was gone. That afternoon Rainville decided to break up the already short-manned Bravo Company into two elements. I was already acting platoon leader (2-6) as Ernst decided that Second Platoon and Third Platoon would make up my contingency of men. Third Platoon would fly out first and secure the LZ for the remainder of us. We soon flew out to an unknown area with no maps and no FO. I was in charge of both platoons as Third also had just an E5 sergeant as its platoon leader.

We landed in a different area of the paddy than did Third Platoon, and as soon as the lead chopper touched down, there were explosions all around us. Men were being hit with shrapnel while still on the choppers. At first I thought we were being mortared as I got off. But then I realized we were hitting booby traps with the Hueys and our feet as we disembarked. We threw some of the wounded back on the ships they were just on. Others never even bothered getting off due to their wounds. The Hueys left as fast as they could, as they were just as confused as we were. They also had their own wounded crewmembers aboard. As things got quiet, I ordered all to freeze and started looking for the booby traps. We still had a Dustoff load of wounded to take care of immediately. Most were lightly wounded in that all were conscious and had their arms and legs. Some were prone and in agony. Doc Harnick went to work, as I did trying to triage for him. I had my RTO call in a Dustoff. I told one of my squad leaders to clear a landing area of any booby traps and we went to work. I had a handful of FNGs on this trip. It was their first mission, and some got their CIB, Purple Heart, and million-dollar wound all in one day. As Doc worked his way through the wounded, he came to one of the FNGs who was prone and writhing in pain. Doc cut off his trousers and checked him out, only to find one small hole in his scrotum. Doc called me over and then pointed to his wound as though it was a major deal. He carried on like he had lost his penis and all. The more Doc carried on, the more this poor guy thought he'd lost it all. The sick fucker thought this was some funny shit for some reason. I put an end to it and told the young private, "It's just Doc's way of having a little fun; you're going to be all right, man."

We soon had all patched up and on the Dustoff as I turned my attention to getting the rest of us into the wood line where Third Platoon awaited us. As I counted the remaining troops of Second Platoon, I realized that I had lost over half my men in one incident. I was now down to only thirteen men. I ordered one of my point men to lead the way and ordered all to walk in each other's footsteps to eliminate any more casualties. As we headed into the wood line in file, I received a call from Rainville. I could now make out his command ship above and at his usual altitude, which was way the fuck up there and away from any small arms fire.

"Who the fuck is the cocksucker in charge down there?" he raved. My RTO handed me the handset as I braced myself for his usual less-than-professional manner. "You dumb fucker! Don't you know that enfilade fire will slaughter your men while in file? Get the fuck on line and now."

"Sir, we're in a heavily mined area, and I have a platoon in the wood line protecting us," I replied.

He just kept raving on as he ignored me and I ignored him. Finally he said, "I'm gonna court-martial your ass." About that time Doc Harnick tore the radio out of my hand and laid into the colonel, calling him everything in the book, telling him to get his chicken-shit ass down here so he can kick the shit out of him. I tried to retrieve the handset, but Doc was having nothing to do with it. We were soon in the mud wrestling for the handset, forcing my RTO in the mud with us as both Rainville and Doc call each other dirty-rotten, mother-fuckin' cocksuckers. Finally, Doc gave up. I chewed Doc's ass out for what it was worth, and we went on our way. We no sooner got to the wood line and Rainville called up again with one short order: "Configure for a PZ."

We were on our way again and were soon reconnected with the remainder of the company. Ernst called me up letting me know that I was in deep shit with Rainville. *No surprise there*, I thought. Oh well, maybe I'll get court-martialed and the fuck out of the field this way.

It was getting late, and we were looking for an RON position, preferably somewhere away from all the water we were encountering. We were now down to about fifty men from all the casualties received since the beginning of the mission, and we were not in any mood to sleep in the goo tonight and face a large force with only fifty of us. We held up in a wood line and waited for dark, as we moved out onto an island of land in the middle of a large rice paddy that had a large hooch between us and a flanking wood line. This position gave us the ability to defend ourselves from a larger force in that they now had to cross open paddies in order to overtake us. However, it also gave the VC a good idea as to where we were.

A couple hours after we settled in, a couple VC, that had crawled to within feet of the CP threw a White Phosphorus grenade and fired into the CP killing one and burning Lt. Ernst on the face. Then we received fire from the large hooch and then the wood line—AK and machinegun fire mostly. We laid into the hooch and wood line with machine guns, sixteens, and grenade launchers. They soon ceased fire but the damage was done. Lt. Ernst was in major pain as others laid dead and wounded. We were now down to about 44 functioning men as I roamed the perimeter checking the field of fire of each position.

Lieutenant Ernst sucked it up and stayed the night; as he decided to medevac out the next morning. As the morning came, a detail of men cleared the hooch we received fire from, and to our amazement, the VC were still there and surrendered without incident. These were the kind of prisoners who received less than Geneva Convention treatment from the angry troops who had just lost their friends. These were the kind of prisoners who often tried to escape, only to be shot by the troops.

Soon we prepared for our incoming resupply ship, which was to bring in 2-6 and our first sergeant (Top) whom we all had a dislike for. He was an old hardcore grunt himself, but he had no respect for us, as he was constantly taking sides with the navy. He would demand that we clean up after ourselves in our berthing areas, previously a job for the ship's crew when we would leave. It was just the little things he would get on us for, as though we were stateside. He seemed to think that he came from the great wars and we were only in a police action. He considered us lesser infantrymen than he.

Two-six arrived as Ernst left. Two-six asked me to take care of Top. Top was told to stay close to me. Top decided to walk behind me as we headed out, staying on the island of land that had two parallel wood lines, but at distance enough not to receive accurate fire. We were ordered to make time to a larger, more defensible paddy for extraction. We had a ways to go, and the morning sun was beating down on us without mercy as we encountered sniper fire and a continuous series of small irrigation canals to cross. Each man had to help the one behind out of each canal. I had to teach Top the right way to grip with his muddy hands, and we were on our way with relentless sniper fire that we just ignored with little more than the occasional hitting of the deck or the lowering of the head. Sometimes we'd throw a round or two in their direction, but would stay the course.

The canals were now taking their toll, and Top became heavier, with less spring to his step. The relentless Mekong sun beat down, demanding a flow of sweat from our muddy bodies.

I could tell that Top wasn't in shape for all this, and the continued sniper attacks were working on him. He was covered in sweat and mud, looking like a beaten man. We finally took a short break when Top said, "Jesus, man, why don't you guys do something about the sniper fire?" I explained to him that it was a daily thing with us and to fire back would only waste good ammo needed for a real firefight. He said, "You mean you guys get shot at every day?" "That's right, Top, every day hardly without exception." We were on our way shortly, and Top was sucking wind again. He couldn't believe that this is what we did every day. When I told him that this was actually a pretty normal hump and not bad at all, he said, "You gotta be shittin' me." He sucked it up as we continue to our PZ and were extracted to a much needed rest.

Two things changed for Top that day: he got his third CIB, and he now had a new respect for us and what we went through. The navy was now on Top's shit list, and we are now prima donnas who could do no wrong. Top wasn't such a bad guy after all; he just needed a little insight. To my surprise, there were no orders for me to report to the stockade to await Rainville's wrath. I would never hear from him again.

I went out on a couple of more missions, but my heart wasn't in it. Then one day we had a few hours in Dong Tam, so I decided to go by the sniper school to say hi, and I ran into Major Powell. He told me that he had made a decision that if I wanted to go back through the testing phase, I would be welcome to do so and that one class was now ending, making for a good time to come in. I made my mind up by the time I got back to the ship to take Major Powell up on his offer. We had recently got a new Lt. (Harold Hector) and I felt better about leaving the Co.. I didn't even ask Ernst or 2-6 for permission. I just told them the Sniper School wanted me to reexamine. I went back into Dong Tam and caught the sniper class in its last three days preparing for the exam. I was given three days to brush up and prepare for the exam. Finally, I passed the exam and was now a sniper. The schooling would be part of my permanent records and DD214.

We had the graduation the next day, and passes for a three-day leave to Vung Tau were handed out. However, I was broke. I had only twenty dollars on me, and that wasn't much for buying beer and spending time in a whore house. I asked if I could go some other time, to which the response was "today or never." So what the hell—at least I could lie around on the white beaches and drink a little beer. It was better than hanging around in the delta. When I returned, I went back to Bravo and picked up my duffel bag and said my good-byes as I left for the *Benewah* and the Sniper Platoon. I was now a sniper and turning my back on Bravo. Had I given them enough? Was this the right thing to do? God, I loved those guys!

***

A couple weeks after I left Bravo they would get hit hard loosing 7 men with many wounded. This would make 34 deaths since I was 1st assigned to Bravo in just over 7 months' time. The WIA (Wounded in Action) casualty rate was well over 200 percent. Many of us had multiple Purple Hearts.

Consequences of loosing at war!

VC prisoner in tow

For Whom The Bugle Sounds
By: Kevin Hussey Jr.
For: John Sperry

I know this place, the peaceful Scene,
The stone, the flags, the grass so Green
A warm May sun, a bright blue Sky,
Beneath this ground, the Heroes lie.

We come to this place every Year,
To visit Them, and shed a Tear
For some were young, and some were Old,
Each with a story that should be Told.

Mothers and fathers, daughters and Sons,
They all remember what these heroes have Done.
Old friends come here to Reminisce,
To talk to old buddies, they dearly Miss.

In Vietnam, the Mekong Delta,
Tall grass and mud, with little Shelter.
The battle ground, the day it Shook,
The enemy, your lives they Took.

The guns, the smoke, the sounds of Screams,
You fought like hell, in the heat and Steam.
You stood your ground, you held the Course.
Proud soldiers of the Riverine Force.

Your name now etched on this long, Black Wall,
For all gave some, but you gave All.
We pass this place in silent Thought,
In dreams the battles are still being Fought.

I come today with my bugle in Hand,
With tears and sorrow I take my Stand.
I press the bugle to trembling Lips,
To honor those on land air and Ships.

Sleep my brothers and be at Rest,
Your brothers of Bravo Co. send you their Best.
Tears now shed, on this sacred Ground,
We know for whom the Bugle Sounds.

Chapter 15

S N I P E R   F U L L   T I M E

USS Benewah APB-35 with River Divisions attached.

I arrived aboard the USS *Benewah* (APB-35), an old WWII barracks ship that berthed the Sniper Platoon and also served as a MRF and 3/60th Battalion base. I found the battalion TOC (tactical operations and command) and was given directions to the snipers' berthing area. Upon arriving, I found a few familiar faces I had gone to Sniper School with or had run into at the Sniper School when visiting. One was Vroman, who also was from Bravo Company, and another was a fellow Oregonian, Larry Haugen. Haugen and I had hit it off in a brief meeting at the school, and he was also the platoon sergeant of the 3/60th Snipers. To my pleasure, Waldron had left as he was being paraded around as the almighty sniper of the army, but his partner Brewer was still with the platoon. Brewer was a good kid—too bad he had gotten hooked up with Waldron. The berthing area was in the bottom hole of the ship, which I hated from my experience with the USS *Westchester*. We shared a space with a navy SEAL team, the likes of which I had never heard of before.

It was afternoon, which was morning for the Sniper Platoon, as they were stirring, getting ready to go above to the galley for lunch leftovers. The food was less than desirable for the sniper teams, as they would usually leave the ship for their mission after lunch and before dinner and then arrive back after breakfast, leaving them to leftovers left out by the cooks.

Larry clued me in as to what their missions of late had been and what to expect. Apparently, they were mainly night missions split into three different missions. A) Mainly they were being attached to the various companies of the battalion at night, usually the ones that were or had been in contact, thusly providing the best opportunities for action. Insertion was usually with the night resupply chopper. B) They were also using Tango boats with the helo pads as a platform, as they would float down the river offshore about two hundred to three hundred meters using the boat's pink infrared light as enhanced illumination for the Starlight scopes.

Heuy landing on Tango with helo pad.

Mission C was the most exciting and the one everybody loved: Night hunter missions. We would board a Huey, employing one sniper on each side of the bird. Two Cobra gunships stacked directly above and behind as the Huey would cruise the endless river systems of the delta. All river traffic hours were well known and published with dropped leaflets to be off limits after dark, making all non-US military traffic fair game. We flew about four hundred to six hundred feet above ground level; all birds would use only their top red lights for visual identity and separation so as to not be seen from the ground. We used tracers (which were frowned upon by the Sniper School) to mark the targets of opportunity. The Cobras would immediately roll out, following the tracers with lights still off. We would immediately grab our PRC-25 radio and give them a brief correction and description of the target, i.e., "Add five zero, right seven five, enemy in two sampans." The Cobras would correct and watch their altimeters as they dived toward the target. Once the minimum altitude was attained, they would turn on their enhanced search lights and destroy the target by dumping their 3.5 inch rockets and miniguns into the targets. It was an exciting show to be a part of.

I was the seventh member of the team and as such there would be some missions in which I would do without a partner or be teamed up with two other snipers. All 9th ID snipers had a code name, and by the time I came aboard, all the really cool ones had been taken such as Eagle Eye, Hawk Eye, Davy Crocket, Daniel Boone, etc. I decided to go with "Bad Eye." Why? Who knows?

I went out that night with Vroman, catching a chopper ride out to Alpha Company without incident. We offloaded and fell in line with the still-moving company, arriving at their RON soon. We sat up on an open paddy and began our vigilance, taking turns every thirty minutes or so in order to keep our eyes fresh. The night was uneventful, as only one water buffalo entertained us throughout the night. Water buffalo were to be watched closely because the enemy liked using them as cover. Haugen once told me a story about when he was on an artillery batteries berm out of the Tiger Lair compound where he had dropped a couple of VC just a couple of nights before. He observed a water buffalo making his way across the paddy in front of the compound. Larry noticed that the buffalo had six legs, so he dropped him at 450 meters, thereby exposing Charlie. It's no easy task killing a water buffalo with match ammunition, especially at that distance. It had to be a heart/lung shot. Larry didn't get Charlie as he was in fifth gear the moment his 1500 lb. shield folded up. A water buffalo will meander if unattended, but has a stride of purpose and direction when used as a shield. There were always rumors of snipers wounding water buffalo and declaring their massive blood trail as proof that Charlie had lost a non-survivable amount of blood, thus indicating a kill. I had to laugh at Haugen's story as I could visualize the VC making a wake on the paddy water as he split the scene. Morning soon came, and we were off on the resupply chopper back to the ship for breakfast leftovers.

I was thinking this was fucking great duty! I loved it! There were three things I perceived as benefits of being a sniper: 1) lower collateral civilian damage, 2) killing the enemy, thus, saving my brothers' lives, and 3) sniper duty is much easier than straight infantry duty. Let's face it; sleeping in one's own rack almost every day was a killer concept to infantrymen, not to mention better food and less ringworm, emersion foot, jungle rot, and physical exertion. Also, at this stage of my tour, my limits of dealing with hard combat were diminishing with every day that I got closer to actually living through my tour. I truly had written myself off as either killed or severely wounded for months now, but now I could see a little, thin, weak light at the end of the tunnel of survival. Maybe, just maybe, I had a real chance of making it. Let's face it; in comparison to an infantry company making its way through the jungle, a sniper makes much less noise and is much harder to see as a result of his element size and the fact he isn't moving to cover ground but to get into position. It's a no brainer; you have a better chance to survive whether you're a sniper, an LRRP, a SEAL, or Force Recon—it's a better deal all the way around. After all, the mission is entirely different; the grunts are the guys who kick in the doors and call names and put themselves on larger forces.

Sniper stories, for the most part, are boring. There is little counter fire and little drama other than the shot itself, and there are many days without any good targets. There's a lot of hurry up and wait and wait and wait. I'm not a patient person by nature, but when the alternative is to be out humping my ass off and staying in the face of the enemy, it's a pleasure to be bored at times.

I went out on a couple more missions with no targets of opportunity. But, finally, on my fourth mission with another of the 3/60th companies, I would have my opportunity. It was early in the night around 2200 hours when I caught some movement in the wood line on the right side of the paddy, I guessed about four hundred meters out. I hadn't been able to range the various landmarks within my field of fire before dark, so ranging was much more difficult with our Starlight scopes, as they would eerily make objects seem closer one minute and further away the next within their haunting green world of visibility. When the objects came a little closer, I could see that it was a party of four. They stopped, and I wait for their next move. One started crossing the paddy from right to left on a paddy dike that ran through a couple of hooch's. I was hoping that they all followed and were out in the open at the same time for my best target opportunities. But the other three held up inside the wood line to await their point man's signal. But they weren't following, and I was forced to make a decision to take him before he made it to the wood line on my left. He was now about 350 meters, and I took my shot. To my surprise, he was still standing there, turning as to ascertain where the noise came from. I assumed I had misjudged the distance as closer in and that my shot was low or else the sonic crack would have made him run or take cover. So I now fire higher and again miss, but this time he hits the mud behind the paddy dike. Fuck! I've over shot him! I was really bummed about now, and his buddies have disappeared within the wood line. I knew that when this guy came up, he was going to be running to the wood line, so I awaited his move, and sure enough he raised his head finally, looking around as though he could see in the night's darkness. I saw his rifle brought forth on the dike as he readied himself for the sprint. As soon as I saw movement, I fired and finally dropped him in his tracks. I was still bummed, however, as I felt I'd given the others an idea as to our location and had probably lost them for good—Bad Eye was right! This was not the way I wanted to start my new job. I was now sure that my Starlight was off zero.

I continued making my sweeping visual probes, and about thirty minutes later I noticed some more movement in the same area as before. As I kept an eye on the enemy, I saw, to my amazement, they were skirting the paddy and coming in closer. They must not have gotten a good reading on the origination of my previous rounds, and I assumed at this time they were going to run right into the right flank of the company's perimeter. I called up the CP and informed them of my observations so they would be ready. Then to my surprise, they started crossing the paddy about two hundred meters out. The first one was halfway across before the other two followed. I waited until the first one closed in on the wood line to the left, and I popped him with one shot. I then turned my attention to the other two. One had hit the mud, and the other was squatting with ears cupped. I knocked him back into the paddy, and both were out of sight. Soon one showed his head, and I fired again, assuming that I got him. No heads, nothing; I was thinking they were all dead but continued to scan. Still watching the right wood line for more action but going back to the dike from time to time, I found movement in the form of low crawling. Both men were still alive, but one was obviously dragging one side of his body. I waited until both were almost back to the wood line and had to expose themselves while crossing the dike parallel to the wood line. I finally got a clear shot at both and put them out of their misery. It wasn't pretty that night, but what the hell? There were four fewer VC to kill Americans!

We were all ordered to take our XM-21s back to the Sniper School as soon as we got a break. I always looked forward to going back to the school, as all the instructors were a great bunch and always welcomed us with open arms, keeping their senior NCO attitude at bay. We weren't allowed to break our weapons down—it was the Sniper School armorers' job. But today, instead of just having my rifle cleaned, the armorers were putting on silencers. I couldn't wait as I enjoyed a ten-cent beer from the iced-down beer barrel as Staff Sergeant Tuck strummed on his guitar with his southern tunes. One of the other snipers came in with his pet spider monkey that was worse than any two-year-old child when it came to minding. The little fucker was bouncing off the walls of the open-air beer patio, knocking over good beers to the point that he finally tied the little fucker up. There was also another sniper in for his silencer from another brigade. Gapol tells me this guy had just made the longest shot in the sniper program: 1200 meters with open sights. I had to ask, and the incredible story goes like this:

It was early morning and he was switching from his Starlight to his daytime ART scope, when someone noticed movement across a small paddy, way the hell and gone out there. He pulled up his (not yet attached) ART scope, and sure enough, there was a VC with a weapon over his shoulder, ready to disappear into the wood line. Not having time to mount his ART scope, he grabbed his rifle and cranked the open sights up as far as they can go (1200 meters). He put his rifle up against a coconut tree and took a crack at him just for fun. To his amazement—and the amazement of those around him—Charlie fell dead in his tracks and didn't move an inch. The CP called in the kill: "Victor Charlie, Black on Black, AK, 1200 meters, open sights." Before the Company could ruck up and move out, they received a call from battalion ordering them to send a squad out to the body and await further orders. Within half an hour, a Huey broke into the company frequency ordering smoke from the location of the shot and another next to the body. It was our general. He was calling bullshit on the shot and was there to call it personally. But after taking out his map and measuring the distance, he just radioed back, "Amazing" and flew off. Truly the most amazing lucky shot I had heard of. But there was one thing I knew from all the shooting I did as a young man: the more you shoot at the impossible, the more likely you are to get in a lucky one now and again.

My rifle was finally ready. I couldn't believe the size of the silencer; it was huge and looked as though it weighed ten pounds or more. I put it up to my shoulder only to find that it was nearly impossible to hold in a standing position with all the weight and leverage. I was thinking this thing must weigh over twenty-five pounds with the Starlight attached! I fucked around enough at the Sniper School to miss any shuttle boats back to the ships, thus weaseling my way back to the beer barrel.

When I got back to the ship, I ran into Haugen, who had just gotten off a night-hunter mission. Seems as though they were going along and had not yet seen anything when he spotted this large vessel. He told Colonel Pete what he saw and that he thought it might be a little big for anything the VC might have. The commander said, "Mark it anyway. It's out after curfew." So of course he did, and down went the Cobras. The Cobras did what they do best, blowing it to hell and gone. They were on their way back to Dong Tam when Colonel Pete got a call on the radio from the brigade commander Rainville. Rainville chewed Colonel Pete's ass up one side and down the other all the way back to Dong Tam because they had just blown up the Mo Cai ferry. When they got off the bird at Dong Tam Colonel Pete said, "Sergeant Haugen, Colonel Rainville is a little upset with us because we blew up the ferry, but don't worry about it. I never liked that damn ferry anyway; the people running it were up to no good." The reality is that the Mo Cai area had the highest concentration of VC in the entire Mekong. They were taking advantage of the ferry; no civilian in his right mind would have been on it that late at night. The Mekong had been saturated with dropped leaflets on a regular basis warning the population about the rules of engagement and the curfews.

***

It was about three in the morning when I saw a file of VC skirting a wood line to my right and in front. The trail they were on would take them to the right of the company, making ambush difficult. In fact, it would give them a flanking position. They just kept on a' coming. I first saw eight to ten of them, and then it was twenty to thirty, then forty to fifty, and still coming. This group of VC reminds me of the group we lost when I was with Bravo, and I didn't want this group to disappear into the jungle like the last. Because they were next to a wood line and would have cover once we started firing on them, it was obvious that artillery and gunships needed to be on this. I alerted the company and asked the CO to make ready for artillery strikes. He sent his FO to our position, who plotted a bracket behind and on the front element. As the first one came into range, he ordered the battery to fire for effect. The FO said, "Shot out." I give it a few seconds and dump the first one on his ass at about 450 meters. He no more than dropped, and the HE rounds started landing, lighting up the entire paddy and wood line. These guys were shittin' and a'gittin' to the rear as the FO made adjustment to his rear bracket and called in the second set of rounds. He nailed it, as the rounds landed perfectly on the edge of the wood line and on the rear element. Then the next volley landed directly where we last saw the leading element, and then he began squeezing the bracket slowly to the center of their position while slowly driving the rounds deeper into the wood line. This fuckin' guy was as good as Ziek and was fucking these VC up. I was elated and felt redemption. Deep inside I was hoping this is the same group that we lost when with Bravo.

Bright and early the next morning, battalion flew in another company a couple of klicks away and on the other side of where we last saw the VC as my company prepared to squeeze the area, hoping to pick up some leftover VC. A resupply chopper soon landed and we boogied out of there for the ship and some sleep, not knowing the extent of the damage. I never did find out how it went, but I know we hurt them badly that night.

We were on our way to another one of the 3/60th companies that was quite a ways east of Ben Tre into the tidal zone. As we approach the LZ, we could tell that the tide was definitely in, as no ground could be seen—only the Nipa palm, a few bushes, and the coconut trees were visible. Then below we could see the company spread out on the dikes and trails. There was no open area (as in a paddy to land on) thus the pilot was forced to squeeze in between some coconut trees. I hated these kinds of insertions because we were forced to hover high and slow, giving Charlie a target, and I was still a little jumpy since my last Huey crash. The LZ was very tight, and the pilot ordered the resupplies to be thrown overboard. But the water containers were bursting open as they hit the water below, forcing the pilot to give it one more try. As he lowered his collective and started his slow descent between the coconuts trees, his blades started hitting the leaves of the trees at a cyclic rate similar to an AK-47's. I thought we were being fired at, and I wanted out of the chopper, so I jumped. Unfortunately, I jumped into a canal hidden by the flooding waters and was stuck up to my knees in mud, and my head was under water! I started thrashing and trying to kick my way free as panic set in. My head was only about six inches under water but enough to threaten drowning if I didn't get out soon. Just as I was about to take in water, I felt a hand; it grabbed one of mine and then the other. I was pulled up enough to catch a breath of fresh air as the men continue pulling until I was free. The chopper pulled up and the men onboard continued throwing out the water, C rats, and ammo, as the grunts went diving for them, and off the pilot went with my partner, leaving me alone with the company. It was another night sleeping in water with the leeches and Mekong mosquitos. Not having a partner is hard on your concentration. It's an eerie feeling looking through a Starlight scope as the shadows move and the distances appear to change as the clouds above hinder and then allow the light from the stars to come and go. Your eyes become fatigued, and you lose your night vision with your right eye. It's necessary to take a break from time to time. I had taken a short break, only to find a couple of VC coming straight at us as I came back to the scope. They were only two hundred meters away in an open break and about to make their way into the wood line. I made a hurried-up shot at the lead one and dropped him in his tracks, only to lose the other. The rest of the night was uneventful. As light broke, we headed out as the company made its way to a more open area, hopefully to complete their resupply, as they were out of water. All the water containers had exploded on the last resupply, and the day promised to be your typical over one hundred degrees, muggy, Mekong weather. As we made our way through the jungle, I fell back with the rear element. I looked to my left through an open area and saw a Vietnamese with a weapon. He looked like an ARVN, but that doesn't mean much around here as Charlie frequently showed a different face now and again. We never operate close to where any ARVN forces are, never, and for very good reasons. I took my safety off and was about to nail this guy when I saw some other movement close by. To my amazement it was an American. Holy shit, he's the lead element and has changed directions and doubled back on his own men. This could have been a disaster had I shot and they then opened up on each other. I'd never seen this before without the lead element notifying all as to their change of directions. Dangerous as hell!

We finally got to a decent-sized rice paddy and set up for resupply. At this point I was not quite sure as to what I should do. So I ask the CO's RTO to ask the resupply ship what its next move is and whether or not their crew will take me aboard. The ship landed and started dumping their water then finally answered our call, telling me to come aboard. As I was about halfway to the bird, all hell broke loose, and I could hear the rounds hitting the bird. For a moment I stopped and thought about turning around, but I really wanted out of this cesspool and kept running as the rounds kept coming. I jumped aboard expecting the pilot to immediately pull his bird into the air, but instead he jockeyed around as though nothing had happened. I was thinking we were going down any time now, but we rise out of the paddy and head west to the MRF ships. I leaned over to the copilot and told him that the bird took quite a few rounds while sitting there, and he turned as though I was bullshitting him and said, "I don't think so" and went back to his duties.

As we landed on the LST where the crew was to pick up its next load of supplies, I let the crew chief know in no uncertain terms he needed to make an inspection. They finally shut it down. I looked up into the cowling area, and the bird was full of holes. The crew chief unbuckled and also realized the truth of the matter. I asked him why they didn't believe me. "Every time we've been hit, we've either felt it or heard it." Looks like they learned something this lucky day.

***

I was in Dong Tam at the Sniper School having my weapon looked at and staying in the lower part of the sniper barracks that night. Another sniper and I had just returned from the NCO club when the sirens went off. There was a large bunker between the sniper barracks and a barracks for in-transit senior NCOs. We went over there and made ourselves at home with the new incoming NCOs as the mortars pounded Dong Tam. Soon the tempo of the strike slowed, and the temperature and humidity in the bunker became almost unbearable. I told my sniper friend that I was going just outside the bunker entrance to the cooler air. My justification for taking the risk was that we could hear the mortar rounds coming in and would have time to duck back inside before they landed. We were outside enjoying a cigarette when out came four of the FNG NCOs. As we were standing there in a circle bullshitting one another, a 122 rocket hit the top level of the sniper barracks next to us. It dropped two of the new NCOs. (You can't hear a short rocket round!) We immediately went to work on them; they had obvious sucking chest wounds. We put cellophane cigarette wrappers on the wounds to stop the sucking of air, but to no avail. They both died within minutes. We felt terrible and wondered if our conversation had been overheard, thus making them feel comfortable enough to come out and away from the protection the bunker provided? It still works on me.

122 Rocket damage to Sniper Barracks   122 DAMAGE TO SNIPER CADRE AREA

I was the odd man out one night, which proved beneficial, as I was given duty on Pink Eye, a Tango boat with a mini-chopper pad on top and a large pink infrared light that looked like a television for light enhancement. I boarded the Tango alongside the *Benewah* around dark, and we headed up river, staying on the right side of the main channel of the Song My Tho. I made myself as comfortable as possible on the steel deck, using some of the sailors' C rats as a build-up for my prone position. We stopped our upriver travel and made a turn downriver and alongside the south bank as the skipper cut his engines and we floated about two hundred yards off the bank. The crew turned on the pink light and lit up the riverbank for me to begin my search for Charlie. We floated until the boat either got too far away or too close to the river and then went under power to regain our position, trying to keep parallel to the bank. This was great duty: I had company to quietly bullshit with, and there was no worry of Charlie sneaking up on me. Best of all, I didn't have to be inserted or picked up by choppers; the insertions and pickups were probably as dangerous as being on the ground in my mind. Soon most of the crew was asleep as we continue our float down the lazy river My Tho. Although boring, it was a wonderfully relaxing night as I clandestinely peer into the private lives of the river frontage inhabitants. Once in a while I caught them sitting on their makeshift bamboo toilets that hang over the river's edge, where the inhabitants of the river's bottom await the nourishment of a recycled rice and fish head dinner. There was activity along the way but no way to tell what kind, as the hooch's are so close. One has to assume it's just neighbors and family going back and forth. Without weapons on them, they are not targets in this neighborhood. I rolled over to stretch from time to time, catching the moon and stars, wondering if someone back home will have the same view in just a few hours. I imagined how great it would be to have a reflector on the moon so we could communicate in some celestial way. The sun soon lightened the eastern sky, and we all return to the *Benewah,* where I caught a hot breakfast for a change in the ship's galley.

We had just came down from the upper decks and were getting ready to go out on another mission when I struck up a conversation with the SEALs who were doing the same. They had been a little quiet throughout our cohabitation of the berthing area, and I thought it was time to find out what a SEAL was. They seemed like a likable bunch, but for some reason didn't feel comfortable hanging with Doggie Snipers. I think that part of it was, that we had given them a little shit about overdoing the camo on their faces and hands, making remarks like "Is that Revlon" But I soon broke the ice, and we were trying to find home state connections in no time. I went back to my area to finish dressing when the SEAL lieutenant came over with a map and spread it out on my rack, asking what we knew of the area they were going to that evening. Soon the other snipers surrounded, and one of the guys asks, "Is this the type of AO you guys deal with?" "Where have you been operating before?" The lieutenant pointed out a few of their past mission AOs and then asked, "Well what do you think?" One of the guys said, "I think you guys should go somewhere that Charlie is instead of hanging around whore houses and R&R centers. That did it. The lieutenant grabbed his map, and they never spoke to us again. I tried to apologize later, but it fell on deaf ears. Oh well! I had to hand it to them though; here's navy guys learning how to be grunts without any apparent infantry training or guidance. I wondered if anything would come of it. Little did I know.

***

I was in transit to Dong Tam and found myself in Saigon when I decided to go out on the town and delay my arrival in the delta. I perused the many shops downtown, looking for souvenirs and gifts for family. I by chance ran into another 9th ID soldier also wearing army issue camos. The issuing of camouflage was a new and rare thing. The only ones I knew of in the 9th ID wearing them were the LRRPs and the snipers, less than .05 percent of the total 9th ID forces. As we approached, I could see that he was indeed a LRRP and a combat medic. We immediately joined forces and continued the recon of downtown Saigon. Soon I was calling him Doc, and he was calling me Sarg.

We soon decided it was time for a beer and entered a small, local bar, ordering some Baa Muy Baa (beer 333), a local Vietnamese rice lager beer. As we turned to find a seat, a couple of Australian sergeants invited us to sit with them. In no time the consumption was at the Aussie level, a level up a notch from the American level, as these guys were used to a much higher content of alcohol than our American beers were made of. Soon the conversation went to our camouflage uniforms and then elevated to their need to have them. We laughed off the thought for many a beer and then soon my medic friend decided he wanted one of those Australian hats with the curved upward brim. The Aussies laughed off this idea for a few more beers. But before long the Aussies came up with a plan my medic friend couldn't refuse. They wanted for the four of us to trade entire uniforms, with the exception of underwear and boots. I just wasn't going for this as I had on my best sniper camos on with all the patches and stripes. Doc relentlessly worked on me until I caved in. The four of us stood up and started stripping, much to the dismay of the Vietnamese bar owner. I don't know what he thought we were doing but he was beside himself. Soon we had made the transfer, and we now thought this was as friggin' funny as it gets!

The Aussies decided to show us the town, now that it was evening time. I soon decided we should grab a taxi as Doc and I already had a few miles on. But the Aussies made the remark that they wouldn't stop for soldiers. We knew better as we had never had a problem. So I started to wave one down, and sure enough, they wouldn't even give me a second look. What the fuck, I thought? So I demanded that one of the Aussies in our uniforms try it, and sure enough, he stopped one, to their amazement. Evidently, they just didn't like Aussies. As the four of us tried to get in, the driver demanded that the Aussies (now Doc and me) must stay behind as he didn't have any room. To which the real Aussies said, "Fuck you" as one of them crawled on top of the Morris Minor, and we three loaded up for the ride. The driver was pissed and cussing in perfect English. After figuring out who was who, he demanded that we two Americans be responsible for payment, to which we agreed. The reason was that the Aussies had a reputation of stiffing the Taxi drivers. As we proceeded to some unknown hotel/whore house, the Aussie on the roof decided he was going to try to make the Taxi roll, and he shifted his weight from side to side while holding on to each side of the Taxi. That didn't work, so he decided to crawl forward and hang down in front of the windshield, further exciting the driver as he couldn't see for shit in the bumper-to-bumper traffic. Doc and I were laughing our asses off over the antics of these allies of ours. These fuckers were crazy, we thought.

SIDE STREETS OF SAIGON

Soon we arrived at a four-story hotel. I paid the driver, and in we went. The Aussies had been here before and went up to the front counter as always, only to have the clerk yelling, "No GI! No GI!" Well this pissed off the Aussies, and the argument began. In frustration, an Aussie slammed down his fist on the glass counter, breaking it in pieces. Immediately the Vietnamese clerk pulled out a .38 revolver and shoved it in their faces. Left speechless, we backed out ASAP, only to find American MPs screeching into the driveway, followed by Vietnamese MPs, followed by Aussie MPs. What the hell was going on here, we wondered? Something big and surely not about us, we hoped. The American MPs grabbed the Aussies as the Aussie MPs grabbed Doc and me. The confusion was on, and there was soon a meeting being held by all MPs as another jeep full of MPs showed up. This time there was an American colonel aboard. The meeting proceeded, and soon the four of us were in front of the colonel. Another jeep full of American MPs roared in. The colonel said, "I don't know what you knuckleheads are up to, but this is your lucky day. We've had this place under surveillance for some time. We're pretty sure that there is MPC (military payment currency) counterfeiting going on here. But because it is off limits to Americans by the Saigon government, we haven't been able to raid the place. We've been waiting for some knuckleheads like you to show up for a long time. You've now given us the right to raid this place. Now get the hell out of here, and get those uniforms changed."

We were on our way in double time, hoping that they didn't change their minds as they surrounded the building. We still kept our uniforms on and continued partying until the wee hours of the morning. As Doc and I didn't have any place to stay, the Aussies felt sorry for us and took us back to their barracks. We found a couple of extra cots and placed them in their room and promptly passed out.

In just a couple of hours, I was awakened by someone kicking the bottom of my boots, yelling "What are these Bloody Americans doing here?" I rolled over, and this crusty, old Aussie sergeant yelled, "Who the bloody hell are you?" The gig was up as we all rolled over with major hangovers pumping through our heads. We were forced to give up our Aussie war souvenirs, and Doc and I were promptly kicked out of the Aussies' base without water or food. It was a long day getting back to Dong Tam. I was actually glad to be back home, even if it meant going out in the field the next day. Those Aussies are brutal drinkers.

***

The season was changing to monsoon season and on this day the cumulus clouds were rising and moving at a rapid rate as my partner and I awaited a Huey on the ship's deck. We had no idea where we we're going or with whom, but that's the way it was with snipers. Sometimes we got good info, sometimes nothing more than orders to catch a ride. The sky was darkening at a rapid rate as the sun dipped and the concentrating clouds blocked what sun there was as the Huey came in for landing. We were soon off and heading due south but at a lower altitude than normal in order to miss the cumulus nimbus and thunderheads directly above. The wind was kicking up in the form of a head wind as we plodded through the night. We had been in the air for forty-five minutes and were still heading south when all hell broke loose as the clouds boomed and clapped, with lightning striking all around us.

The ship started going into uncontrollable yaws and pitches, but we continued to beat our way through it as the blades started popping and whopping to the violence of the winds and the sheets of rain. Finally, after an hour of this and no end in sight, the pilot decided to abort the mission, and we made a 180 degree turn to our relief. I had long left my normal position of hanging my feet out while sitting on the edge of the cargo floor, and I buckled into a canvas seat, but the sideways sheets of rain still managed to penetrate and were helped with the constant turbulence within the fuselage. I've never experienced anything like this in my hundreds of hours of chopper time or, for that matter, any fixed-wing time. I was fucking scared as hell as the blades start popping more and more loudly, and the pilot is unable to control the involuntary forty-five degree angles of attack. The worse it got, the lower we were flying and the slower we were going. It was obvious that the chopper crew was scared as hell also as they hung on.

The pilot couldn't take anymore and attempted a landing, but to no avail, as he just couldn't control the pitching of the bird, and the blinding sheets of rain continued with intermittent lighting strikes. We were now down to tree-top level, and the gunners were at ready positions with one hand on their M-60s and the other wiping their goggles. One moment it was dark as hell and the next it was lit up by the lightning as though it was noon as we continued to rock and roll. The pilot tried to put it down once again, and this time he succeeded, although it was a hard landing that smashed my already weak vertebrae together. There are few large paddies down here like in the northern delta, just little five-acre patches of paddies. There was a sense of relief once we were on the ground but only for a moment as we realized that we were close enough to the surrounding wood lines to be within small arms fire.

The blades continued to pop and whop as the bird bounced and threatened to go airborne due to the wind gusts, as the pilot kept his rotor RPMs up for quick takeoff! We could see the constant bending of the blades by the wind gusts when the lightning struck. It was now a game of how big are your balls! Do you stay here and await the inevitability of Charlie laying into you, or do you take your chances in the air? We also had a fuel problem that helped make that decision for us as we took off again, only to be beaten up some more by the constant, uncontrollable pitching, rolling, and yawing of the bird in the blinding monsoon rains. We went only a couple of miles and sat it down again until our nuts shrank again thinking of Charlie, so within five minutes we were off again, This time we were almost thrown into the wood line by a lateral gust before we could get out, but the pilot managed to grab enough collective to pop above the trees as we continued our rollercoaster ride north. The next hour would go the same, puckering our asses awaiting a blade to fly off or bust in two, taking temporary refuge on the ground from time to time. Then finally we could see some clearing to our northwest, and we headed toward Can Tho, where we touched down and fueled up for our return to the ships anchored off Dong Tam. It was a relief, to say the least. Although the weather there was still less than desirable, we were safe at last. We refueled, the crew checked out the bird the best they could in the dark, and then we all started to laugh as we settled down for some C rats inside the bird. We were like a bunch of kids talking about the scariest carnival ride we had ever been on. I will never forget it!

***

It was my first night on a night hunter mission. We were cruising rivers and canals close to Mo Cai and having a fairly good night as we had caught two different sampans with a handful of VC in each. My partner marked them and then the Cobras dived, dumping on them with everything they had. There was one fantastic secondary explosion that lit up the river. I loved the fireworks on these missions. Even without the secondary explosions, the Cobras were fun to watch all by themselves. I then came upon a small sampan with only one occupant traversing the river. I shot out my tracer round and called in for "no need for adjustment," as I felt my round was right on. The two Cobras rolled out and dived on the tracer as we veered out of their path. They turned on their Xenon lights and instead of a volley of rockets and miniguns, they cut the lights off with no firing on the target. They then stacked themselves back up and behind us as we hunted until midnight and then went on into Can Tho for refueling and a lunch break. After the birds were refueled, I strolled over to the Cobras and asked one of the pilots why he never fired on an obvious target. "Was it a child or woman?" I asked. The answer I got was "No reason to waste rounds on a guy who has a hole through his chest and is hanging head first in the water. That was one great shot, sniper." Cool, I thought, one lucky shot anyhow! How I loved this form of employment. Staying clean, dry, and high! Not to mention the excitement as to what was around the bend and the fireworks the Cobras had to offer.

Heuy Cobra over Song My Tho
Heading out for Hunter Killer Mission

I'd just finished an uneventful night alone with one of the 3/60th companies and was airborne in the resupply chopper heading for Dong Tam, cruising at about 1500 feet, high enough to be safe from small arms fire, when sonic cracks from a .51 caliber got our attention, and then we felt one hit the bird and immediately we started losing altitude. The pilots were busy as we were now auto rotating to terra firma. One was on the radio with his Mayday and the other busy trying to figure out our LZ. Soon the pilot was yelling at me, wanting to know where to land, as though I knew where we were any better than he did. All I could think was to tell him to land next to a wood line so that we could easily disembark and find cover. "Which wood line?" was his response. Mine was "Fuck if I know!" We were soon approaching the ground as the door gunners started strafing the nearby wood lines. Then the pilot in his uneasiness started his auto rotation landing as he grabbed the collective. But he misjudged the distance and took too much of a bite out of the air as the craft stalled and fell. With a bang we were on the ground, the force jamming my vertebrae again and banging my head on the side of the fuselage. But we were down, and all disembarked with expedience and headed for the wood line.

It was immediately made clear that I was in charge. I ordered the men to retrieve the remaining rounds and smoke grenades from the bird and to make one last radio call explaining our intentions and the color of smoke we would use when needed. We had landed so hard that the bird's floorboards were level with the rice paddy mud and the skids were sprung out to the side. Recovering the ammo and smokes, we took up a defensive position not far into the wood line and awaited help. My back was killing me. I had a goose egg on my head, and the others weren't much better off. I felt as though I was with a bunch of FNGs, as these guys had never been in the bush before and weren't mentally prepared for it. However, we had more than our share of ammo and two M-60s manned by men who knew how to use them. We weren't going down easy!

About the time everyone settled down, we could hear Vietnamese from a distance and so the tension rose again. But we were soon visited by two Cobra gunships overhead, giving us a big sigh of relief, as we now knew they had spotted the downed Huey. We popped smoke to give them our position so that they wouldn't mistake us for Charlie. Soon one dived right at us, and I thought we were fucked because I thought this pilot assumed we were the bad guys. But he was diving short as he unloaded some 3.5-inch rockets and a burst of minigun fire. He found the VC that was talking earlier. All was quiet as they stayed on top of us until a platoon of grunts came to save the day. We jumped on the now waiting, empty birds, and away we went with smiles on our faces and a ride to Dong Tam, where I immediately went to the Sniper School beer barrel prior to taking a shuttle back to the *Benewah* and calling it a day!

Ed at Bn. TOC

I went to Battalion TOC for our evening orders now that Haugen had left the Sniper Platoon. I was told that there would be two teams of us inserted with one of the companies that had been in tough action all day. As we started our descent, we could see the smoke from burning hooch's, and smoldering remnants of napalm and arty strikes. However, as we landed we could see by the demeanor and actions of the awaiting troops that everything was in control. The company had already formed a RON perimeter as patrols came in from body searches. The perimeter was on the corner of a large rice paddy. My partner and I took the open side of the corner as the other team took the side that had a hard-ball trail leading directly into their position, where they also set up an ambush with a grenadier and a machine gunner as added beef. The evening was upon us soon as the glowing embers from fires burned themselves out. About 0300 hours, we heard a noise behind us, which raised temporary concern, as the nearest position behind us was forty to fifty feet. At first we thought it was someone crawling to our position for conversation, but he crawled on by us toward the other sniper position, which was only fifteen to twenty meters from us. We thought nothing about it, as it wasn't all that unusual for men within a perimeter to shuffle around for one reason or another. Soon we could see the eastern sky lighten as dark skies gave way to dawn, and then there was a loud *boom* with a flash, followed by moans of pain and agony coming from team two's position. The first thing coming into everyone's mind was attack. Was it a mortar, grenade, or an M-79 round? But that was it—nothing more. We then all agreed it sounded like and probably was a grenade, as the wounded were patched up, including both snipers and the grenadier. They confirmed a grenade landed right in front of the grenadiers' M-76, tearing into the weapon, which took the brunt of the blast, it then threw shrapnel into the rest of the men of the position. The medics immediately patched them up, called for a medevac, and soon they were gone. The question of where the grenade came from then arose. The only conclusion was from within our perimeter. As each position was questioned, a closer search of the perimeter area revealed a VC only two canals/four meters behind my position hiding in the water with debris covering his head. This I thought, had to be the cause of the early sounds behind us. He must have chosen the other position instead of ours because of the increased opportunity for casualties. I felt terrible for not questioning the noise earlier and thanked God for no deaths.

Rumors were running rampant within the battalion that soon we would be pulling out of the delta and that the 9th ID would be going home. What a wonderful rumor, I thought. Too good to be true I was sure, but they were strong rumors, and, best of all, it was also rumored that the 3/60th would be the first to bring home unit colors. The rumors continued and didn't let up. I had cause to go into Dong Tam, and the rumors were even there. God, could this be true? Could I possibly make it after all? My mind was abuzz with possibilities tempered by doubts. I tried to not think about it, but the rumors were just too strong. I went over to the Sniper School and hung with the cadre over a beer. They told me that the school had received orders to prepare for dismantling the school and moving it to the 25th ID in Cu Chi. Many of the cadre were closing in on having been in Vietnam for a year and would go home. The idea was to send some home and keep others to get the 25th ID Sniper School up and running. The plan was to use some of the existing snipers as cadre also. This information did it for me—I believed. The light at the end of the tunnel was now a little brighter. I went back to the ship with a smile and an alcohol weave. I awoke a different person. The possibility of me making it was real, and my cup of combat soup was running over! My balls shrank immensely, and I didn't have the same sense of doom within. I made it a point to pull rank and be the one always going to TOC for the evening's orders so that I could choose the best form of employment available for my survival.

My next employment was on a Tango boat/pink light mission. I considered this to be the safest form of employment available. It started off as usual, making time up the river for the float down. The monsoons were with us now, and the skies started dumping an inch an hour on the cold, steel deck. I piled up as much gear as the crew would allow me to get wet so that I could have a supported sitting position, thereby keeping more of my body away from the cold, wet, steel deck. My position also gave me a larger area vulnerable to enemy fire, but I felt the trade-off to be worth it. I borrowed a helmet to help keep the rain off my face and out of my eyes, and we floated down the river.

The problem with rain is that it limits the distance of your field of fire, so I asked that we get a little closer to the riverbank for a better view. It wasn't long before the skipper of the boat ran into a sandbar. Being stuck in the boat reminded me of being stuck in mud with my pickup when the skipper threw the transmission into reverse and then back into forward, only to hit another sandbar and then another. The noise of the large diesel engines increased, letting Charlie know we were in trouble. To make things worse, we were getting even closer to the riverbank than before. This back and forth movement of being stuck then free, lasted for nearly a half hour before it was evident we were screwed and stuck for good. The skipper called for help, and another Tango headed our way to hopefully tow us from the mud. The crewmembers were now behind their guns, preparing for the worst as the skipper killed the now worthless engines. There was no doubt in our minds that Charlie had heard us and would take advantage of the stationary target.

A half hour went by as I continued to scan the riverbank for any sign of movement. Then just as we heard the other Tango coming up river I saw movement directly to our front. It was erratic, and the enemy was obviously trying to conceal their movement. I was not getting any solid shots because they showed for a second or two and then disappeared either because of concealment or because of the rain. I went ahead and started firing to alert the crew and to possibly delay any attack by forcing the enemy to move more slowly. The crew held fire while yelling at me to explain myself, and then all hell broke loose as rockets were fired that broke at the last second above our heads, overshooting the boat. The crew started pounding with their Quad 50s, twenty-millimeter guns, and their automatic grenade launcher. These guys blew the shit out of the riverbank, creating a light show to behold and gave me a sigh of relief as it was obvious we had the power to sustain ourselves. That was it. Charlie had blown his wad, and his balls were shrunk to raisins. The river became quiet as the other boat approached. We still weren't out of the woods and feared another attack as I continued to scan. The other boat approached, only to get stuck temporarily himself as he rocked back and forth, trying to get close enough to throw a line. This thing was turning into a circle jerk and looking worse instead of better, I'm thinking. But he finally made it close enough to throw a line, and the pull was underway, as both boats continued to temporarily get stuck while yanking on one another. But soon we were underway and called it a night as the monsoons continued their pounding of the delta.

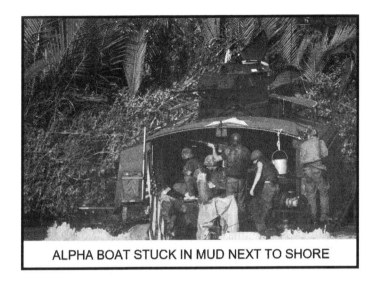

ALPHA BOAT STUCK IN MUD NEXT TO SHORE

***

It was always easy to get to your next location/mission, but not always easy to get back. This was especially true when with one of the companies. There weren't always supply choppers every morning to return on; therefore, sometimes I had to hang with the company the next day and take whatever came along that was going back to either the ships or Dong Tam. This could be in the form of a Riverine boat or any chopper coming in. Sometimes when the company was being reinserted on an Eagle flight/sortie, I would just stay on the chopper and go back with them, but even then they didn't always return to base immediately, and I would be part of the next sortie and insertion, only to stay and wait for my turn to get off. After all, the choppers had to refuel sometime or another. The same would apply when being transported by Tangos. No one in the rear seemed to give a shit about where we were anyhow, as we were a pretty loosely run organization with no real command within. Haugen seemed to be the platoon sergeant when I got there, and now, either by osmosis or time in rank, the job was mine. I was by myself this day, and I decided to stay on the Tango and catch some sleep while going back to the ships. But to my dismay, these guys headed out deeper into the delta on their own mission, weaving in and out of various canal systems looking for trouble. This went

205

on all day, and then they picked up another company to insert. Once again I stayed aboard, hoping for a ride back home. The boat crew knew nothing of their schedule other than they had an idea as to when they would need refueling and resupply themselves, but they had just resupplied prior to me boarding, so I was looking at maybe another three days with these guys.

I was all alone in the cargo deck of a Tango with just the old WWII .30-caliber machine guns mounted on the gunnels, a few rat-infested mattresses, and some picked over C rats. These guys didn't seem to ever want to come out of their protected positions of weaponry, and it took all day before I even met one of them. They were nice guys, but they didn't seem to give a shit about my dilemma, and I wasn't getting any sleep with the threat of ambush from the canal banks only feet from us. But I was thinking that this wasn't so bad since I was cruising around the delta in a fortified boat that only B-40 rockets could penetrate. I wasn't trudging in the Mekong mud, and, besides, being stuck on this boat gives me an excuse not to be in the field.

Late in the day, the monsoon rains started pounding, and I decided to go to the top deck for a shower, only to find that these monsoon rains weren't your normal rains. They came down with brutal force and tried to rip my eyelashes off while re-circumcising me at the same time. Bad idea! Now I was cold with nothing but a cold steel deck to warm me. We set up in the main channel for the night, but there were no barracks ships around, so I was stuck. The crew took turns sleeping on the filthy three-inch mattresses, leaving me the steel deck. I awoke at dawn after maybe two hours of sleep as the crew re-manned its stations. I could smell the coffee coming from the inside, but I have nothing but turkey loaf for breakfast and water tasting like diesel for me, as I earlier took provisions for only twelve to eighteen hours when being inserted. I want off this fucking thing! Finally I get good news—we're heading back to the Song My Tho and the *Benewah*. But to my dismay, the boats turned up the canal cutting through Ben Tre. This meant that they were to go through some of the nastiest canals in the entire delta, including the infamous Crossroads. The Crossroads were famous for the intensity of the ambushes, and to this day the Vietnamese have statues there of ambushing VC.

I had already been on many Tangos being ambushed. I watched as Alpha boats (ASPB—Assault Support Patrol Boat) were blown completely out of the water, falling back to the river as a crumpled piece of steel, dividing the entire Riv-Div and forcing them to stay and fight. The Riv-Div always won in time, but the damage would be done.

ASPB-- Assault Support Patrol Boat's tied to barge.

ASPB on the move.

One of my favorite boats was a converted Tango boat with two large Caterpillar diesel engines with water pumps in the cargo area. The crew would hose down the banks through the nozzles with great pressure. These things would knock over coconut trees, blow up bunkers, and trip booby traps so prevalent in landing areas. Due to the amount of pressure these things put out, they had to balance the boat by washing down both sides of the river at the same time. The nice thing was that they had continuous ammo, (water) tempered by the amount of fuel on board. However, one day as the Riv-Div slowed down in a narrow canal, the powerful engines sucked up the water so fast that they denied the boat any water to float on, so it began sucking mud, which in turn killed one of the engines, which in turn denied the boat balance. The remaining nozzle pressure turned the boat on its side. Apparently, the brilliant engineers hadn't put in an engine cutoff system for such an event.

ZIPPO BOAT PREPPING LANDING AREA

Another of my favorites was the Zippo boat. It had a super large fuel tank of napalm set in the cargo space. It was a flamethrower on steroids. These guys could maintain a 150- to 200-foot stream of flaming terror for about twenty minutes. They would lay the flame on the landing area or ambush area with great effect. I only remember one time when disembarking that the flames were still burning, making walking a little uncomfortable. However, we had smoke for cover, so all wasn't bad.

As we plied our way up the canal and got deeper into Charlie's stronghold, the radio chatter quieted as all manned their positions. I charged all the 30s in the lower deck with crusty belts of ammo and prepared myself for a lonely experience.

To our amazement we cruised through the Crossroads and headed north without even a sniper round. But now we were going up a canal that was so tight, the boats couldn't make a U-turn. The banks were only ten feet away. The high tide had given these guys access to a seldom traveled canal. At times like this, you understand why the plastic PBRs and aluminum Swift boats weren't allowed to operate down here. They wouldn't last a day!

Alpha Boats (ASPB) leading Riv-Div formation

Monitor Boat leading Tangos down river.

The slow growl of the diesel engines was soon broken by the sound of rockets being fired and the crushing explosions that followed. The .51-caliber machine guns soon started their chatter, followed by impotent AK chatter hoping to find an open spot in the armor. Tracers and rocket exhaust filled the sky, and I started burning off the .30-caliber belts into the unknown underbrush lining the canal. There was a constant rumble with no waning as bullets ricocheted and smacked into the side as rockets flew short, splattering their shrapnel against us. I moved to another 30 caliber machine gun and burned up its belt. Then finally the incoming ceased as soon as it started. The gunners, however, still laid into them as though they were still receiving fire, just to make sure that they got the message. Soon the order was given to cease fire, and the demand for damage reports could be heard from boat to boat. The skipper of my Tango yelled down to make sure I was all right, and then the cheers and laughing started as all realized not a single soul was seriously hurt. The slow rumble of diesel engines resumed as I reloaded the 30s and tried once again to get some sleep, but to no avail as there was now a bond between myself and the crew, and now they wanted to have a conversation. We as grunts had always had an affection for the Brown Water Sailors and their job. They were the only navy personnel we trusted, and conversely they trusted us more than the ship's personnel. That being said, they still were very protective of their privacy and their gear. We were, after all, in their house and next to their personal belongings.

Curtesy of: Mobile Riverine Assn & Albert Moore Pres.

Sikorsky Sky Crane overhead.

When I arrived at the *Benewah*, the stories of a pullout were ramped up as never before. The other snipers were already being reassigned, and it looked like the end of the 3/60th Sniper Platoon. In general nobody had a real clue what for sure was going on. Will they be going home, if so when? Will they be reassigned? I figured this was a good time to make a break for it. I told TOC that I too have gotten reassigned, and with no questions, I decided to pack up and head over to B Company's ship. I was probably AWOL but didn't really give a shit anymore. It was all about that light at the end of the tunnel now. If the fuckin' government wanted to pull out of the delta and leave the Vietnamese people to an inevitable butchering after all the hard work and lives spent, then I'll be a son of a bitch if I'm gonna give them anymore of my life. That was now my way of thinking!

Mobile Riverine Force on the move.

Navy Crewmember taking a break.

Chapter 16

P U L L   O U T

I caught a shuttle boat to Bravo's ship. There I find Bravo in total disarray as some of the old-timers are staying, and some going home with the 3/60th, while the others are being transferred to various other battalions. It was apparent that these battalions were being bolstered by transferees who had approximately the same amount of tour time left. Men who had just a few days left in their tour and from other battalions were being transferred to the 3/60th. So only short-timers were to go home with the flags? Others were being transferred around the division, so I decided that I was going to find one that was going home soon and then try to find a way to integrate myself with them. I was convinced that battalion thinks I'm under the Sniper School command and that the Sniper School thinks I'm under battalion command. With no place to call home, I caught a shuttle to Dong Tam and immediately took my rifle to the armorer at the Sniper School, grabbed a beer, and called the sniper barracks home. I told them I was awaiting orders and was hoping for an early DEROS (Date of Eligible Return from Overseas). Then a bomb was dropped, as I was told that all snipers would not get an early out. Some would stay with the 9th ID, and others would go to the 25th ID's (25th Infantry Division's) new school. I was then asked if I would be interested in moving north with the 25th ID contingency. "Hell no" was my answer, and I popped another ten-cent beer.

I ran into some of the guys from Bravo at the NCO club and got the latest pullout news. I was totally jealous of those leaving. There weren't many of Bravo actually going home with the 3/60th as the battalion was being remade of short-timers of all different kinds of MOSs from around the division. The ships were a constant revolving door for those coming and going. The next shortest guys went to other Second Brigade battalions for redeployment to the States soon after the 3/60th. I ran into Doc Schuebel, and he told me that he was on the 3/60th roster, along with Lieutenant Wolfer, my first platoon leader. This surprised me because Doc wasn't that short and technically was from a medical battalion and not 3/60th. Someone in battalion was watching out for Doc. Probably Wolfer was my guess.

The Sniper Commandant Major Powell started to question my hanging out, and I realized that I had to come up with a plan, or at least make myself more scarce. I started hanging out at Anh's Steam Bath and the NCO club, and I started eating at different mess halls to make myself a little scarcer. I then started sleeping in the Sniper School's bunker, which was hot and stuffy, but no one went in there unless there was a mortar attack, which of course was only a matter of time, and I then I had to make up suspicious excuses. Major Powell came to me and let me know that he could get me assigned to a Sniper Platoon if needed. I agreed that if orders were not forthcoming I'd agree to his offer. I was fast running out of money and had to resort to waiting for mortar attacks at the NCO club in order to steal chit books from the hated REMFs. As soon as the mortar rounds landed or the sirens went off, I hid and waited for all to leave and then rounded up all the chit books lying on the tables. This gave me more drinking money and some trading stock. After all, when we were mortared in the field, we didn't have warning sirens and had only our fatigues to protect us from the shrapnel. Fuck 'em and feed 'em fish head was my attitude.

Dong Tam was overpopulated due to the pull out, and, therefore, so was the NCO club. The tension was sharp between the REMFs and the grunts. It had always been that way because the REMFs thought of the club, as their private club and had their special tables and stools. The bartenders gave the REMFs the cold beer, more ice in their drinks, and in general, better service. The difference in uniform wear, filth, worn boots, our reaction to loud sounds, et cetera, set us apart and reminded them of the reality of why they were there. The fact that they were apart from the real war was something they didn't want to be reminded of, and we paid for it. They acted as though we didn't exist and looked right by us. On top of that, the REMFs were in much better shape than we were, and there were more of them. We were all underweight and malnourished, and as such our chances in fist fights were diminished. I didn't even want to get to know any of the fuckers. They were pathetic fucks as far as I was concerned. While we all realized that it took a team effort to prosecute a war and that the REMFs were an important part of it; their attitude was toward us was less than stellar.

Soon I ran into more of the guys who had been reassigned to a Third Brigade battalion. They told me they saw my name on their orders for reassignment to the same company as themselves. They wanted me to go to the new CO and ask him if we could create our own platoon of just Bravo guys, as they wanted to stay together and wanted me as their platoon sergeant. I packed up and moved into their rear area not far from the NCO club (my new office). We were awaiting the rest of the company to come in from the field, and then I would make my pitch to the CO. However, I was now confused. Should I go back into a line company and face more combat? Do I let the new CO know I'm a sniper, and let my men down by going to the Sniper Platoon? Do I continue hiding in the shadows awaiting the unknown? Day by day, beer after beer.

We met every day at the NCO club awaiting the arrival of the company. I started realizing that I had changed. I was short fused, punchy, gave less of a shit than ever before, and the anxiety was almost overwhelming. Drinking seemed to be the only medicine.

The CO finally came in, and so I went to the first sergeant and asked for a meeting with the CO. Top was very protective and wanted to know why. I explained and he told me there was absolutely no way. I demanded that the CO be the one to make the decision, and he relented to asking the CO. I came back that evening only to receive a rude rejection once again from Top and no meeting with the CO. The guys were bummed, and I could understand why. They, after all, knew each other's abilities and moves and wanted to keep the unity within. We all got shit-faced.

The next morning I went to Top and told him I was a sniper and that I was going to the Sniper Platoon. "That's fine with me," he said, and I was on my way. However, once there, I didn't feel comfortable with them the minute I met them. They acted as if I was going to pull rank or something. They were overstaffed, and I was the odd man. So I just disappeared and went back to the Sniper School.

I bounced around a couple other battalions with no feeling of belonging or desire to belong. Besides, I really didn't know what the hell I was looking for anyhow. Being a sniper wasn't so bad, after all, I determined, as no one really knew what to do with you or who controlled you. I was able to just come and go as I pleased. No one checked for orders coming or going. But I needed to find a home and soon, as I was broke and I needed to get on a payroll somewhere.

I went to the Sniper School only to find that they had bugged out and moved to Cu Chi. There was a note on the door explaining that a lieutenant in Tan An was now in charge of the division snipers and was calling Tan An home. Tan An is north of Dong Tam and the home of the Third Brigade. So I caught a chopper to Tan An and started my recon of the area. I liked what I saw. It was obvious to me that this was a much more secure area in that the defensive demeanor was much more lax, which meant to me that these guys had little enemy pressure. As I questioned my new drinking partners in the NCO club, I liked what I heard: fewer mortar attacks, closer to Saigon, on the main highway, cleaner, and better smelling. I found that the 5/60th was the farthest northern battalion at base camp Rach Kien. I decided that that was my new home, the closer to Saigon, the safer was my point of view. I had a brief meeting with the lieutenant who was now in charge of the Sniper School and told him I had lost my orders and asked him if he could assign me to the 5/60th and that I also just wanted to check in and say hi. That was all fine with him, and he really didn't seem to give a shit what I did, but he didn't know what he could or couldn't do about orders. He explained to me that he would probably be going to Cu Chi himself and that the Third Brigade would be the only brigade of the 9th ID left in Vietnam and that they were soon going to be under the command of the 25th ID as our division commander from the 9th ID, Major General Hollis, was taking over the 25th ID command.

I caught a ride to Rach Kien, not knowing what I was really getting into. I was at first amazed that the travel on Highway 1 was so loose. Nobody was in convoy, and I'm seeing personnel in jeeps with no apparent weaponry. This was a different world, no doubt.

As I was traveling, I was wondering what Doc and the guys were up to? Were they in the States yet? Were they still processing out of country? I was so happy to know that at least some of those who deserved to live got to. I could just imagine the smiles on their faces as they paraded with the battalion's flags and behind Pistol Pete.

The reality was that they were being humiliated in Seattle by firecrackers thrown at them. While in formation they were pummeled with garbage, unable to fight back. Doc Schuebel was hit in the face with a tomato, knocking his glasses off, while the cadre frantically tried to hold the men in formation. Welcome home, men!

Soon we took a hard right off Highway 1 into a small village and onto a dirt road heading to Rach Kien. We stopped and bought a cold Coca-Cola, a novelty to me. As we proceeded, I was at first very paranoid because the wood line was so close to the road, inviting ambush, but the driver seemed not to be concerned in the least. In just a few miles, we approached this dilapidated ill-planned base camp that seemed to be sitting on a swamp. But most important was the lack of visual defense and perimeter bunkers. What the fuck was this, I wondered? Once inside the perimeter, I saw that the camp took on a more military look, and I disembarked for a closer look. I found the NCO club and had a drink with the battalion Chaplin, a Catholic priest with a great personality and a wealth of information.

*The sniper program was now considered a profound success and now had wheels. The school would go on to Cu Chi with the 25th ID, and from there, schools would spring up in various infantry divisions throughout Vietnam. Although the caliber of the instructors and weaponry weren't up to 9th ID standards, it was still a worthwhile program that made a difference in the prosecution of the war.

The army, however, didn't learn its lesson very expeditiously as the war ended. It took the army years to make a sniper school available to its infantry. The Special Forces, however, knew the importance and would be the first to implement a sniper school in the army years later.

Chapter 17

R A C H   K I E N

After an info recon at the NCO club, I found the transit barracks and made myself at home. I finally write a letter to home as it has been a while since I had a place to call home. I inform them as to my new address and wellbeing.

The next day I tried to find the Sniper Platoon, as that was where I asked to be assigned by the lieutenant in Tan An. I only found the acting platoon sergeant, who didn't seem to care if I was there or not and seemed to be offended. He seemed to feel as though I was trying to take someone's job, and I assured him that I was not. I changed gears here as there seemed to be no real structure, and it was a great opportunity to make a change. I told him I was actually off line because of three Purple Hearts and a ninety-day profile. I headed to the NCO club and mulled over my new off-the-cuff plan. I also realized that none of the officers I've come across seem to care who I am or what I'm doing. I was thinking that if I could just hide and keep moving around from company area to company area that I just might be able to keep under the radar.

This was my new plan, but I had one problem. I needed to somehow sign in so that I could start being paid without bringing too much attention. I went to the HQ office and told them I was a new sniper and that I needed emergency pay. It worked! I was off to further recon this shit hole of a base camp. I was further perplexed by the lack of perimeter protections and the willy-nilly construction. The place looked like a squatter city with tin, plywood, cardboard, wire mesh, and whatever making up the construction of various buildings. There were small sloughs of water intermittently scattered and built around. There were, however, all the basics: an HQ company building, artillery battery, ammo dump, supply company, medical dispensary, EM, NCO, and O clubs, a two-bit PX, and a large mess hall that stunk to high heaven along with all the rest the place.

I was starving as I'd only had some C rats since my arrival, so I went to the mess hall, only to have my appetite diminished by the heat and rancid smells emitting from the area. There would not be any weight gain. I was going to go home a skinny, malnourished, beat-up drunk.

The next evening I crawled out of the NCO club and ran into a first lieutenant who asked me if I was on duty. I told him "no." He then ordered me to go get a weapon and come back. Perplexed, I returned with an M-16 in hand from supply and followed him behind this dilapidated, vacant small building next to the camp's perimeter where I found this E-4 guarding a VC prisoner in a makeshift jail. He told the E-4 that he was relieved and left me there to guard the prisoner. I figured the E-4 must have needed a break for dinner or something and that he or someone else would shortly relieve me. The POW camp here was nothing but an open area covered with a tin roof, open on two sides with no door. The two open sides were only lined with concertina wire. It reminded me of a pigpen without the pig shit.

This VC just sat there, unrestrained and staring me down unflinchingly with hatred in his eyes. We stared each other down for an hour in a game of who's going to flinch first. I finally had it with this fuck and took the rifle off safety and aimed it between his eyes. He finally gave up and moved to the shadows in the back corner of the enclosure. I was now getting a little pissed, as I hadn't eaten and it was getting dark, with no light in the cage or flashlight on me and there was nobody around to run a message for me, no chair, no comforts at all. I was starting to think I was the prisoner here. Hours went by and no fucking lieutenant and not a soul has checked on me or gotten close enough to yell at for help. This lieutenant was going to get a piece of my mind. Even if it costs me, it's going to happen. Finally I'd had it and ordered the little fuck out of his cage. I was going to take to him to my hooch and tie his ass up while I got some sleep. He just sat there and acted as though he didn't hear a thing. So once again I put the 16 off safety and pointed it at him. Still no reaction. He just sat there staring at me with contempt. This guy wanted me to come in there after him. I thought this over, but it just was not a good idea. No way was I going to give this guy a chance to get to my weapon or escape, so I just sat there hour after hour all night long thinking about getting even with the lieutenant. I may even punch the son of a bitch I was thinking. Despite my drowsiness and thirst, I made it through the night, and soon the sun rose, but still no relief. I decided that I was going to fire off a couple rounds and end this shit when about that time; a detail of men came to take the VC and transport him to brigade. I asked these guys who the lieutenant was that left me here, but they knew nothing of him or the E-4—just that they were to take this guy to Tan An. Oh well, I was out of here. I'll find the son of bitch one day and get even.

I managed to keep under the radar for only a few days when I was approached by the Headquarters Company commander. I lied to him also as to why I'm off line. (It, however, was not really a lie as most units put personnel in the rear who had three or more Purple Hearts, and I still had a little of my medical profile left. It was just that I took myself off line as opposed to being put off line as I had insinuated. I went further and told him that my battalion commander was friends with his battalion commander, and that was how I got here. He informed me that since I was no longer a functioning sniper, I was not authorized to wear camouflage uniforms and that I need to start showing up at the morning formations for daily orders. We saluted, and I went back to the far end of the base camp where there was an NCO barracks and forced myself on the population, taking the first available bunk. I found a hole in the wall (illegal) beer club and made it my home as the NCO club was too close to the HHC (Headquarters of Headquarters Company). My attitude was shitty, as I was now a fucking REMF myself, and I was not taking shit from anyone. Fuck the morning formations. I was sleeping in. This would give me a week away from the captain. When I ran into him again, to my surprise he was cordial and said nothing about me not making any of the morning formations or about my camo uniform. However, I was given a job as night CQ (Charge of Quarters) of Headquarters Company, and I had to report to work that night.

When I got there, the place was empty, and all but one had gone home. The clerk informed me that my only job was to watch the place and answer the phone. I sat around for a few hours and then got bored as hell, so I rifled through the place, out of curiosity, went back to my desk and fell asleep. I awoke at dawn and wrote a note letting whomever know that all was well, and there were no calls to report. As soon as the clerk came through the door, I walked out the back door. This was the way it was every night, not even one visitor or phone call. I was just a security guard. So I started coming to work after all had left, fully tanked from the NCO club. I brought a pillow and slept all night with my head on the desk, and this was the standard drill until I was given the new job of supply sergeant of Headquarters Company.

It was a nice little setup with two personal rooms for me and my Doofus Specialist E-4 who had a supply MOS. There wasn't shit going on there; seldom did we issue any weapons or clothing. We had one day when we went to Dong Tam to get clean sheets and deposited the dirty ones. Then we issued sheets, and that was about it. This was one sack job, and I figured that the E-4 could handle it all. So I used this place as nothing but a flop house and came and went as I pleased. A few days went by and the specialist complained that I was not doing my share. I explained to the fucking REMF that I was the sergeant, and he was the worker. He could close down for lunch as far as I was concerned, but I saw no reason to help. He wasn't working more than two hours a day, and the rest of the time he was just there to keep the door open. I did, however, tell him that I would now do the drive to Dong Tam myself once a week. I figured that would be a welcome break and that I could fuck around in Dong Tam and Tan An on the way. He really squealed at this, as he always looked forward to the trip himself. Oh well. I still didn't go to any morning formations.

I further reckoned the base camp in depth when I heard a volley of 105s and decided to go over to the battalion artillery battery to check out how these guys operate. I already knew that they had it dicked compared to the guys we worked with in the delta, as these guys fired less in one day for an entire battalion than Bravo Co. required all by itself. I was watching these guys go through their disciplined procedure as they fired, and to my amazement and pleasure, there stood Ziek. As soon as the mission ended, I surprised him with my presence. It was all smiles as we squeezed the shit out of each other's hands. I now had a friend in the area and was tickled pink. These guys had a nice setup with screened porches and ice chests full of beer, which we got into immediately as we caught up on all that had happened to us since Bravo. Ziek had been feeding these guys full of shit, as they all know who I was from his stories. They were a great bunch, and I felt very welcome there. As the time passed by, I was oblivious to the yelling of orders outside the porch, and soon there was a volley that sent me halfway through the screen door. I stretched the shit out of the screen and was embarrassed as all laughed their asses off at my extreme reaction. I was thinking, haven't these guys ever been around a grunt before, and how in the hell did Ziek get used to these explosive sounds? It would be a while before I came back and got over the embarrassment of my overreaction. But this was the first of a lifelong short circuitry within that I would have to deal with. I would be jumpy for the rest of my life.

***

I came down with some kind of crud that had me bedridden. I couldn't eat, and I was constantly in the latrine. It took me a week to get over it, and when I did, I found out I'd been fired as the supply sergeant. Seems as though my pansy-ass specialist went to the CO and whined about his abuse.

I was sent to the NCO barracks and told that I was now in charge of battalion Details, what the fuck ever that is? I showed up after morning formation and was given a list of things to do and told to go over to the dispensary and pick up the walking wounded who have limited profiles and use them to complete the details. What I have are all grunts. Most have ringworm, emersion foot, or some kind of dysentery. The details were light and just busy shit, but it pissed me off because most of these jobs should have been done by the lazy-ass REMFs. These grunts finally had an excuse for a day off, and they had to do this shit? Just wasn't fair. This went on every day, and I enjoyed the conversations with my fellow infantrymen and learned the differences in their employment up here. We shirked our responsibilities and didn't always get everything done. I felt it was more important to protect my grunts than pretty up the base camp.

One day I was given a group of mostly rear echelon personnel, a change I'd been looking for. I split the group up and put the grunts on an easy detail and gave the REMFs the shit work. In fact, I made up shit just for them. My evil little plan gave me a smile, and I let the grunts in on it. They loved it, and it was good for a giggle or two and their morale.

Another day I was given the task of recovering some insulated food containers that were left in the field by one of the infantry companies. I was given just one jeep and my choice of men from the detail to accomplish the task. The problem was that most all of the grunts had foot issues, and I wasn't too keen on taking a bunch of REMFs with me who had never been in a firefight. I found two grunts who could walk and took four of the REMFs who looked like they might have something going. We armed ourselves with 16s, grabbed some ammo, grenades, smokes, and a PRC25 radio. I was given a map with the guesstimated grid coordinates, and off we went.

We headed south on Highway 1 and stopped due east of the destination on the side of the highway. This was nice country, I was thinking—large paddies dotted with nicely thatched hooch's; the trails were clean and used heavily. We only had about four to five klicks to go. But as we lost sight of the highway and the foliage thickened, I realized these guys were scared shitless, they weren't keeping a proper distance between one another, and in general not looking like grunts. When we cleared a hooch, they had no idea as to how to back one another. About two klicks in, one of the grunts came up to me and made his distaste for the mission known. He just didn't like the fact that there were only three of us who had CIBs. He was right, of course. This piddle-ass mission had disaster written all over it. If there were any VC watching our movement, they could tell that we were not a force to be feared. We were easy pickings for a small group of VC. I plodded on, taking point to the grid coordinates given as the area got uglier and more threatening.

We arrived and there was no sign of any grunts having been anywhere around. I called HQ and explained to them that there were no signs at the coordinates. They asked us to cloverleaf the area. "The containers must be close by," was their answer. I remind them of the quality of men I had with me, but there was no response. I took the two grunts off to the side and asked them how they felt about things. They explained to me that hot food in the field was a rare thing for them, but that the quality of food by the time it got to them was shit anyhow. I never did have hot food in the field myself while in Vietnam. They were wanting to get the fuck out of here, as did I.

So I called everybody together and asked for a show of hands as to who wanted to walk point—no response. Then I asked them who wanted to continue aimlessly walking in circles looking for the containers—no response. I told them I was going to abort the mission and make up a lie for command. I further told them that if anybody here said anything that got back to any of us, the others were to kick the shit out of that person. All agreed and took the pledge. I called HQ and told them we found the site where they had lunch, but that there was no sign of the containers. They told me to search the surrounding hooch's; I lied and agree. We took a break to fill in the time and then returned to base camp. I was totally pissed and figured that one of these fucks was going to get me busted. Oh well, who really gives a shit at this point!

Then one day I was given a job to make a new fuel bladder pad outside the base camp perimeter. They wanted me to use old fifty-gallon drums for a foundation and place them in the wet rice paddy. The location was fifty meters from the barracks and only one hundred meters from some civilian hooch's. I determined that this was a stupid idea and told my CO that it was a job for engineers, that most of my men had foot issues caused by paddy water, and that the bladder, once ruptured could flow dangerously close to a barracks and/or a civilian population. He was not happy and told me that if I was to refuse an order that I must put it in writing. I took me four pages and a full day to do so. I handed my written report to him, and the next day I was relieved of my duties as sergeant in charge of details. They did, however, rethink the location of the bladder.

So now, I am just hanging around the NCO barracks with nothing to do each day. This was such a fucking joke. No Article 15s as of yet were given. It seemed as though these guys bought my story about having some kind of connection with the battalion commander. So it was back to the NCO club.

Today man 1st landed on the moon, and as I was using the piss tube outside the NCO club, I looked up in wonderment. What an accomplishment, I was thinking. I imagined once again that somehow my thoughts of family were being reflected off it and back to them in Oregon. Then it hit me hard that all Americans were looking at the moon. It was taking their minds off Vietnam and our struggles. We were now on the back burner. We already felt so alone and left to die by our country anyhow, and now here was a way for people to further put us and the Vietnam War out of their minds. I sank to an all-time low and forgot that I was a short-timer REMF.

I finally found the whore houses outside the perimeter. One has a kitchen with steaks and cold Budweiser! And it was run by a Southern man in his forties. He had about ten girls working for him at various times throughout the day. He opened for lunch and beer at noon, and the girls started straggling in slowly throughout the day. I got to talking to this guy, and it seems as though he was running from the law back home and had been in Vietnam for over fifteen years. I further found out that the mess sergeant was a daily patron, which explains why he had good beef steaks and the mess hall didn't. The building was made of plywood and scavenged lumber, something an American would piece together and it looked like it. There was a large back room with beds lining the wall, and some beds are above one another (as in bunk beds). All have a pull curtain for some privacy. It was a scummy place, but what horny hormone filled nineteen-year-old really gives a shit?

The next day I went over to the other whore house. It was a large bamboo-thatched hooch with about four separate rooms in back and had a small bar in the front that only seated about six guys and it only has Vietnamese beer. There were also some tables and chairs sprinkled around the front room. When I got there, only a couple guys were hanging around, and one girl was working all three of us for some action. Soon the two guys started standing in front of one of the rooms, as if in line. Soon the line grew and grew as more guys came in. Now there were about ten guys in line. I finally asked what the hell was going on. I was told that they were all waiting for Lin. Who the hell is Lin, I asked. "Just get in line, and you'll find out." Well, I was not about to take fifteenths, but it did get my curiosity up, and I kept up my questioning. I figured this gal must be one great piece of ass but soon found out that all the money in the world couldn't get her panties off. She's the blow job queen of the delta, I'm told. She has hair down to her knees and wears only a bikini that you can't get off. She gets on top, splits her hair and wraps it around your unit in a crossing manner. Then she crosses it again and wraps it around your scrotum, crosses it again and then brings it up the crack of your ass and around your waist, to where she then grabs a hold of her hair and pulls it tight. The back and forth crisscrossing motion is more than you can handle, I was told.

Finally, she arrived, went to her bamboo room, and in no time the line is moving. These guys weren't lasting two minutes, and some were getting back in line for seconds. I was friggin' amazed at how fast she went through twenty guys. She was making a friggin' mint, no doubt. I was going to have to try that someday, but I was going to be first in line when I did, I was thinking.

A week later, I awoke and jumped out of bed, only to pass out and fall back on the bed. I tried to get up, and it happened again. Now I was scared shitless, as I couldn't take in a deep breath without passing out. Nobody was around because they all had jobs. I slowly dressed myself in the slowest way possible so as to not increase my respiratory rate as I started making my way to the dispensary. It was one step at a time, and I didn't dare try to talk to anyone for fear I'd pass out again and fall on the rocky street. I contemplated lying down on the street and waiting for some help, but I was making it one step at a time, so I continued. It took me over a half hour to go a hundred meters or so but I made it. After a checkup the doctor determined that my liver was enflamed and that when my diaphragm expanded, it pressed on my liver, causing the pain and thus the passing out. He gave me some morphine, and I was able to get around better so that I could make the trip to Saigon and the Third Field Hospital. Upon arrival, it was all I could do to get in bed, as the morphine was no longer doing its job. I now couldn't even talk in a whisper or raise my arm as the fear threatened to increase my breathing rate. I had to concentrate on keeping my shit together. A doctor finally came around and figured out that I could only communicate with my eyes and raised fingers. He soon gave me another dose of morphine, and I was able to tell him what I knew. IVs were put in, and I felt much better soon. The doctors started drawing blood and asking for any urine or stool sample that I may be able to give. After checking my blood, they gave me antibiotics. They just didn't know what the deal was and made no bones about it.

The ward I was in was full of unknown diagnoses. This is where they put all who haven't been diagnosed yet, and it was full of guys in the early stages of malaria. My bed was up against a small wall next to only one other bed against the wall. The young private next to me was a great kid but scared as hell as he has been in this ward for a month and with no answers. He was a wealth of information and made me comfortable with the scenario. A week later, I felt much better and was given lower and lower pain medications and was even allowed to eat a restricted diet. Soon I was running around bored, looking for some trouble. The tests, however, continued. One day I was put on a table and told to get on my hands and knees. About that time the most beautiful nurse in the hospital comes in with a large glass tube about eighteen inches long and about three inches wide. She prepared it with some Vaseline. The doctor told me to put my head between my legs and the self-conscience mortification of the penetration began. What a way to meet beautiful women!

Soon the private got a visit from two doctors, a major, and a full-bird colonel. They told him that they had good news and bad news. "The good news is that you'll be going home to your family tomorrow. The bad news is that you have a rare neurological disease that is not treatable and is fatal. You will probably have three to six months to live." They answered his few questions and were on their way with condolences.

I couldn't believe my ears. This poor son of a bitch! I was the only friend he had, so I did my best to try to be pragmatic and at the same time upbeat by talking about those things he would want to do when home. To my surprise he was taking all this fairly well and told me that he had a bad feeling about his sickness all along. It was a long day and night being with him. The next day he shook my hand and promised to write. That was the last I heard from him.

I was now a little shaken up, even though I was feeling better. However, my doctors still had no answers for me. I was down to 138 lb. and looked like I'd been in a German concentration camp. I feared the possibility of the day that the colonel comes in the room and walks toward me.

However, within a couple of days, my doctor came and told me that there was nothing more for him to do, that I seemed to be in pretty good shape now, and should start gaining weight soon. He apologized for not having a concrete diagnosis, let alone a prognosis. He did, however, tell me that he believed that I had an amoebic infection of the liver and possibly some other organs and to watch myself closely.

I was off and I had some pay, so I walked over to Tan Son Nhut to find the BX (Base Exchange) at the base. It was an amazing place, I find. These air force guys knew how to live. There were picket fences surrounding the small lawn in front of each barracks. The BX was a store better than any we had in my little hometown. I bought a new Kodak Instamatic and some personal items and searched out the NCO club.

I found some air force guys with three stripes on their shoulders entering an airman's club and figured that this was the place for me. However, the doorman told me that I couldn't come in. "What the fuck is this?" I said. "Army guys aren't allowed in air force clubs, bullshit!" He was not a man of many words and just told me I'm not allowed. I was fucking pissed! An army grunt wasn't allowed to have a beer on an air force base? I demanded to talk to the club manager. He told me to go outside and wait. I did, and soon two APs (Air Police) pulled up in their jeep with clubs drawn. Fortunately, they figured out the problem: three stripes in the air force was only an E-4; I had assumed that sergeants were going in. I needed to go to the NCO club down the street. However, they didn't like my uniform and told me that I was out of uniform and must leave the base. When leaving Rach Kien, I grabbed a shabby camo uniform that had only one set of sergeant stripes, a CIB, and no name tag. As soon as they were out of sight, I did a 180 and headed for the NCO club. I was starving for a good meal and a beer. Come hell or high water, I was going to get me some!

I couldn't believe this NCO club. This place was a Garden of Eden with tropical landscaping, an outdoor patio, dance floor, bandstand, and all the amenities one could hope for. There wasn't a place like this anywhere back home close to Walla Walla or Pendleton. I received some unaccepting looks as I strolled out to the patio. I took a seat under a banana tree and was soon greeted by a beautiful Vietnamese girl in her long, flowing Ao Dai attire. She soon brought me an ice-cold beer and a menu. Once again I was taken aback by how these guys lived. The menu was full of wonderful things that I yearned for and many that I had no idea what they were. The T-bone soon struck my eye. I was in heaven—cold beer, T-bone, tropical atmosphere, and good music topped off with a beautiful waitress.

I followed up the steak with a large salad and more beer. The day was starting to get a little hot, so I went inside for another beer, only to have the bartender inform me that I needed to be in proper uniform to further enjoy the premises. I go off on these fucks. "You fucking REMF motherfuckers, you lavish yourselves daily in good, cold beer, good food, air conditioning, and swank surroundings, while I go out and get my ass shot up while eating C rats, drinking warm, shitty water, sleeping in mud, and all in one hundred-degree weather. They didn't ask me to be in proper uniform when they sent me to the hospital. And you fucks can't even allow me a cold beer. Eat shit and die Mother Fuckers!" I was out of there before the fucking APs showed up again. I was ready now to go back to Rach Kien, where the REMFs have at least a little couth.

I was told that there were water trucks leaving Ton Son Knut every hour for Dong Tam. I could at least catch a ride as far as the Rach Kien road with one of them. I walked outside the busy main gate and was awaiting a water truck when one of the APs at the main gate ordered me to come over to them. Not thinking much of it, I went on over. There were two of them: one E-2 and an E-3. "Where are your orders?" one asks. I told him I'd just gotten out of Third Field, and that they hadn't gave me any. "You're out of uniform—get up against the wall!" the airman says "You're shittin' me, flyboy," was my remark. And they threw my scrawny ass up against the concrete abutment. I swung around with my elbow

230

only to find myself on the ground hard and with a knee in my neck. My struggling was useless, but soon the pressure was off me, as I heard someone berating them. I turned to see a colonel kicking them like they were dogs. "What the fuck do you guys think you're doing? Can't you see he's a goddamn American? These poor grunts don't have a fucking Vietnamese hooch girl to do their laundry and sewing. He's a fucking sergeant, and not once did you address him as such. Your job is to keep the traffic going and keep unwanted forces out, not to give shit to grunts hitchhiking. Now get back to your posts and do your job!" The colonel apologized and informed me that he was in charge of Ton Son Knut security. He promised me that they would be taught a lesson and that if they gave me any more shit to get ahold of him.

I went back over to my hitchhiking post and started fucking with the Mosquito Wing (one stripe) Flyboys. I started with flipping them the bird then I grabbed my crotch and pretended like I was bending them over. I didn't let up. I had gotten hotter under the collar instead of getting over it. This went on for a half hour before I caught my ride down Highway 1, now with a smile on my face.

I got back to my barracks only to find that my bunk was taken and that all my personal belongings from my foot locker had been stolen. It had my extensive collection of rare camouflage fatigues that I'd been working on for months. But what was worse was that someone had the balls to steal my private photo album. It had all the best of my pictures and many that I just couldn't send home because of the bloody nature of them. Practically all my pictures of my sniper days were gone also. I was infuriated, and no one seemed to know what happened or cared. Once again my love of the REMFs took another dive. Who the hell would want another man's private photos? A wannabe fucking REMF, that's who! Some son of a bitch is going to take my pictures home and show them to his friends and family and make like he's seen some shit. I was in a rage, but no one seemed to want to get to the bottom of it. God, I hate these fuckers! The whole time I was with Bravo I never had anything stolen.

Someone had set up a makeshift illegal beer club behind S-4. It was a dump of a place with about three makeshift barstools and a couple of plywood tables. There was a piss tube made from an old ammo tube with a broken shard of mirror above it. Beer was the same price as at the NCO club, but it was invisible from those at headquarters, keeping me out of sight and out of mind. There were also a couple of other grunts who were off line hanging out, making my visit more amiable. Visiting Ziek and hanging at the illegal club seemed to be my only salvation as I became more and more anxious about going home soon. I was now a short–timer, and the reality of really making it was more and more on my mind every day.

A Lieutenant Trujillo, also an off-line grunt, approached me one day and asked if I would be his driver the next day for a trip to a place called Thu Thuh. I agreed and grabbed a jeep the next day along with some weaponry and ammo, and we were off. It was a beautiful day, and I really liked this guy. He had about the same respect for the REMFs as I did and sounded like he was a true platoon leader with some decent combat experience. We headed east toward Cambodia after a short southerly drive down Highway 1. I was blown away at what we are doing. If we tried this down where I came from, we'd be dead meat in no time. The dirt road was a little bumpy with the occasional mud hole and lined with idyllic Vietnamese hooch's and paddies. It was midafternoon, and we had gone about ten miles east when we arrived at what looked like an old ARVN compound without the protective berms, no bunkers, just trenches and wire, and it was sitting out in the middle of a large paddy with hooch's in line on two sides.

Battalion wanted us to recon the compound, and so we walked through the open buildings with concrete floors and tin roofs. It looked like the civilians took most of the siding off the buildings, but other than that it looked fine. There was concertina wire around the two-acre perimeter and no signs of booby traps. All seemed well. I guarantee you, this compound would be full of booby traps, having been abandoned, if it were down in the Kien Hoa Province.

We went back to the jeep, and I decided to check the fuel, as I hadn't when we left. In my past construction world, we always fueled vehicles at the end of each shift or day, and I had assumed that this was also the situation and SOP within the army. But to my amazement the tank was on fumes. I felt terrible and apologized immediately. To my surprise, Trujillo blames the previous driver. This doesn't, however, rectify our immediate problem. It was getting late, and we needed fuel soon. We called into battalion and gave them a situation report (sit-rep). Battalion said they were moving to Thu Thuh first thing in the morning for operations and that we could wait until then. We asked for a chopper to bring in some fuel, but they told us "no can do." We looked at one another with amazement. These guys think that it's safe for us to be here all by ourselves, out of artillery range, with limited armament, no food, no medical, not shit. I'll admit it was not Mo Cai or the Kien Hoa province, but this was going a little far, I was thinking. There were at least twenty hooch's within two to three hundred meters of us, and the entire village knew we were here. There had to be at least one VC sympathizer within that was going to rat us out?

We rummaged through the jeep to get a grip on our actual gear. We had only two bandoliers of twenty-round magazines, our M-16s (not zeroed), two grenades, two smoke grenades, and a trip flare under one of the seats. We had no food and very little water. We talked about our defensive strategy and decided to place the trip flare across the open entrance and made like we were setting up in the center of the compound. As soon as it was dark, we moved to the shallow trenches next to the wire and camps entrance, figuring that if we had any company, they would choose the avenue of least resistance. Every half hour or so, we moved. It was dark with little moon but good starlight, and our visibility was no more than thirty to forty feet. We were damn scared and realized that we could be easily taken by very few VC. I was damn glad Trujillo was a grunt as was he of me. There was no sleep or even talk about taking shifts. All four eyes were needed. But to our amazement, the eastern sky was getting lighter, and we were now thinking it was now or never for Charlie. But it was now getting lighter, and our view was out to fifty meters or better. Then I come up with a theory of why we weren't fucked with; Charlie thinks it's a trap, and as soon as they started something, the artillery was going to rain down on their parade. The lieutenant and I started laughing our asses off; thinking that must be it? We jumped up, exposing ourselves laughing and dancing, waving our arms challenging Charlie to come for us. We'd made it! If we had been further south, there is no doubt that the VC would have at least probed us and found out whether or not it was a trap and damn the civilian casualties.

Soon the battalion convoy showed up, and the men set up their temporary headquarters. I fueled up the jeep and prepared to go back to Rach Kien when I was approached by a captain who informed me that I had duty in the communications trailer. Fuck! No sleep and now I have to sit in a fucking com room with no air conditioning all day long and with no personal provisions for the next three days. I had become a whining REMF!

***

Next to our barracks in Rach Kien was the ammo dump. It had a high roof and overlooked the entire base camp and afforded a decent view of the sunset. As I'm close to going home I decide to use the roof as a place to sun bath and get some color for my homecoming. I'm up there with a friend drinking cold beer and watching an insertion of grunts from afar. They are accompanied by a couple Cobra gunships and the CC ship, they are all circling the infantrymen. Then for some reason the CC ship decides to change course and altitude and runs straight into one of the Cobras. An explosion is immediate and the two balls of fire plummet to the earth with no chance of survival. A sad sight and a deadly error on the CC ship pilot's part. We hear later it's a Bn. Commander from another Bn. who was in the CC ship. It's hard enough to watch death due to Charlie, but when it's caused by one's own, its double hard.

A master sergeant I had met a few times in the NCO club asked me if I wanted to go to Saigon with him as his driver. Seems as though he needed to make an impression and wanted to look important. I grabbed a jeep, checked the gas, went over to his room, and we filled the back of the jeep with presents. But instead of leaving via the regular road to Highway 1, he had me take a left toward the whore houses and the surrounding hooch's. I pulled up to a bamboo hooch, and to my surprise out comes Lin, the long-haired blow job queen of the delta. She made herself comfortable in the back with all the presents, and off to Saigon we went. We went to her parents' apartment in a nice area just outside downtown Saigon. She went up to prepare her family for the guest, and then the master sergeant turned to me and said, "I know what you're thinking; what's he doing marrying a whore? But have you ever thought about how much one could charge for such talent in America? Hey, I'm getting ready to retire; I can use some added income." I said nothing but was totally blown away that the guy was marrying the girl and going to pimp her out once home. Oh well, different strokes for different folks.

***

I had only a few days in-country left when I headed over to the NCO club. As I entered, out came a guy with a piece of metal stuck in his forehead, bleeding like hell. As I went in, the whole place was laughing their asses off. Seems as though this dumb shit came in with an old pineapple grenade that he had taken the explosives out of, but had left the blasting cap in. He set it in front of him at his table, announced he was going to pull the pin, and did, as everyone scrambled for cover. He sat there laughing for about five seconds, and then the grenade went off. But to his surprise, the blasting cap itself had enough explosive power to blow a couple of segments of the casing away and into his forehead. Obviously, this guy didn't have both oars in the water. But what the hell? He spiced up the day of a few bored men—guess he was good for something.

***

Finally, I receive DEROS orders and pack my bags for processing in Tan An. I can now start filling in the last sections of my Short Timers Calendar. It's a drawing of a woman sitting with legs crossed and spread, exposing all. There are 100 segments in all and the last three include both nipples and the most important segment is the last one between the legs. But first I have to find the lieutenant who put me on POW watch. I scoured the base camp one more time, but to no avail. The anxiety of imagining my homecoming caused sleepless nights for the rest of my tour. Anxiety was now my brother as I imagined a stray bullet or mortar round finding me before I could get out of this shit hole. Once I get to Oakland, I'd have to process once more—the termination of my active-duty obligation (ETS). It was going to be a double whammy of smiles and jubilation—getting home and out of the army at the same time!

They processed me a day late, and my last day in Vietnam was the longest day of my life. There was dead silence as the 707 rotated off the Bien Whoa runway.

I lifted my butt off the seat to make the plane a little lighter for just a second as my sphincter muscles tightened. The silence within the plane continued until we were out of range of small-arms fire, and then all hell broke loose as the yells, whoops, and hollers broke out as we celebrated our departure.

I was now thinking the airplane was going to go down in the ocean. This couldn't be for real! Where was Ziek, I wondered? What was it going to be like once I got home? I was now twenty-one and could legally drink with my buddies. What would the single female situation be? For the first time in my life, I was not thinking about any long-term goals. I didn't really give a fuck what career was awaiting me—I was just looking forward to the next beer, my friendship with my buds, and the next piece of ass. Life was going to be great!

Chapter **18**

C O M I N G   H O M E

The flight home was a joyous one. Although I was sleep-deprived, I couldn't catch a wink as we landed in Guam for refueling. We disembarked to the terminal, which was full of green marines heading to Nam. I was immediately surrounded, as were other men with CIBs. The questioning was rapid-fire: What's it like? Got any tips on how to stay alive? Where was your AO? On and on they questioned. They didn't care that I was a Doggie; they just wanted to talk to a grunt, and that much was obvious to the REMFs, who were left alone by the young Marines. It was an observation I couldn't help but revel in. I tried to be as positive as I could be to these young marines, as I saw myself in them only one year ago. As I boarded the plane, I couldn't help but thank God that I'd made it, and I wondered how many of those young men wouldn't.

As we flew into Honolulu, I overheard a lieutenant colonel sitting close to me. He was talking about how to get to the bar once on ground and seemed to know his way around the airport. We were given thirty minutes on the ground. I followed this guy like stink on dung once we offloaded. He was setting a fast pace and making a beeline to the terminal via a small gate in the cyclone fence. I stayed on his heels, and we were leading the pack. As we headed into the lounge, I made a move to pass him, only to crowd him into the door jamb, without any regard to his rank. We were so intent on beating the crowd to the bartender that neither of us seemed to care about the incident. He ordered two vodka tonics, and I did the same as we were surrounded by soldiers trying to get in their drink orders. I pounded my drinks down within seconds and ordered again. Finally, I apologized to the lieutenant colonel for my actions. He just laughed it off and ordered again.

We were soon back on the flight, and I had a definite buzz going as the excitement mounted as to our next destination: "The World". We had been dreaming and talking about the world for a year now. As my excitement wore off, I finally caught a couple of hours of much-needed sleep and awoke to the morning sun rising, just hours away from our destination: Travis Air Force Base in California.

As the plane landed, all aboard were fully awake. Cheers dominated the moment. It was a beautiful California day as we disembarked to the open tarmac that was void of any celebration or welcome. I chose to get on my knees and kiss the concrete, as did some others.

Although my concept of humanity had been totally degraded because of the war, I was elated about my prospects. I'd made it home, though I was a little beaten up. I was home! I was now a man, a leader of men, and I had no fear of pursuing the American Dream after what I had been through. Life was mine to cherish and pursue. What I didn't know then was that my now-degraded concept of mankind would be my main impediment to fulfilling my dreams.

I was to be discharged during my processing in Oakland, and I was hoping to be back in Oregon by day's end. But this being the army, it was a long, drawn-out process, and I was delayed by the fact that most workers go home at 5:00 p.m. We were given Class A green dress uniforms, but to my disappointment, the army didn't have all the ribbons and badges for me. I was especially bummed that they didn't have any dress CIBs or blue infantry shoulder rope. After all, that is what I was most proud of. It distinguished me from the fucking REMFs, and now I had to look like one of them. I was not happy: dirty, rotten fuckers anyhow! And, because it was late, there were no doctors to process my discharge physical. So we filled out the paperwork ourselves with the help of a medic giving us the proper passing information needed, and so we all signed the form stating that our physical being was good, regardless of the realities. Those wanting to see a doctor had to stay and go through some unknown process. Fuck—I was home and wanting to see my family and friends, not hang around an army depot awaiting whatever kind of hoops the discharge folks wanted to put me through. With one quick signature, I could be paid all my back pay and be on my way. It was dark now and getting late. Forgoing the doctor's physical was a no-brainer.

Ortz, my old platoon sergeant and friend, was living in Oakland. He had been discharged early and was now a civilian working for a California-based airline. I called him for a ride to the airport, and he was soon on his way. He got me an early morning flight to Portland, where I could catch a flight to the Tri-Cities, Washington, or Pendleton, Oregon; both were close to my home of Milton-Freewater, Oregon. With time to kill, Ortz took me out on the town, where we met some of his friends for drinks. As I walked into the crowded bar, I was immediately picked up by the eyes of most; then, just as suddenly, they looked away. The table was full of friends of Ortz and some other vets, so I was feeling good as I pounded down the Budweiser's in a state of euphoria. I couldn't friggin' believe it: here I was back in the world, drinking in a bar legally and with friends. I was discharged honorably, with the GI bill for education, and I was free to enjoy the great American Dream. It just doesn't get any better, I'm thinking.

Ortz took me to the airport, and after some discerning looks followed by a discount, I was soon on my way to Oregon. It was 1:00 a.m. now, and I was still too pumped to sleep, as my stewardess poured the Bloody Mary's freely. Once in Portland, again the looks were there, followed by disregard. I decided it (the looks) were because of the beaten-up pair of combat boots hanging from my duffel bag. I threw them (a piece of me) into the nearest garbage can. I couldn't get a flight into Pendleton until morning, and I'd now hit the wall of exhaustion. I took a taxi to the nearest cheap hotel, where I crashed and didn't awaken until afternoon.

Finally, I was in Pendleton, and my mother and her sister Diane were there to pick me up. The looks in their eyes were so precious and joyful that I wanted to tear up, but I couldn't as I remembered how I left her crying at the airport one year ago. I would cry only once for another fifteen years or more.

Mom wanted to parade me around town in my uniform, as her pride was so obvious. But, for some reason, I now wanted the uniform off, and our priorities collided. My sister, Karen, and brothers, Gary and Billy, were such a joy to see, as were my old friends. Everyone wanted to know what the ribbons on my chest were for. I gave them a very brief, dismissive description.

Coming home had great hope in and of itself. In fact, I thought things were going to be better than before. I recalled my father telling me how he kept his

Marine Corps uniform on for over a month once home and how it garnered free drinks and toasts to his coming home, not to mention easy looks from the women. It was only because he wore out the uniform that he finally started wearing civilian clothing.

I really wanted the uniform off, however—but none of my old clothing fit, as I was now thirty pounds lighter. The next day I bought a car from my uncle Merlin and went to Walla Walla, where I could get some new clothes. Once again in the public eye, I got the eye of discernment and dismissiveness. I knew that public support for the war had diminished since I went into active duty, but I couldn't quite understand the reaction toward me as a soldier who had only done what his country asked him to do. Hell, I didn't even get to vote while overseas. These people did get to vote; they had the opportunity to change things. And now they wanted to look down on me? Fuck them and the donkey they rode in on! Maybe I would move to Australia!

Once in civilian clothing and having said hello to all the family, I was now wanting to party with my friends. My pockets were loaded, and I was ready to go. I got a carload of friends together, and the party was on at a local tavern, as they all questioned me about my time in Nam. Some had recently been discharged, too, and the conversations were wild. Life was good, and the beer was cold: it just didn't get any better! We soon decided that we needed to go to Walla Walla to chase some skirt. On the way over, one of them said to me, "Ed, no talking about Vietnam tonight, or we're not going to get lucky." WTF? No pussy for the vets? Can't be! My attitude took a diversion as I was now not even thinking about girls but about what had taken place in my own country. I was now pissed, and it showed. I didn't think I liked being an American anymore.

I couldn't talk to my nonmilitary friends like I used to; they either didn't understand or didn't want to hear about Vietnam. One night I tried to tell my two best friends in life about April 3. I hadn't even gotten halfway through the story when one said, "Ya, right, Ed" and changed the subject. It was the only time I ever even tried to tell the story to anyone for forty years.

Elk season soon came, we had the usual crew and we were on our way to the old cabin in the Blue Mountains. I was excited, here was something that would take my mind off of the bullshit. I loved the mountains and had many good memories of them. The first night was great as we sighted in our rifles and proceeded to get full of bad food and good beer. The next morning we all went out for the hunt behind the cabin. As we followed our designated paths for the drive I began getting very anxious and start looking for Booby Traps and then areas of possible ambush which in turn made me look for areas to defend and take cover. I stop and reassure myself that I'm not in Vietnam anymore. Then I realize that if anyone was to accidentally shoot near or at me; I'd probably shoot back with intention. I turned and returned to the cabin where I would stay for the entire Elk season before returning home. I had lost my mountains and I was sick about it.

Retuning to town, every day was the same; I got up around noon, went to the tavern in the afternoon, played some pool with friends, drank some beer, went to the nightclub, drank some beer, bullshitted with my vet friends, drank some beer, danced with a girl, drank some beer, got into a fistfight, went to breakfast, went to bed, and then started it all over again. This pattern went on for weeks, and then I realized I needed to sign up for the next semester at the local community college. The problem was that now I had no idea about what I wanted to do with my life. Absolutely none! But I knew I needed to at least get a start and get some required classes out of the way, so I enrolled in an effort to do the right thing and break my pattern of self-destruction.

I found that there were a fair number of vets also enrolled, and soon we were meeting for a beer or two after classes. This routine progressed into drinking all night and ignoring my homework. The next thing I knew, someone suggested that we have a vet meeting first thing in the morning, and soon we were drunk on our asses before noon.

One day while having lunch in the Cafeteria some firecrackers were thrown under my seat as a prank. I ran through the table I was sitting at, knocking everyone backwards as their lunches were thrown up into the air. I had made it all the way to the door when I got a grip on myself. I stopped and turned around as all were in disarray but eerily silent, and looking at me as I was some kind of idiot.

I was finding that I was very anxious when sober, to the extent that anxiety was almost overwhelming me. I looked up Mike, an old friend and Nam vet;

I tried to explain to him the feelings and overwhelming sense of losing control. Mike was not much help and only said that time would make things easier. Alcohol, drugs, and sex become my only means to any enjoyment. Deep down inside, I wanted to fall in love and straighten my life out, but I didn't seem to know how to keep a relationship going. This, combined with not having much money left, kept me from getting serious, and so I went through women at a rather rapid pace, as I missed out on some great gals. My entire semester was soon a waste of time, and I found myself working construction because I'd run through all my savings.

Now my pattern was going to work with a hangover, partying all night, and doing it all over again. I didn't seem to give a fuck about much of anything anymore, and my anger was now at a rage with those I didn't know. I only cared about my friends and made no new friends unless they were combat vets. I was getting into way too many fights in the bars, and part of the problem was that I was winning most of them. Soon I was in six fights in one week in one bar.

Things were spiraling down at a rather rapid rate when I got into a drinking contest and downed twelve double shots of Old Crow whiskey. On my way home, I mouthed off to the wrong person and got my ass kicked badly. I awoke naked in my bathtub, with my eyes crusted shut from blood and puke. It took me two days to get over the hangover, and in the meantime, I'd made a decision to leave the United States. The problem was that I was broke, so I decided that Alaska was where I needed to go to get my shit in order and obtain a bankroll. One of the guys I went to Sniper School with was a guide in Alaska and worked for the world famous bear guide Bill Pinnel. I called him just as he was ready to leave for Alaska, and he told me that if I could make it up there in four days, he could put me to work. So I threw some shit together, temporarily traded use of my Chevelle SS-396 for a beat-up Volkswagen bug with my roommate, and I was on my way within one day. The problem was that I need to make 2800 miles in less than three days, and 1195 miles of the trip were gravel.

My roommate Gary's VW was a piece of shit, but I didn't want to drive my Chevelle over the 1200 miles of gravel Alcan road. The VW didn't have a radio antenna, the tires were less than desirable, and Gary had rolled it through the main gate of Camp Pendleton prior to getting discharged from the corps.

The officers at the Canadian border were less than kind to me, as they were convinced I was a draft dodger, even though I wore an old camo fatigue shirt. They told me later that the camo was one of the reasons they thought I might be a draft dodger—go figure. After five hours of holdup, they finally let me go on my way.

Just as I got to Dawson Creek, my generator went out, and I had to wait until morning to get a new one put in, which put me further behind and left me with few funds.

I was finally making some time on the Alcan and picked up a hitchhiker, only to find this fuck was a draft dodger and was ranting about going back to the United States to overthrow the government. Mile after mile, I listened to this fuck rant and rave, justifying his inability to serve his nation. I was so pissed at this punk that I entertained the thought of killing him and leaving him to the Yukon grizzlies. Instead, I determined where the most desolate place was on the Alcan, and at about 1:00 a.m., I kicked his ass out of my car with a berating for his actions. It made my day, and I was off again hauling ass as fast as I could to Alaska. I'd had very little sleep and soon fell asleep at the wheel, running off the road at the most advantageous spot. Had it been anywhere else, I'd have run into a ditch, a tree, a river, a bank, and a million other spots that would have been disastrous. But the scare gave me an adrenaline boost, and soon I was at the US border east of Tok, Alaska.

As I rolled my window down, I started shaking due to the cold temperature and my lack of warm clothing. The border agent took this as something other, and soon I was being grilled like never before. Seems as though these guys also think I'm a draft dodger trying to get back into the States. The VW was torn apart, with all my belongings thrown on the greasy asphalt. I was freezing my ass off, and they wouldn't let me in the building or the car. Now I was getting pissed and let them know about it, which only aggravated them into holding me up for hours more. I now couldn't make it to Bill Pinnels in Palmer or the plane to the Brooks Range, and they didn't give a fuck. I now, more than ever, wanted to leave the States for Australia.

I finally make it to Bill Pinnels home in hopes that they hadn't left, but his wife confirmed my worst fears. I now had less than twenty dollars left and nowhere to go. I headed for Anchorage and drove around a little before heading to Homer, where my mother's old boss ran a seafood cannery.

It was a beautiful drive down to Homer, and overall I was very impressed with Alaska and was looking forward to enjoying its recreational opportunities before moving to Australia. The day was waning, I finally got to Homer and I found a high spot a hundred yards off the beach out on the Homer Spit. I threw my sleeping bag out and soon took a much-needed sleep, only to be awakened by the tide slapping my sleeping bag. I knew nothing of the giant Alaskan tides, and soon the tide had risen to the floorboards of the VW, and I was now on top of it, getting ready to swim the one hundred yards to the Spit road. As the sun rose, everybody and their dog was stopping to look at what appeared to be a VW floating in the bay with someone on top of it. If any had a camera, they were taking a picture. Fortunately, the tide receded, and I was able to make it to the cannery the next morning.

I filled out my job application and asked for Bill, the owner. He was at first scolding and asking why I hadn't contacted him prior to my arrival. He explained that the pay was little, but he'd put me to work with the canneries plumber for now.

I still was broke and only had canned peas from home to eat. I slept on the beach at night in a higher, more close in area, and spent my last dollars on a shower in town. Finally, payday came around, and I celebrated by having a decent meal and a few beers, as I had the next day off. Being a little drunk, I didn't feel like setting up my tent, so I just threw my sleeping bag in it and crashed on the beach again.

Early the next morning, I was awakened to someone lightly kicking me, telling me to get up. An older gal in her seventies laid into me. "I've been watching you, and I know you have a job. There is no reason to be living like a bum when you have honest employment! Get in your car and follow me! I've got a place for you."

She just wouldn't listen to any of my excuses and demanded that I follow her. What the hell, I was thinking; I have nothing to lose. With hangover, I followed her into town and to her place, which was a piece of property that was scattered with a handful of one-room log cabins. She explained to me that I could pay her when I had some extra money. I tried to give her my .300 Win Mag. rifle for collateral, and she just remarked, "A man needs his rifle in this part of the country; you keep it." After some wrangling, I convinced her that it would be better off with her than in my cabin for security reasons.

Bill gave me a new job for my second week and asked me to have a chat with him. He wanted to know if I really had worked at all the canneries that I had listed in my job application and if my intentions were to stay the summer. I assured him that all was correct. He then told me that he had plans for me and that he was going to give me a different job each week until I fully understood the workings of Alaskan Seafoods.

Around the seventh week, Bill asked me to lunch at the Porpoise Room, a restaurant and cocktail lounge owned by the cannery. He was impressed with my work ethic and wanted me to run the docks for him. It entailed managing the crew, unloading and loading the boats, transferring the product to the cannery, and, most important, repairing the relations between the cannery and the fishermen. There had been a breakdown in relations, and the product presented by the fishermen was less than desirable as a result. I was told my most difficult skipper would be John Hillstrand of the fishing vessel the *Invader*. Bill and I, from here on out, were to meet once a week.

I was jacked! I just wanted a chance to show my abilities and grow, and here it was. I talked to the skippers and found out that they felt as though they'd been cheated by the weighing process when delivering. Because the prices were so low, I rounded up the weight of each lift of product from the crane to the docks. Immediately, the fishermen started to relax and come around—all except John Hillstrand. He was a tough customer and tough on his crew, so I didn't take it too personally. John ran a day boat for shrimp and usually filled the boat with an average of eighty thousand pounds a day. He was picky and precise, but soon, even he cracked a smile. He and his men worked long hours each day, and often his wife came out in her Chevy Travelall with their kids, whom I had to watch carefully as they had the propensity to crawl around everything in sight. They were the same Hillstrand boys who now captain the *Time Bandit* on *The Deadliest Catch* television show.

I soon met John's father, Earl, who came out now and again to meet his son. He was a great man who had an interest in my Vietnam experiences and thoughts. Earl was a businessman who had the famous Salty Dog Saloon and Land's End hotel at the end of the Spit. As Earl and I became friends, so did hard-ass John and I, and life was soon as good as it gets out on the docks.

I found a girlfriend, and life got even better. She was a local and very beautiful. The relationship kept me out of the bars, and my mind was on her and my work.

I renewed my interest in flying and restarted my flying lessons. I didn't have much money left over each week, so I could only purchase an hour a week on the Cessna 150. I spent much of my time across the bay gliding inside the glaciers, enjoying the view of Homer and Kachemak Bay.

At my next meeting with Bill, he asked me to redefine and reinvent the entire product unloading and transferring process. It was a great challenge and an opportunity to be creative. It was a challenge I grabbed by the horns, and all my waking hours were spent thinking about the possible changes. Even though my back injuries were making things difficult, life was good!

I often wore my camo sniper shirt when the weather was good, and most around the docks were aware of my service in Vietnam. One evening I was having a quick beer with a friend from home at the Porpoise Room, when one of the crewmembers from the company's fishing boat approached me and publicly got in my face about serving in Vietnam. He was, in fact, outraged and called me everything in the book from "baby killer" to "murderer." I immediately flushed with anger and started shaking with the urge to rip this guy's head off and shit down his neck. The fact that this was company property and involving another company employee was all that kept me from it. Fortunately for him, he left, but the damage was done. I started pounding down the drinks like there was no tomorrow.

I started planning his demise and couldn't keep it off my mind. It haunted me every hour of the day and I became a changed man. I didn't give a fuck about anything but putting this guy out of his misery. As time went by, I got a grip on myself and realized this scum wasn't worth any possible legal repercussions should I fail to pull it off cleanly. But I was still not getting him out of my mind. Who says capital punishment doesn't work? I was now destroying my relationship with my girlfriend as my anxiety increased; I now realized I was not good for this girl, and she deserved better. I was drinking too much and not paying attention to my job as I should. The anxiety was overwhelming as I realized I was not the same person I once was. All it took was one person to put me over the edge.

Fall came, and the snow started to fly. My friends from home were getting ready to head back south. John wanted to take some pictures of the glaciers before leaving and asked me to take him up in the Cessna 150. I was not yet a pilot, so I suggested that he meet me in Anchor Point where there was a strip shown on the map. The strip was parallel to the beach near the mouth of the Anchor River. I asked John to go there in his car and get to the upwind end of the runway. As I flew over, I could see John standing there next to his car at the south end of the runway. He was waving his arms as if to say, "Here I am—land here." John was in navy communications, so I assumed that if the conditions were bad he'd wave me off with hands pushing off to the side.

Without flying low and getting a closer look at the runway, I went ahead and set up for a standard left turn pattern. The runway had cliffs on both ends, so I set up a reference point on the far end as I brought the nose up and bled off as much speed as I could in a nose-high attitude with the stall buzzer intermittently buzzing. In final, I couldn't see the runway for my nose-high attitude, and as I touched down, I took a peek to my left and realized I was in deep shit. The gravel I saw on the runway from altitude was really huge rocks with no gravel in between them. As I started to shove the throttle in, my main gears hit, breaking and driving my nose into the rocks, breaking off my nose gear, throwing the plane forward on its lateral axis and tearing the engine off to the side 90 degrees. As I was thrown up in the air, I was also thrown upside down and out to the ocean. While upside down, I had the wherewithal to turn all the electrical switches off as the plane hit the shallow water, breaking the fuselage. The next wave pushed me ashore upside down. I popped my seatbelt, shoved the door open, and crawled out.

For some reason, I started laughing my ass off and couldn't even stand due to the laughter. John ran through the jagged rocks to save me from a potential fire. Out of breath and with torn up legs, he finally got to me only to realize I was not down on the ground from injury but from laughter. John was mad as hell at me now and wanted to hit me, but he couldn't dredge up the energy due to his exhaustion. As we both lay there and laughed, my stomach finally turned sick with anxiety, and I just wanted to disappear as I realized this was an accident that could have and should have been prevented. It was pilot error!

My self-worth was diminishing as my anxiety increased, only to be quelled by alcohol and drugs. As Gary and John prepared to leave Alaska, I brought myself to believe that my leaving would end my problems. I told my girlfriend that I would soon be out of work and that it was time for me to go. Life was not good; I didn't even have the money to move to Australia and I'd begun a long-lasting pattern of self-destruction and had an "I don't give a shit" attitude that would last for decades as I went through bouts of depression, anxiety, good jobs, and good women like they were used underwear. Fighting the Veterans' Administration for acknowledgment of my wounds would further contribute to my anxiety and depression and lack of respect for my country.

Time does help heal all wounds (to a certain degree), as does a "fuck it and fuck them" attitude helps mask them. However, I would receive help from the most unlikely of sources in 1994. Ziek and I went back to Vietnam in '94 along with two ex-army officers. It was not a trip I planned or even looked forward to. In fact, I was pressured to go and lost several nights of sleep just thinking about it.

The anxiety was enormous as we landed at the old Ton Son Nhut airport in what is now called Ho Chi Minh City; it however will always be Saigon to me. We first hung out in Saigon for a couple of days, planning our trip to the Mekong Delta region in which we fought. We finally got to the village of My Tho on the northern banks of the river My Tho, where we were met by a contingency of active and retired military personnel wanting to know our plans in the area. After a lengthy conversation over tea, we were finally allowed to go further south to the city of Ben Tre, which was our old brigade HQ and now the HQ of the current military command of the delta. We met another contingency of military, consisting of General Vi, (retired), and the current commander and colonel of the region. We meet at a building used as a veterans' club and the American War Museum. The men were cordial, and we donated one hundred dollars to their veterans club as a bribe to further our mission of attaining access to the battle site of February 20, 1969. They agreed to take us there and also agreed to find and gather officers and men who were there that day. We hung out for a couple of days awaiting the gathering of the troops and were usually met by the general and the colonel for a meal or two each day during this time. General Vi was a very statuesque man and looked like a general, whereas the colonel was more common in looks, riddled with shrapnel scars. Whereas General Vi was very amicable, however one could tell that the colonel wasn't very happy to be there and seemed to be very distrustful, making me very uneasy. Both fought in the American War. The general was a general when we were there during the war, while the colonel was a platoon sergeant then.

The night before our excursion, we had a large dinner party for approximately twenty, including those going to the battle site with us, with live local music and a menu fit for a king. It was a surreal evening, watching the men in their communist uniforms down a meal that none could probably afford. It was a party atmosphere as we all rose and spoke, explaining who we were and where we were from. The room was a mess, as the Vietnamese threw their chicken bones on the floor out of custom, the beer bottles cluttered the table while the live Vietnamese folk music played on.

The next day we rented a large boat of thirty-five feet and boarded with approximately six ex-VC who were at the battle of February 20, along with the general and an interpreter. As we approached the infamous Crossroads, our bones chilled at the site of fifteen-foot white statues aiming B-40 rockets and AKs right at us. The Vietnamese had made a monument of this famous ambush site for all to remember. My acuteness of watching the shoreline increased as though we were in Tango boats twenty-five years earlier. It was as if nothing had changed. The same hooch's, the same rice paddies, the same water buffalo, and the same ambush sites.

As I was riding in the bow of the boat, I looked back at the VC, only to see one of them shaking uncontrollably in fear of returning as he was comforted by the others. This was going to be a long, ugly day, I was thinking.

We finally got to the battle site, which was now more densely populated. The area's children had sent word out to all that we were in the area, and they all wanted a peek at us. I really didn't want to deal with the history of the battle as it was where I had lost my best friend, Roniger, and so I chose to spend time with the children. Although very timid, they were also very curious, and I was able to lure them next to me with some lame magic tricks. They all wanted to pull on my arm hair as though it was something rare. My camera was especially interesting to them. As time went on and the others perused the battle site, the children had further increased in numbers, and the new members demanded to see the large, hairy man and his magnetic finger trick that was now the talk of the area. It was a blessing to see the children with their smiles and without the knowledge and fear of war. I was thinking Vietnam was a beautiful country now, with beautiful people—a thought I had never thought possible.

As we gathered to leave, the children followed me like the Pied Piper, taking turns holding onto my hands and touching my body hairs.

Ed, Gen Vi, Ziek 1994

As the boat left, I sat up in the bow once again with Ziek, as the children ran alongside the boat waving good-bye to their new friend. My smile was as big as it had ever been. As soon as the children were out of sight, General Vi came over and sat next to me with the interpreter. He placed his hand on my knee, looked me straight in the face, and told me the following:

> "I have fought all enemies of Vietnam throughout my life, and I am most proud of calling myself an American war veteran than anything, as you Americans were the bravest and most honorable of them all. But the reason I'm here is because I have wanted for the longest time to thank the American soldiers, and this may be my only chance to do so. I want to thank them for going out of their way to save the women and children. I know that you did so at the cost of your own lives, and I just want to thank you all from the bottom of my heart."

My emotions were overwhelmed as the tears flowed down my face, and I tried to hide them with eyes forward. I cried more at that moment than I had in twenty-five years while cussing Jane Fonda and John Kerry for their words of damage. This experience would end my inability to cry from then on.

As I left those men (my former enemy) in the delta, I couldn't help but think how odd it was that I now felt more comfortable with them than the average man at my local pub.

This would begin my healing, and I would, in time, seek help for PTSD, go to my military reunions, lose my hatred for REMFs by realizing their much needed contributions, find my balance, and find a good woman. I've settled down on the Oregon Coast with my wife Donita, and life is now good.

***

PTSD was and is nothing more for me than losing hope with mankind and thusly not giving a shit within.

The reality of how low man will go to get his way and mistreat his own while attaining that goal breaks ones heart. Your concept of mankind takes a huge hit. You are raised to believe in your country, your fellow man, freedom and liberty and then; the reality of your own country fucking you over (i.e. Johnson stopping the bombing and causing U.S. casualties) while you're in combat to preserve those ideals rips you a little harder. Then the compounding reality of being treated like shit once home, really hits double hard. And even worse; they put you down lower than the draft evader and draft Dodger. Your local VA Hospital treats you like you're a con man asking for food stamps you don't deserve. Many VFW clubs wouldn't allow you to join because you came from a "Police Action" and not a "Foreign War". Go figure as they say?

A nation that continues down this path has a shortcut leading to its destruction and the ensuing hell that it comes with. It really hurts to know it's your nation that you fought so hard for that is doing all this! The more time passes and you dig into the reality of mankind's actions, how you were treated and how politicians overloaded your Generals with BS rules of engagement (and continue to, to this day) digs a hole within that's hard to get out of! And so; life is less and means less for you than it does others.

This is why PSDT destroys: Overtly you know what is best and right to do for your continuing existence, but it seems that once you've perfected or done 90% of the project/job/obligation/class/next step/relationship/what's expected of you; you ask yourself within and with no conscious thought: "Why bother, it doesn't mean shit anyhow"! And so you don't!

America needs to dig within and ask; who is going to fight for us in the future? We are poisoning another generation (and their families) of protectors as I write! There is a limit as to what a man can take and there is a smaller percentage of real men being raised this day and age in the U.S. that can take on the hell this world has to offer

***

As time has gone by, Captain Perkins would write stories about me and in particular about April 3, 1969. The History Channel produced a special called *Snipers' Deadliest Missions* that highlighted the April 3, 1969, story. The NRA's lifeofduty. tv also released a film called *Choosing Honor*, and my life would change forever. I became involved with AmericanSnipers.org, helping the organization raise monies for our active-duty snipers overseas, and I also became more involved in the military and law enforcement sniper community. I found comfort as a motivational speaker, talking about how to improve one's abilities through the power of the inner mind.

Ed: During filming of Choosing Honor

***

As of this writing, there is a pending recommendation for the Medal of Honor for Ed.

GLOSSARY

Airmobile: Helicopter-borne infantry.

AK-47: Soviet-manufactured Kalashnikov semi-automatic and fully automatic combat assault rifle, fires a 7.62-mm at 600 rounds per minute; the basic weapon of the NVA & VC. It has a distinctive popping sound.

AK-50: Newer version of the AK-47. Some have a permanently mounted "illegal" triangular bayonet which leaves a sucking wound that will not close.

AO: Area of operations.

ARVN: Army of the Republic of Vietnam; the South Vietnamese Regular Army.

ASPB: Assault Support Patrol Boat, AKA--Alpha Boat.

ATC: Armored Troop Carrier, AKA--Tango Boat.

Bac-si: Vietnamese for doctor; also used to refer to medic in the U.S. Army.

Bandoliers: Ammo belts for rifles.

Base camp: A resupply base for field units and a location for headquarters of brigade or division size units, artillery batteries and air fields. Also known as the rear area.

Battery: An artillery unit equivalent to a company. Six105mm or 155mm howitzers or two 8-inch or 175mm self-propelled howitzers.

Beehive round: An artillery shell which delivered thousands of small projectiles, "like nails with fins," instead of shrapnel.

Bird: Helicopters or any aircraft.

Bird dog: Forward Air Controller, usually in a small fixed wing aircraft.

Blood trail: A trail of blood left by a fleeing man who has been wounded.

Body bag: A plastic bag used to transport dead bodies from the field.

Body count: The number of enemy killed, wounded, or captured during an operation.

Boo-coo: Vietnamese slang for many or much.

Boom-boom: Vietnamese slang for sex.

Boonies: Infantry term for the field; jungles or swampy areas.

Bouncing Betty: Antipersonnel mine with two charges: the first propels the explosive charge upward, and the other is set to explode at about waist level.

11-Bravo: (11B) Army designation for an infantry man.

Bronco: Twin-engine observation aircraft equipped with rockets and miniguns.

Bronze Star: U.S. military decoration awarded for valor or meritorious service.

Bush: Infantry term for the field.

C-4: A plastic, putty textured explosive carried by infantry soldiers. It burns when lit and would boil water in seconds instead on minutes, used to heat C-Rations in the field and to blow up bunkers.

C-7: A small cargo airplane; the Caribou.

Cache: Hidden supplies.

CAR-15: Carbine- M-16 rifle with a telescopic butt and short barrel.

CCB: Command & Control Boat.

Charlie: Viet Cong or NVA.

Cherry: Slang for a soldier who has never been under fire.

Chicom: Chinese communist.

Chieu Hoi: Vietnamese "open arms" to give up.

Chinook: CH-47 cargo helicopter.

Chopper: Helicopter.

Chuck: The Viet Cong or NVA.

CIB: Combat Infantry Badge - Army award for men assigned to the infantry for being under enemy fire in a combat zone, worn on both fatigues and dress uniforms.

Claymore: An antipersonnel mine when detonated, propelled small steel projectiles in a 60-degree fan shaped pattern to a maximum distance of 100 meters.

CMB: Combat Medical Badge. Awarded to medics who served with the Infantry while under direct enemy fire.

Cobra: An AH-1G attack helicopter, armed with rockets and machine guns.

Code of Conduct: Military rules for U.S. soldiers taken prisoner by the enemy.

Compound: A fortified military installation.

Concertina wire: Coiled barbed wire with razor type ends.

Conex container: A corrugated metal packing crate, approximately six feet in length.

Contact: Firing on or being fired upon by the enemy.

CP: Command Post.

CQ: Charge of Quarters..

C-rations: Combat rations. Canned meals for use in the field. Each usually consisted of a can of some basic course, a can of fruit, a packet of some type of dessert, a packet of powdered coca, sugar, powder cream, coffee, a small pack of cigarettes, two pieces of chewing gum, and toilet paper.

CS: A riot-control gas which burns the eyes and mucus membrane.

DEROS: The date of expected return from overseas. The day all soldiers in Vietnam were waiting for.

Det-cord: Detonating cord used with explosives.

Deuce-and-a-half: Two-and-a-half ton truck.

Didi: Slang from the Vietnamese word di, meaning "to leave" or "to go."

Didi mau: Slang Vietnamese for "go quickly".

Dinky dau: To be crazy, from "dien cai dau".

Distinguished Service Cross - The Nation's second highest medal for valor.

DMZ: Demilitarized zone. The dividing line between North and South Vietnam established in 1954 at the Geneva Convention.

Doc: Medic or corpsman.

D-ring: A D-shaped metal snap link used to hold gear together, used in repelling from choppers.

Dust-off: Medical evacuation by helicopter, or term for Medivac helicopter.

Eagle flights: Large air assault of helicopters.

Early-Outs: A drop or reduction in time in service. A soldier with 150 days or less remaining on his active duty commitment when he DEROS'd from Vietnam also ETS'd from the army under the Early Out program.

Eleven Bravo: 11B - the MOS of an infantryman.

EM: Enlisted Men (E-1 – E-4).

ETS: Estimated Time of Separation from military service.

Fatigues: Standard combat uniform, green in color.

Field Surgical Kit: Carried by medics for small surgery and suturing.

Fire base: Temporary artillery encampment used for fire support of forward ground operations.

Firefight: A battle, or exchange of small arms fire with the enemy.

Flak jacket: Heavy fiberglass-filled vest worn for protection from shrapnel.

Flare: Illumination projectile; hand-fired or shot from artillery, mortars, or air.

FNG: F--king New Guy.

Forward Observer. A person attached to a field unit to coordinate the placement of direct or indirect fire from ground, air, and naval forces.

Frag: Fragmentation grenade.

Freedom Bird: The plane that took soldiers from Vietnam back to the World.

Free fire zone: Free to fire upon any forces you may come upon...Do not have to identify. Sometimes called free kill zones. Everyone is deemed hostile and a legitimate target.

Friendly fire: Accidental attacks on U.S. or allied soldiers by other U.S. or allied soldiers.

Gook: Derogatory term for VC; derived from Korean slang for "person".

Green Berets: U.S. Special Forces.

Grids: Map broken into numbered thousand-meter squares.

Grunt: Infantryman.

Gung ho: Enthusiastic.

Gunship: Heavily armed helicopter.

Hamlet: A small rural village.

HHC: Headquarters and Headquarters Company, higher up: the honchos; the command.

Hooch: A hut or simple dwelling, either military or civilian.

Hot: Area under fire.

Hot LZ: A landing zone under enemy fire.

HQ: Headquarters.

Huey: Nickname for the UH-1 series helicopters.

Hump: Grunt term to march or walk carrying a rucksack in the field.

I Corps: The northernmost military region in South Vietnam.

II Corps: The Central Highlands military region in South Vietnam.

III Corps: The densely populated, fertile military region between Saigon and the Highlands.

IV Corps: The marshy Mekong Delta southernmost military region, mostly below Saigon.

Immersion foot: Condition resulting from feet being submerged in water for a prolonged period of time, causing cracking and bleeding.

In-country: Vietnam.

KIA: Killed in Action.

Kit Carson scout: Former Viet Cong who act as guides for U.S. military units.

Klick: Kilometer, (1000 meters).

L: A type of ambush set-up, shaped like the letter 'L'.

LAAW: A shoulder-fired, 66-millimeter rocket. The launcher is made of Fiberglass, and is disposable after one shot.

LBJ: Long Binh Jail, a military stockade in Long Binh.

Loach: A LOH (light observation helicopter) sometimes used to draw enemy fire so cobras can come and make the kill.

LP: Listening post usually a two to four man position set up at night outside the perimeter away from the main body of troops, which acted as an early warning system against attack.

LRRP: Long Range Reconnaissance Patrol. An elite team usually composed of five to seven men ....who go deep into the jungle to observe enemy activity without initiating contact.

LSA: Small arms lubricant.

LST: Landing ship Tank.

LT: Lieutenant.

LRRPs: Members of Long Range Reconnaissance Patrols also dehydrated food package replacing c-rations.

LZ: Landing zone. Usually a small clearing for the landing of helicopters or the area of the beach used for a Naval/Tango boat landing.

M-14: A 7.62mm Cal. Rifle that fired semi and full automatic. Used in early portion of Vietnam conflict.

M-16: The standard U.S. military rifle used in Vietnam from 1966 on. Successor to the M-14.

M-60: The standard lightweight machine gun used by U.S. forces in Vietnam.

M-79: A U.S. military hand-held grenade launcher, which used a 40 mm shell.

MARS: Military Affiliate Radio Station. Used by soldiers to call home via Signal Corps and ham radio equipment.

MASH: Mobile Army Surgical Hospital.

Marker round: Usually the first round fired by mortars or artillery. Used to adjust the following rounds onto the target. Sometimes an airburst White Phosphorus round.

Med Cap: Medical Civil Action Program in which U.S. medical personnel would go into the villages to give medical aid to the local populace.

Medevac: Medical evacuation from the field by helicopter.

MIA: Missing in Action.

Minigun: Rapid fire machine gun with multi-barrels that is electronically controlled, capable of firing up to 6,000 rounds a minute primarily used on choppers and other aircraft.

MOH: Medal of Honor. The highest U.S. military decoration awarded for conspicuous gallantry at the risk of life above and beyond the call of duty.

Monitor: An armored metal patrol boat. Sometimes armed with Tank Turret w/105 Howlitzer.

Mr. Charles: The Viet Cong or the NVA.

Mortar: Consisting of 3 parts, a steel tube, base plate, and tri-pod. A High Explosive round is dropped in the tube, striking a firing pin, causing the projectile to leave the tube at a high angle.

MOS: Military Occupational Specialty.

MP: Military police.

MPC: Military Payment Currency. The scrip U.S. soldiers were paid in.

MRF: Mobile Riverine Force (Army-Navy contingency).

Nam: Vietnam.

Napalm: A jellied petroleum substance which burns fiercely, used against enemy personnel.

NCO: Noncommissioned Officer.

NLF: National Liberation Front.

Number one: The best.

Number ten: The worst.

NVA: North Vietnamese Army.

OCS: Officer Candidate School.

OD: Olive Drab,

P-38: A tiny collapsible can opener.

Perimeter: Outer limits of a military position.

PF: Popular Forces. South Vietnamese National Guard- type local military units.

Point: The forward man or element on a combat patrol.

Poncho liner: Nylon insert to the military rain poncho, used as a blanket.

Pop smoke: To ignite a smoke grenade to signal an aircraft.

POW: Prisoner of War.

PRC-25: Portable Radio Communications, Model 25. A back-packed FM receiver-transmitter used for short-distance communications. The range of the radio was 5-10 kilometers, depending on the weather, unless attached to a special, non-portable antenna which could extend the range to 20-30 kilometers.

PSP: Perforated steel plate.

Puff the Magic Dragon: AC-47 AKA; Spooky: is a propeller-driven aircraft with 3 Miniguns - capable of firing 6,000 rounds per minute per gun for a total of 18,000 rounds per minute - The mini guns were on one side of the plane. The plane would bank to one side to fire.

Punji stakes: Sharpened bamboo sticks used in a primitive but effective pit trap. Often smeared with excrement to cause infection.

Purple Heart: U.S. military decoration awarded to any member of the Armed Forces wounded by enemy action. Any soldier who was awarded three Purple Hearts was allowed to leave Vietnam.

QUAD-50s: A four-barreled assembly of .50 caliber machine guns.

RA: Regular Army, prefix to serial number for enlisted men.

Rack: Bed or cot.

R&R: Rest and Recreation. Two types: A three day in country and a seven-day out of county vacation.

Rangers: Elite commandos and infantry specially trained for reconnaissance and combat missions.

React Force: A unit to come to the aid of another unit under enemy fire.

Recon: Reconnaissance. Going out into the jungle to observe for the purpose of identifying enemy activity.

Red alert: The most urgent form of warning. Signals an imminent enemy attack.

Red Legs: Slang for men in the Artillery.

Riv-Div: River Division. Contingent of Navy river vessels.

Rock'n'roll: Firing a weapon on full automatic.

RON: Remain Over Night.

RPG: A rocket-propelled grenade. A Russian-made portable antitank grenade launcher.

RTO: Radio Telephone Operator.

Ruck / Rucksack: backpack issued by infantry in Vietnam.

Saddle up: Put on one's pack on and get ready to move out.

Salvo: Firing an artillery battery in unison.

Sapper: A Viet Cong or NVA solder who gets inside the perimeter, armed with explosives.

Satchel charges: Pack used by the enemy containing explosives that is dropped or thrown and is generally more powerful than a grenade.

SEAL: Highly trained Navy special warfare team members.

Search and destroy: An operation in which Americans searched an area and destroyed anything which the enemy might find useful.

SEATO: Southeast Asia Treaty Organization.

Shake'n'bake: Officers who were commissioned after a few months training in O.C.S. This term could also be applied to sergeant who attended NCO school and earned rank after a few months in service.

Shithook: Chinook, CH-47 helicopter.

Short: Tour of duty being close to completion.

Short-timer: Soldier nearing the end of his tour in Vietnam, usually with 100 days or less left.

Shrapnel: Pieces of metal sent flying by an explosive bomb, artillery shell, grenade or M-79.

Silver Star: U.S. military decoration awarded for gallantry in action.

Six: any Unit Commander, from the Company Commander on up.

SKS: Simonov 7.62 mm semi-automatic carbine.

Sky crane: Huge double-engine helicopter used for lifting and transporting heavy equipment.

Slack man: The second man back on a patrol, directly behind the point.

Slick: A UH-1 helicopter used for transporting troops in tactical air assault operations. This helicopter had little armament thus it was called a "slick".

Smoke grenade: A grenade that released brightly colored smoke. Used for signaling choppers or masking movement. Yellow, Purple, Green and Red was a hot LZ.

SOP: Standard Operating Procedure.

Spec-4: Specialist 4th Class. An Army rank immediately above Private First Class.

Spec-5: Specialist 5th Class. Equivalent to a sergeant.

Spooky: AC-47 is a propeller-driven aircraft with 3 Miniguns -capable of firing 6,000 rounds per minute per gun for a total of 18,000 rounds per minute - The mini guns were on one side of the plane. The plane would bank to one side to fire.

Stand-down: An infantry unit's return from the boonies to the base camp for refitting.

Starlight scope: A night scope to intensify images at night by using reflected light form the moon, stars or any other source of light.

Steel pot: The standard U.S. Army steel helmet.

Strobe: Hand held strobe light for marking landing zones at night.

Syrettes: A hypodermic needle connected to a collapsible tube. Contained morphine in most cases. After inserting the needle in the body one would squeeze the morphine tube like tooth paste.

Tango Boat: ATC(H) - Armored Troop Carrier (Helicopter)

Tet: Buddhist lunar New Year. Buddha's birthday.

Tiger Scouts: Ex VC and NVA who became scouts and interpreters for the infantry.

Tiger Fatigues: Camouflage fatigue uniforms.

Top: A top sergeant, usually 1st Sgt of the Company.

Tracer: A round of ammunition chemically treated to glow so that its flight can be followed.

Triage: The procedure for deciding the order in which to treat casualties.

Trip flare: A ground flare triggered by a trip wire. Use to notify the approach of the enemy.

UH-1H: A Huey helicopter.

USO: United Service Organization. Provided entertainment to the troops.

VC: Viet Cong.

Victor Charlie: the Viet Cong; the enemy.

Viet Cong: South Vietnamese Communist.

Vietnamese Popular Forces: South Vietnamese local military forces.

Vietnamization: U.S. policy initiated by President Richard Nixon late in the war to turn over the fighting to the South Vietnamese Army during the phased withdrawal of American troops.

Wake-up: The last day of a soldier's Vietnam tour. Example for 6 days: 5 days and a wake-up.

Walking wounded: Wounded who are still able to walk without assistance.

White phosphorus: (Willy Peter) an explosive round from artillery, mortars, or rockets, grenades. Also a type of aerial bomb. When the rounds exploded a huge puff of white smoke would appear from the burning phosphorus. The round was used as marking rounds and incendiary rounds. When phosphorus hit the skin it would continue to burn. Water would not put it out. It had to be smothered (mud was used to seal off the wound) or it would continue to burn until it exited the body.

Willy Peter: White Phosphorus.

Wood line: A row of trees at the edge of a field.

The World: The United States.

WP: White phosphorus.

Xin loi: A Vietnamese meaning "sorry about that".

XO: Executive officer; the second in command of a military unit.

Zippo Boat: Monitor Boat with flame thrower capabilities.

A SPECIAL THANKS TO:

Chris Cook
Ed Ziek
My wife: Donita
Albert Moore
Dona Shockman

***

John Beck
Nick Betts
Bob Cruz
Leon Edmiston
Joe Gapol
Larry Haugen
Dan Hendricks
Chris Jacky
Eric Mattingly
Chuck Mawhinney
Dan Middendorf
Debra Omundsen
Willy Perez

A SPECIAL THANKS TO:

Mike Perkins
Larry Reed
Zack Reese
Jerry Richards
Jerry "Doc" Schuebel
John Simpson
John Sperry
Rick Stewart
Erol Tuzo
Judy Wiese
Greg Williams

MEKONGMUDDOGS.COM
&
EDTHESNIPER.COM

Made in the USA
Lexington, KY
04 January 2015